PRAISE FOR *CHRISTIAN ETHICS AND NURSING PRACTICE*

"*Christian Ethics and Nursing Practice* makes a thought-provoking and unique contribution to the nursing literature. Its detailed exploration of the linkages between the *ANA Code of Ethics for Nurses* and the scriptural strands of law, holiness, wisdom, and prophecy provide a robust framework within which to consider the realities of nursing practice. The culminating explication of moral maturity in the Christian nurse is particularly instructive. This team of scholars provides a vital resource for nurses."

—MARY MOLEWYK DOORNBOS, Registered Nurse; Chair and Professor of Nursing, Calvin University; author of *Transforming Care: A Christian Vision of Nursing Practice*

"Within healthcare and nursing there has been a growing emphasis on the importance of spirituality. Models of spirituality are wide and diverse as they try to encompass dimensions of caring that focus on meaning, purpose, love, hope, and God. However, sometimes in the quest to find common ground between different viewpoints, the particularities of religious traditions get lost or are downplayed in ways that can strip the unique power of religious traditions to bring healing to vulnerable people. Similarly, within healthcare ethics, there is a push towards values that are universally acceptable. Again the particularities of religious traditions can easily be occluded to the detriment of our moral formation. This book helps to move us beyond the general to the particularities of the Christian tradition and asks and seeks to answer the question: what might it look like if we took biblically based Christian ethics seriously within a nursing context? The result is a deep, rich, challenging, and potentially healing book that offers an important contribution to the ongoing conversations around the role of spirituality and religion within healthcare. This is an important book that deserves serious consideration."

—JOHN SWINTON, Registered Mental Nurse; Registered Nurse for People with Learning Disabilities; Chair in Divinity and Religious Studies, University of Aberdeen

"Drs. Steele and Monroe have articulated a masterful and scholarly treatise on one of the recurring conundrums in a Christian's delivery of ethical health care, i.e., 'Which comes first, "my sacred" or "my secular" Being?' Their text undertakes a systematic and rational discourse prodding the reader to consider the distinctiveness, the interrelatedness, and the imperative amenability of these two seemingly opposing elements; and yet, ultimately, to draw the indisputable reasoning that, from a Christian's standpoint of ethics in health care, the sacred and the secular are one and the same. Case vignettes from graduate nursing students supplement each chapter, providing circumstances and practicalities to support the authors' premises for finite empathy and infinite spirituality as the ultimate persuasions for prioritizing and proffering ethical and selfless clinical service to humankind. This is a must read for both the health professions student as well as the seasoned practitioner."

—SAMUEL LIN, Rear Admiral and Assistant Surgeon General (Retired),
US Public Health Service; Deputy Assistant Secretary for Health (Retired),
US Department of Health and Human Services

"Steele and Monroe provide an exquisite text connecting four strands of moral discourse found in the Bible to the professional *Code of Ethics for Nurses*. Deep, contextual analyses of biblical texts are presented and compared to the moral values, character, and ethical comportment required of the professional nurse. Each chapter culminates in current illustrations of the relationship of moral discourse in the Bible to the virtuous practice of today's nurse through clinical stories. Additionally, the authors provide excellent reflective exercises that may generate group discussion or personal reflection to enhance understanding of the significant connections between Christian faith and the practice of professional nursing."

—CHERYL B. CROTSER, Registered Nurse; Nurse Executive-Board
Certified; Dean and Director of Graduate Programs,
School of Nursing, Roberts Wesleyan College

"Steele and Monroe attempt to negotiate two interpretive frameworks of caregiving and succeed in doing so. They describe the various aspects of the nurse's professional roles, while always acknowledging that for the Christian practitioner the moral life is defined as imitation of Christ expressed in habits of holy living and obedience to standards of goodness. They, then, provide analytical mechanisms for the Christian practitioner. In doing so, they offer an overall model for the nurse in a clinical setting to fulfill 'vocation'—in both the narrow sense of professional vocation and broad sense of living for God. The work is obviously meant as a text but can well serve the veteran nurse addressing seemingly endless morally complex circumstances."

—JAMES R. THOBABEN, Dean, School of Theology & Formation, Asbury Theological Seminary; author of *Health Care Ethics: A Comprehensive Christian Resource*

"Steele and Monroe have done a superb job in presenting the *ANA Code of Ethics for Nurses* within a solid biblical framework. This gem of a book informs ethical nursing practice from a clearly articulated Christian worldview. The theology and nursing expertise of the authors blend a scholarly and professional aspect to ethical practice that is both intellectually sound and readily applicable to patient care situations across the lifespan and in diverse practice settings. As a nurse educator, I find the tips and strategies embedded in each chapter especially helpful for enhancing the student learning experience. A wonderful resource for both undergraduate and graduate nursing courses."

—VALORIE ORTON, Registered Nurse; Clinical Nurse Leader; Assistant Professor of Nursing, George Fox University

Christian Ethics and
Nursing Practice

Christian Ethics and Nursing Practice

RICHARD B. STEELE
HEIDI A. MONROE

Foreword by Lorie M. Wild

CASCADE *Books* · Eugene, Oregon

CHRISTIAN ETHICS AND NURSING PRACTICE

Scripture quotations are from the New Revised Standard Version Bible, copyright © 1989 National Council of the Churches of Christ in the United States of America. Used by permission. All rights reserved worldwide.

Cascade Books
An Imprint of Wipf and Stock Publishers
199 W. 8th Ave., Suite 3
Eugene, OR 97401

www.wipfandstock.com

PAPERBACK ISBN: 978-1-5326-6504-2
HARDCOVER ISBN: 978-1-5326-6505-9
EBOOK ISBN: 978-1-5326-6506-6

Cataloguing-in-Publication data:

Names: Steele, Richard B., 1952–, author. | Monroe, Heidi A., author. | Wild, Lorie M., foreword.

Title: Christian ethics and nursing practice / Richard B. Steele and Heidi A. Monroe ; foreword by Lorie M. Wild.

Description: Eugene, OR : Cascade Books, 2020 | Includes references and index.

Identifiers :ISBN 978-1-5326-6504-2 (PAPERBACK) | ISBN 978-1-5326-6505-9 (HARDCOVER) | ISBN 978-1-5326-6506-6 (EBOOK)

Subjects: LCSH: Nursing. | Christian ethics. | Nursing ethics.

Classification: R725.56 .S74 2020 (paperback) | R725.56 .S74 (ebook)

Manufactured in the U.S.A.   06/02/20

In Loving Memory
OF
Sarah Lynn Steele
(December 23, 1984–November 14, 2017)

Contents

Figures

Tables

Foreword

Nursing has been defined in a variety of ways over the centuries. Few would dispute that nursing is a relational profession. Nurses, as they tend to the well-being of others, often at the most critical times of life and death, confront difficult choices. As such, nursing is an ethical business. In fact, year after year, the trustworthiness of nursing continues to outrank other professions in public polls.

Building trust among the public does not happen by accident. Nursing education, built on a foundation of the liberal arts and sciences, involves teaching the art, science, and skills of nursing. Yet beyond the fundamentals, nursing education plays a central role in character formation as well as cultivating professional and ethical comportment.

Within this context, Richard B. Steele and Heidi A. Monroe offer a new framework to understand ethics in nursing and, more broadly, in healthcare. These authors bring a pairing of theological (Steele) and nursing and bioethics (Monroe) experience and expertise to this work.

The authors developed and use the framework detailed in this text as part of a required graduate nursing course designed to "explore the discipline through a theologically informed set of values." The university policy provides direction, explaining that

> in some cases this engagement will result in an alignment with key movements of a particular discipline. In other cases it may lead to a critique of some of the discipline's foundational assumptions. But in all cases the engagement will reflect both a deep knowledge and proficiency in the discipline itself and a rigorous and sensitive application of relevant theological principles and values.

Steele and Monroe have taken this mandate to a higher level by working together in the classroom and in crafting this text. The theological grounding and their interdisciplinary partnership are what distinguishes their course and this text from being simply another course in nursing and bioethics. Their deep commitment, not only to the course but most importantly to students, provides a rich perspective for teaching, learning and professional development.

Initially, when planning the course, the simple goal was to have graduate nursing students think about their clinical practice differently by understanding and applying a new paradigm for professional nursing values and ethics. What Steele and Monroe have accomplished is to provide a framework that helps Christians appreciate a new way to integrate elements of biblical guidance with practice. At the same time, those professing other faiths, or those who do not claim any faith tradition, gain an understanding of the biblically grounded "strands" of moral discourse that shape our laws and ethical practice. They artfully align the four strands—law, holiness, wisdom and prophecy—with the American Nurses Association's *Code of Ethics for Nurses with Interpretive Statements*. Rather than compete with other ethical theories and decision-making models, their unique approach to the *Code* complements rather than supplants these classic frameworks, providing a fresh perspective.

The authors bring experience, expertise and a deep commitment to their disciplines to the course and, most important, to their students' learning and professional development. Each is a gifted teacher. Yet, one of the most exciting and novel features of their text is the way in which, along with the course as a whole, it reflects the shared endeavor of teaching and learning. In the classroom and through online discussion boards, Steele and Monroe engage students by inviting them to share exemplars from their own practice that illustrate the themes embedded in the *Code* along with the norms of Christian discipleship mapped out in the Bible. In short, they recognize that each person in the classroom—whether student or teacher—contributes to the experience of learning. In doing so, the principles and practices come alive.

The clinical exemplars shared throughout the text will resonate with the nurses or other practitioners who read this book. Too often, texts regarding ethical conflicts feature profound ethical dilemmas such as euthanasia, assisted suicide, abortion or organ transplant, to name a few. Most clinicians will encounter few, if any, large-scale ethical dilemmas. In contrast, the exemplars included here reflect the countless real-life, day-to-day situations that nurses and other clinicians confront in their practice that demand ethical comportment and decision-making. Nurses from all specialties will recognize the scenarios shared precisely because the authors of the exemplars are practicing, bedside nurses.

Another feature of this work that sets it apart from other ethics texts is the inclusion of classic works of art to convey the central themes. The selected images add another layer of depth to a very rich narrative. Taken together, the art, along with the biblical and professional narratives, illustrate the human experience that grounds and frames nursing practice.

Any ethics text runs the risk of becoming a discussion of ethical dos and don'ts. Here, Steele and Monroe elegantly weave a narrative that builds a foundation for understanding the ANA *Code* as well as providing guidance for action in alignment with the same. One perspective shared as a part of a student's course feedback offers a succinct summary not only of the course from which *Christian Ethics and Nursing Practice* was born but also of the gifted teaching and writing of Steele and Monroe:

> While this course served as a religious requirement, the course as a whole beautifully integrated faith with the nursing profession in a seamless manner. The readings and in-class discussions emphasized the overlap and sparked rich dialogue between a diverse religious cohort.

To create a tapestry of such varied backgrounds, perspectives, and goals for learning and nursing practice demands gifted teachers, wise scholars and committed professionals. As readers, we are fortunate beneficiaries of what I hope will become a valued resource for nursing ethics for faculty, students and practicing nurses alike.

—Lorie M. Wild, PhD, RN, NEA-BC
Dean, School of Health Sciences
Seattle Pacific University

Acknowledgments

We are grateful to the following colleagues at Seattle Pacific University (SPU), Seattle, Washington, for their gracious help, through gifts of time and talent, with this project: Katie Bennett, Administrative Assistant, Graduate Nursing; Carrie Fry, Sciences Librarian; Kristen Hoffman, Psychology and Scholarly Communications Librarian; Kieran Jackson, Computer and Information Systems Helpdesk Lead Technician; David Nienhuis, Professor of New Testament; Steve Perisho, Theology and Philosophy Librarian; Frank A. Spina, Professor Emeritus of Old Testament; Lorie M. Wild, Dean of the School of Health Sciences and Professor of Nursing; and Dominic Williamson, Senior Instructional Designer: Graphics/Illustration. Special mention must be made here of our dearly departed colleague, James O. Mitre, Instructor of Psychiatric Nursing, who deeply cared for others and often shared the story used in chapter 3 to help students learn. Jim's untimely death in 2014 brought sorrow to our campus and to the wider Seattle healthcare community.

Our special gratitude goes to the graduate nursing students at SPU in the autumn 2017, spring 2018, and spring 2019 sections of NUR 6301 Values, Faith and Ethics, who used early drafts of this work as a course text. Their "clinical voices" can be heard throughout the book. We also wish to thank the following student workers in the SPU School of Health Sciences for their logistical assistance in the preparation of the manuscript: Sophia Hamann, Rachel Johanson, Caitlyn Schnider and Michelle Anastacio Trujeque.

Two colleagues from other institutions—Valorie Orton, Assistant Professor of Nursing at George Fox University in Newberg, Oregon, and Gerald Sittser, Professor of Theology and Senior Fellow in the Office of Church Engagement at Whitworth University, Spokane, Washington—carefully reviewed the manuscript and offered many kind suggestions for its improvement. We are deeply in their debt.

We also wish to express our appreciation for the assistance given us by Meghan Brown, Permissions Associate at Art Resource, New York, New York, and Zhanna Etsina, Manager, Rights and Reproductions Office, The State Hermitage Museum, St. Petersburg, Russia, in securing licenses for and high-resolution images of several of the pieces of artwork used in this volume.

Finally, we wish to thank our spouses, Marilyn Hair and Joseph Monroe, for the countless ways in which their love blesses our lives daily, and particularly for the patience and support they unfailingly offered us as this book grew from dream to reality.

Abbreviations

GENERAL

ANA	American Nurses Association
APRN	Advanced practice registered nurse
Code	ANA *Code of Ethics for Nurses with Interpretive Statements*
NRSV	New Revised Standard Version
NT	New Testament
OT	Old Testament
RN	Registered nurse
RSV	Revised Standard Version
SPU	Seattle Pacific University
V. (vv.)	Verse (verses)

SCRIPTURE

Hebrew Bible / Old Testament:

Gen	Genesis
Exod	Exodus
Lev	Leviticus
Num	Numbers
Deut	Deuteronomy
Josh	Joshua
Judg	Judges
Ruth	Ruth
1–2 Sam	1–2 Samuel

1–2 Kgs	1–2 Kings
1–2 Chr	1–2 Chronicles
Ezra	Ezra
Neh	Nehemiah
Esth	Esther
Job	Job
Ps (*pl.* Pss)	Psalms
Prov	Proverbs
Eccl	Ecclesiastes
Song	Song of Solomon
Isa	Isaiah
Jer	Jeremiah
Ezek	Ezekiel
Dan	Daniel
Hos	Hosea
Joel	Joel
Amos	Amos
Obad	Obadiah
Jonah	Jonah
Mic	Micah
Nah	Nahum
Hab	Habakkuk
Zeph	Zephaniah
Hag	Haggai
Zech	Zechariah
Mal	Malachi

New Testament:

Matt	Matthew
Mark	Mark
Luke	Luke
John	John
Acts	Acts
Rom	Romans
1–2 Cor	1–2 Corinthians
Gal	Galatians
Eph	Ephesians
Phil	Philippians

Col	Colossians
1–2 Thess	1–2 Thessalonians
1–2 Tim	1–2 Timothy
Titus	Titus
Phlm	Philemon
Heb	Hebrews
Jas	James
1–2 Pet	1–2 Peter
1–2–3 John	1–2–3 John
Jude	Jude
Rev	Revelation

Apocryphal / Deuterocanonical Books:

Tob	Tobit
Jdt	Judith
Add Esth	Additions to Esther
Wis	Wisdom of Solomon
Sir	Sirach (or Ecclesiasticus)
Bar	Baruch
1–2 Esd	1–2 Esdras
Ep Jer	Epistle of Jeremiah
Sg Three	The Prayer of Azariah and the Song of the Three Jews
Sus	Susanna
Bel	Bel and the Dragon
1–2 Macc	1–2 Maccabees
3–4 Macc	3–4 Maccabees
Pr Man	Prayer of Manasseh

Introduction

"[Jesus is] our nurse . . . our healer."

EPISTLE TO DIOGNETUS 9.6, IN RICHARDSON, 1953, P. 221

THE AIM AND STRUCTURE OF THIS BOOK

The aim of this book is to show how the religious and moral teachings of the Christian Bible compare, contrast and correlate with the ethical standards of modern nursing, as stated in the *Code of Ethics for Nurses with Interpretive Statements* (hereinafter referred to as the *Code*; American Nurses Association [ANA], 2015). We intend it to be used as a textbook for courses in nursing ethics at Christian colleges and universities, and it is likely that many of our readers are themselves Christians, who have devoted their lives to caring for the sick, the injured, the elderly, the disabled and the dying as a way of living out their commitment to Jesus Christ. Such readers will presumably have a deep personal interest in knowing how closely the teachings of the Bible match the provisions of the ANA *Code*. But we recognize that many nursing students at Christian educational institutions belong to other religious traditions—or to none at all. We cherish the hope that this book will be useful to these readers as well. For we hope that they at least feel an interest in the general question of the relationship between "religion" and "health care," even if they feel no need to reconcile the provisions of the *Code* with the norms of Christian discipleship mapped out in the Bible.

To accomplish our aim, we distinguish four main types or "strands" of moral discourse in the Bible—law, holiness, wisdom and prophecy—and correlate each of these strands with two or more of the nine provisions

1

spelled out in the *Code* (ANA, 2015), as shown in Table 0.1 below. The left column lists the four strands and offers a "theme verse" for each strand. The theme verse for each strand is taken from one of the scriptural passages that will represent that strand later in the book. The relevance of the four theme verses to nursing practice may not be immediately obvious at first glance but will become clear as we proceed. The right column lists the nine provisions of the ANA *Code*, arranged in four groups, with each group bearing a general thematic correspondence with one of the four strands of biblical moral discourse.

Table 0.1. The Four Strands and the Nine Provisions

The Four Strands	The Nine Provisions
Strand 1: Law: "Keep the commandments . . . for your own well-being" (Deut 10:13).	Provision 1: The nurse practices with compassion and respect for the inherent dignity, worth, and unique attributes of every person. Provision 2: The nurse's primary commitment is to the patient, whether an individual, family, group, community, or population. Provision 3: The nurse promotes, advocates for, and protects the rights, health, and safety of the patient.
Strand 2: Holiness: "Be holy, for I am holy" (Lev 19:2; cf. Matt 5:48; 1 Pet 1:16).	Provision 5: The nurse owes the same duties to self as to others, including the responsibility to promote health and safety, preserve wholeness of character and integrity, maintain competence, and continue personal and professional growth. Provision 6: The nurse, through individual and collective effort, establishes, maintains, and improves the ethical environment of the work setting and conditions of employment that are conducive to safe, quality health care.
Strand 3: Wisdom: "God's works will never be finished; and from him health spreads over all the earth" (Sirach 38:8b).	Provision 4: The nurse has authority, accountability, and responsibility for nursing practice; makes decisions; and takes action consistent with the obligation to promote health and to provide optimal care. Provision 7: The nurse, in all roles and settings, advances the profession through research and scholarly inquiry, professional standards development, and the generation of both nursing and health policy.
Strand 4: Prophecy: "No prophet is accepted in the prophet's hometown" (Luke 4:24).	Provision 8: The nurse collaborates with other health professionals and the public to protect human rights, promote health diplomacy, and reduce health disparities. Provision 9: The profession of nursing, collectively through its professional organizations, must articulate nursing values, maintain the integrity of the profession, and integrate principles of social justice into nursing and health policy.

We recognize that the Bible says little if anything about many of the specific activities performed by modern registered nurses (RNs) and that many of the activities performed by persons named in the Bible as "nurses" would rarely, if ever, be performed by modern RNs. When the word *nurse* appears in the Bible as a verb (Hebrew: *yānaq*; Greek: *anatrephō* = nurture; *thēlazō* = give suck; *trephō* = feed), it often refers to breastfeeding, either by a child's mother or wet nurse (Gen 21:7; Exod 2:7, 9; 1 Sam 1:23; 1 Kgs 3:21; Song 8:1; Isa 66:11; Wis 7:4; Luke 11:27; 23:29). In one remarkable instance, God himself enables his people, wandering in the wilderness, to "suck" nourishment from their surroundings: "he nursed [them] with honey from the crags, with oil from flinty rock; curds from the herd, and milk from the flock . . ." (Deut 32:13b–14a). As a noun (Hebrew: *yôneq*; Greek *trophos*), "nurse" usually refers to a woman who cares for another's child as a wet nurse or nursemaid during the child's infancy (Num 11:12; Ruth 4:16; 2 Sam 4:4; 2 Kgs 11:2; 2 Chr 22:11; Isa 60:4), though she might stay on as a chambermaid after her charge grows up (Gen 24:59; 35:8). Saint Paul once uses the word in this sense, when he likens his apostolic work to that of "a nurse tenderly caring for her own children" (1 Thess 2:7).[1] And the *Epistle to Diognetus*, an anonymous Christian writing of the second century, exhorts the reader to regard Jesus himself "as Nurse [*trophos*], Father, Teacher, Counselor, Healer [*iatros*], Mind, Light, Honor, Glory, Might, Life" (Richardson, 1953, p. 221). It is noteworthy that "nurse" heads this list, and that "healer" (or "doctor") is included as well.[2]

---

1. In the Revised Standard Version (RSV) translation of 1 Kings 1:1–4, we read of a young woman who was hired as a "nurse" for the elderly King David. But the Hebrew term used there, *sākan*, is better translated as "attendant," per the New Revised Standard Version (NRSV). Her assigned duties include those of a "concubine," although David's impotence prevents her from exercising them. We therefore exclude this passage from the list of biblical references to "nurses," though we mention it here in passing because older concordances sometimes cite it.

2. The Old Testament also refers several times to midwives (Hebrew: *mᵉyalledet*; Greek: *maia*). These were women whose chief responsibility was to assist pregnant women in childbirth (Gen 35:17; 38:28; Exod 1:15–22). Those named in the Bible as midwives do not seem to have performed any other "nursing" functions, nor is midwifery listed as a function of those who are named as nurses. It is possible, of course, that some ancient women served both as nurses and as midwives, but there is no direct textual evidence to that effect.

Figure 0.1. Anonymous, *Salome and midwife bathing the infant Jesus* [fresco]. (Twelfth century). Dark Church, Open Air Museum, Goreme, Cappadocia. This fresco illustrates a scene from the *Proto-Gospel of James*, chapters 19–20 (Ehrman, 2003, pp. 69–70). The *Proto-Gospel of James* is a mid-second-century apocryphal writing that was crucial in the development of Christian Mariology; this particular scene became a popular subject in Eastern Christian art.

We also recognize that the *Code* (ANA, 2015) in its current form is a thoroughly secular or "nontheistic" document. That is, it makes no claims about the existence or nature of God. That does not mean that it directly denies or expresses doubts about the existence of God. It simply brackets out the question of God and assumes that the validity of the ethical standards it upholds does not depend on the validity of any given system of religious beliefs and practices.

Thus, we cannot read the Bible as a manual of nursing (cf. Verhey, 2003, pp. 32–67), nor do we find any explicitly "religious" content in the *Code* (ANA, 2015). Nevertheless, we argue that the Bible's ways of structuring the character and conduct of Christian individuals and communities can richly inform the way nurses and healthcare facilities (or at least Christian nurses and church-affiliated healthcare facilities) do their business. We argue further that the nine provisions of the *Code* are in many respects congruent with the moral and religious values of Christian Scripture, and stipulate qualities of a nurse's personal character and professional practice that resonate closely with the complex account of godliness found in the Bible. Indeed, as Marsha Fowler (2015) argues, several of the *Code's* key concepts, such as compassion and human dignity, have their roots in one or more of the world's great religions and reflect the Christian convictions of Florence Nightingale and other founders of modern nursing (pp. 1–3, 41–42).

The book contains five chapters. Chapters 1–4 follow the pattern shown in Table 1 above. Chapter 5 discusses their interrelationships.

Chapter 1, "The Nurse as Citizen, Professional, and Public Servant," examines the legal strand of Scripture, with special attention to the Ten Commandments of Moses and the so-called Love Commandment of Jesus. It then correlates these texts to Provisions 1–3 in the *Code* (ANA, 2015), which deal with human dignity and patient rights. This analysis is followed by a discussion of the theme of law in the theological writings of Florence Nightingale (1992, 2002).

Chapter 2, "The Nurse as Healing Presence," relates the biblical theme of holiness, as delineated in the Levitical Holiness Code and Jesus' Sermon on the Mount, with Provisions 5 and 6 in the *Code* (ANA, 2015), which deal with the personal and professional virtues required for skillful and ethical nursing practice.

Chapter 3, "The Nurse as Savvy Problem-Solver," looks at the wisdom strand in Scripture, as exemplified in passages on healing from the book of Sirach and the letter of James. It then compares these texts with Provisions 4 and 7 in the *Code* (ANA, 2015), which focus on professionalism in nursing and the skills required for effective problem-solving and decision-making in clinical situations.

Chapter 4, "The Nurse as Patient Advocate and Social Critic," focuses on the prophetic strand of biblical moral discourse. This strand is exemplified by Jesus' programmatic sermon in the synagogue of Nazareth, and by two stories that Jesus mentions in that sermon about healings performed by Old Testament prophets. These prophetic texts are then correlated with Provisions 8 and 9 in the *Code* (ANA, 2015), which pertain to human rights, social justice, health diplomacy and health policy.

Chapter 5, "Moral Maturity in Christian Nursing," summarizes and synthesizes what we have learned in chapters 1–4 about the congruence between faithful Christian discipleship, as delineated in Christian Scripture, and the vocation of nursing, as normed by the *Code* (ANA, 2015).

SIX POINTS OF CLARIFICATION

We must clarify several matters before we proceed. First, the translation of the Bible that we use throughout this book is the New Revised Standard Version with the Apocrypha. Some readers may be unfamiliar with the Apocrypha, or suspicious of them, so a few words about them are in order. The Apocrypha are a group of sixteen books written between the fourth century BC and the first century AD, that is, *after* most or all of the books of the Old Testament (OT) had been composed, but *before* most of the books of the New Testament (NT) had been composed. Their authors were Jewish (like the authors of the OT), who wrote in Greek (like the authors of the NT) and concerned themselves with the problems faced by Jews living in the heavily Hellenized culture of that period. The Apocrypha certainly provide indispensable information about the historical, religious and political background of the NT—but do they belong in the Bible itself? Should they, in other words, be regarded as "canonical"? The term *canon* refers to the list of books that a particular church body accepts as its scripture. The problem is that different church bodies have somewhat different canons. Virtually all churches accept the thirty-nine books of the OT and the twenty-seven books of the NT as canonical, but opinions differ on the Apocrypha. Roman Catholic and Eastern Orthodox Christians generally accept them as sacred Scripture but often regard their religious authority as inferior to that of the original Hebrew Bible. Their secondary ("deuterocanonical") status is disguised a bit in Catholic and Orthodox Bibles, however, because they are interspersed throughout the OT—apocryphal history books with canonical history books, apocryphal wisdom books with canonical wisdom books. In sharp contrast to Catholic and Orthodox practice, many Protestants and Evangelicals reject the canonicity of the Apocrypha altogether and exclude them from their published editions of the Bible. The New Revised Standard Version takes a middle way between these extremes. Reflecting contemporary ecumenical sensibilities, it *includes* the Apocrypha, but represents their *deuterocanonical* status by placing them together in a separate section between the Old and New Testaments. One of the OT Apocrypha, the book of Sirach, features prominently in chapter 3 below, and we will treat it as deuterocanonical Scripture.

A second important clarification pertains to the relationship between the *books* of the Bible and the *strands* of biblical moral discourse. In the OT and the OT Apocrypha, the relationship is quite close. For example, Strand 1 predominates in the five books of the Law, namely, Genesis,

Exodus, Leviticus, Numbers and Deuteronomy. There are no OT books in which Strand 2 is dominant, but there is a long block of holiness material, known as the Holiness Code, found in chapters 17–26 of Leviticus. Strand 3 comes to the fore in a cluster of books known as the OT Writings, which include Job, several of the Psalms, Proverbs, Ecclesiastes and the Song of Solomon, as well as the apocryphal books of the Wisdom of Solomon and Sirach. Strand 4 predominates in the Former Prophets (Joshua, Judges, 1–2 Samuel, and 1–2 Kings) and the Latter Prophets (Isaiah, Jeremiah, Ezekiel, and the Twelve Minor Prophets). We must bear in mind, however, that even when a given strand of moral discourse "predominates" in a given biblical book, traces of the other strands may also be found there. For example, Moses, the lawgiver of Israel, is also called a "prophet" (Deut 18:15–22); conversely, Daniel the prophet gives thanks to God that he has been granted "wisdom and power" (Dan 2:23). With respect to the New Testament, the relationship between the books and the strands is still more complex, and the interweaving of the strands even more pronounced. The Gospels, for example, sometimes feature Jesus as a lawgiver (Strand 1), sometimes as a sage (Strand 3), and sometimes as a prophet (Strand 4); and his Sermon on the Mount (Matt 5–7) quite explicitly harkens back to the Levitical Holiness Code (Strand 2). Again, the letter of James, which represents the wisdom strand in chapter 3 below, also has many features of biblical prophecy (D. Nienhuis, personal communication, July 9, 2018). It is important, therefore, not to overidentify any one strand of biblical moral discourse with any one book or group of books in the Christian Scripture.

This leads to a third clarification. Not only are multiple strands sometimes found together in a given biblical book, but the simultaneous presence of multiple strands in many biblical books, taken one by one, and in canon of sacred Scripture, taken as a whole, provides a depth and richness of ethical insight that none of the strands by itself could offer. True, the representative texts we have chosen for each strand differ markedly in literary form and even to some extent in religious outlook. Yet these differences do not reflect contradiction. On the contrary, they demonstrate the variety of ways in which the Bible, in its rich diversity-amidst-unity, seeks to shape the lives of its readers. The four strands supplement, reinforce and enrich each other, and each strand helps to correct the excesses and deficiencies to which each of the others, taken by itself, might be prone. One way to visualize this is shown in Figure 0.2, which illustrates the technique of braid-making:

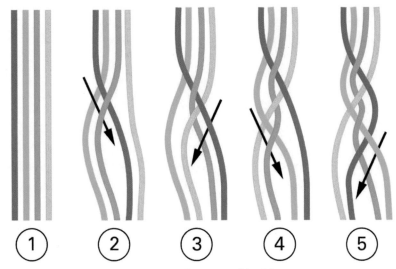

Figure 0.2. *Four-strand braid*

Strand 1: Law

Strand 2: Holiness

Strand 3: Wisdom

Strand 4: Prophecy

We start, as shown in step 1 above, with four colored strings or strands—purple, green, red and gold. When we interweave those strands, as shown successively in steps 2 through 5, we get a braid. Now the canon of Christian Scripture is like the completed braid. If we then ask how it tries to shape the character and conduct of its readers, we discover that it does so in four somewhat different ways. Sometimes the Bible lays down laws (Strand 1). Sometimes it promotes virtuous habits or morally praiseworthy character traits (Strand 2). Sometimes it recommends sensible strategies for making decisions, solving problems and interacting with others (Strand 3). Sometimes it sharply criticizes behaviors and social institutions that cause people to forget God or oppress others (Strand 4). Different as these modes of moral instruction may seem, however, they all serve a common purpose: to increase readers' love of God and neighbor. To grasp the Bible's overall moral vision, therefore, we must not merely analyze its separate strands of moral discourse: we must correlate and coordinate their respective concerns and insights. We must let the Bible's rich complexities, subtle nuances and diverse perspectives all have their say in shaping our character and conduct. In chapters 1–4, we take the four strands one by one; then, in chapter 5, we put the four strands into direct conversation with each other. We argue that people attain moral maturity when they hold the distinctive approaches of all four strands in dynamic tension, allowing each strand to have its say, and braiding them together into a strong, supple, integral whole.

Fourth, we sometimes distinguish between the ethics of *conduct* and the ethics of *character*, as shown in Table 0.2 below. Strands 1 and 4, which emphasize what people should *do* and how they should *act*, represent conduct-focused ethics. In contrast, Strands 2 and 3, which emphasize who people *are* as moral agents, represent character-based ethics. This distinction between conduct-focused and character-based ethics is also discernible in the *Code* (ANA, 2015). Thus, Provisions 1, 2, 3, 8, and 9 (which correlate with Strands 1 and 4, as shown in Table 0.1 above) stress the personal and professional conduct of nurses, whereas Provisions 4, 5, 6, and 7 (which correlate with Strands 2 and 3) focus on their moral virtues and professional skills. Yet it is important not to push the distinction between conduct-focused and character-based ethics too far. People's behavior usually reflects their selfhood in its entirety, and their selfhood is only knowable to others (and often to themselves) by their concrete actions in the world. We may distinguish character and conduct for purposes of ethical analysis, yet we recognize that they are really *aspects* or *dimensions* of the moral life in its entirety.

Table 0.2. Conduct-Focused Ethics vs. Character-Focused Ethics	
Conduct-Focused Ethics: Emphasis on laws, regulations, rules, policies, procedures or protocols	**Character-Focused Ethics:** Emphasis on virtues, habits, skills, disposition, motives, moral sentiments, emotional intelligence
Strand 1: Law	Strand 2: Holiness
Strand 4: Prophecy	Strand 3: Wisdom

Fifth, as previously noted, we argue in this book that ethical nursing practice involves obedience to laws, regulations and protocols; the cultivation of virtuous habits; decision-making procedures based on evidence, insight and experience; and advocacy for the rights and needs of patients, and that these differing emphases parallel the dominant themes of the four strands of biblical moral discourse, respectively. True, the *Code of Ethics for*

Nurses with Interpretive Statements (ANA, 2015) does not explicitly invoke the Bible as a moral authority, nor does it imply that a person must be a Christian in order to practice nursing ethically. Yet the norms for the character and conduct of nurses set by the *Code* do correspond closely to the overall picture of godly living delineated in the four strands of biblical moral discourse, and our task is to explore these parallels. The way in which the four biblical strands and the major objectives of the corresponding provisions in the *Code* collectively contribute to moral maturity in Christian nurses is illustrated in Figure 0.3.

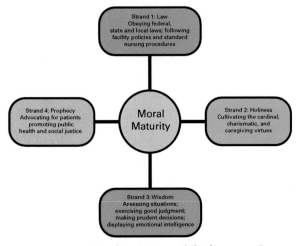

Figure 0.3. *Moral maturity and the four strands*

Our sixth clarification has to do with how we refer to "the nurse." We acknowledge that the history of modern nursing has been heavily female-dominated, but the 2017 National Nursing Workforce Study (Smiley et al., 2018) reports a welcome, steady increase in the numbers of men in the nursing profession. Additionally, we acknowledge that there is now much dialogue about gender identity and the use of preferred pronouns, which may apply to some of our readers (Turner, 2014). In view of these facts, we generally speak of "nurses" in the plural. Wherever we must refer to "the nurse" in the singular, we alternate the usage of male and female pronouns, rather than constantly using awkward or ungrammatical constructions such as "he or she," "s/he," or "they" in a singular sense. We ask the reader to understand that such singular pronouns are intended to apply to every nurse, regardless of gender or sexual orientation.

TWO CAUTIONARY NOTES

Here we must interject two cautions. First, we raise the possibility that Christian nurses might experience a conflict of conscience when reading the *Code* (ANA, 2015), which regards itself as the "nonnegotiable" (p. vii) ethical standard of the profession. We assume that the supreme moral authority for every Christian is the Bible and that one of the chief ways in which thoughtful Christians put their respect for the Bible's moral authority into effect in their personal and professional lives is by using it to test the adequacy of any other proposed moral standard. As it happens, we see nothing in the *Code* that flatly contradicts the moral teachings of the Bible, such that Christian nurses would be obliged in conscience to disobey the former in order to remain faithful to the latter. Nevertheless, Christian nurses cannot accept the *Code*'s claim to be "nonnegotiable in any setting," if that implies that its text is perfectly unambiguous throughout, that its implications for clinical practice are always self-evident, or that questions can never be raised about its adequacy and relevance to specific cases. Yet we presume that the ANA does not intend its members to regard the *Code* in such a "fundamentalist" fashion. For the *Code* itself has a long history of development, which reflects the changes that have taken place in health care and in American society generally over the past century (pp. xi–xiii; Fowler, 2015, pp. vii–ix). Nurses have been asking tough questions of their *Code* since they first had one, and we presume that the ANA intends them to keep doing so. In that case, the *Code* serves as an indispensable working norm for nursing practice, a norm that should not be violated by individual nurses in their daily work but that is always subject to constructive critique, and that can be revised as necessary through due process by the ANA. No Christian nurse should have trouble accepting *that*.

Second, even if Christian nurses can accept the *Code* (ANA, 2015) as morally binding upon their character and conduct, given that the *Code* itself is always revisable and that—for Christian nurses, at least—its moral authority is always subordinate to that of the Bible, there remains another problem. The ethical texts of the Bible are not always self-evident in meaning, nor is the precise manner of their application in specific cases always clear. Thus, although the moral teachings of the Bible are certainly indispensable for Christian nurses in interpreting the *Code*, those teachings themselves require careful theological interpretation and ethical reflection. The method we use here for interpreting our chosen biblical passages is both theological and historical-critical. A few words about these two features of our method are in order.

On the one hand, we read the Bible theologically, that is, as Christian *Scripture*. The church throughout the ages has regarded the Bible as God's authoritative word for God's faithful people, as a testimony to God's sovereign love and redemptive power in (or "behind") human affairs. We are not committed to any particular theory of *how* the human authors of the Bible derived or experienced divine "inspiration." We do, however, affirm that the church, under the guidance of the Holy Spirit, has recognized the voice of God in (or, again, "behind") the writings included within the Bible and regards these writings as uniquely "useful for teaching, rebuking, correcting and training in righteousness" (2 Tim 3:16). Furthermore, we are guided in our reading of the church's sacred *book* by the church's *rule of faith*, that is, the cluster of doctrines and religious practices deemed orthodox by the ancient ecumenical councils and held in common by the Roman Catholic Church, the Eastern Orthodox Church, and most mainline Protestant and Evangelical churches. On the other hand, we read the Bible historico-critically, that is, in light of contemporary research into the history and culture of ancient Mediterranean societies. To interpret a passage of Christian Scripture faithfully obliges us to consider the circumstances under which it was originally written and the needs, problems and worldview of the people for whom it was originally written, at least to the extent that these can be reconstructed through research into the histories, cultures, languages and literary conventions of the ancient Near East. In interpreting Scripture, we regard theological reflection and historical criticism as friendly yokefellows, not fierce adversaries, and virtually all the secondary sources we cite share that view.

The strategy for reading Scripture that we have adopted here draws heavily upon two sources. The first is *The Art of Reading Scripture*, coedited by biblical scholars Ellen F. Davis and Richard B. Hays (2003). Particularly useful is the book's programmatic essay, "Nine Theses on the Interpretation of Scripture" (pp. 1–8). Our second major resource is *Reading the Bible in the Strange World of Medicine*, by theologian and bioethicist Allen Verhey (2003), and particularly *his* programmatic essay, "The Bible and Bioethics: Some Problems and a Proposal" (pp. 32–67). It must be stressed, however, that our reading of the texts we have selected to represent the four strands of biblical moral discourse is sharply focused by an objective that is not envisaged by the essays in the Davis and Hays volume and is only indirectly related to the purpose of the work by Verhey. Our objective is to show how the complex picture of Christian discipleship displayed in the Bible compares with the ethical responsibilities of professional nurses prescribed by the *Code* (ANA, 2015).

THE ORIGINS AND DISTINCTIVENESS OF THIS BOOK

As noted above, we intend this book to be used as a text for nursing ethics courses at Christian colleges and universities, and that is indeed how it came into being in the first place. The authors are faculty members at Seattle Pacific University (SPU). SPU is a church-related institution; its faculty and staff are required to be professing, practicing Christians; its curriculum and campus life are regulated by an official Statement of Faith. Undergraduates are required to take at least two, and usually three, courses in theology and Bible, and all graduate professional programs include one course (or short modules distributed over several courses) in discipline-specific theological reflection. The course from which this book originally sprang, NUR 6301 Values, Faith and Ethics, satisfies this requirement for the Master of Science in Nursing and Doctor of Nursing Practice degrees. It has .been co-taught annually by Steele, a moral theologian, and either Wild or Monroe, both professors of nursing, since 2014. As our curriculum requires, and as our own consciences dictate, we teach the course from an explicitly Christian standpoint, but we neither proselytize our students nor penalize those whose religious views differ from our own. The present book, which arose from the lectures and class discussions for that course, takes the same approach. We try to show how Christian moral and religious convictions match up with the current ethical standards of the nursing profession, as stated in the *Code* (ANA, 2015), and we seek to highlight the spiritual and professional advantages for Christian nurses, who conscientiously apply their faith to their practice. Yet we do not claim that Christians somehow make "better nurses" than non-Christians (cf. Doornbos, Groenhout, & Hotz, 2005, 1–8). We write from a faith perspective, just as we teach. Yet we have no hidden evangelistic agenda and we intend no censure of those whose religious views differ from our own.

The origins of this book help to explain its distinctiveness. On the one hand, little if any attention is given to Christian Scripture in the standard textbooks of bioethics and nursing ethics, such as Beauchamp and Childress (2013), Jonsen, Siegler, and Winslade (2015), Grace (2018), or

Fowler (2015). On the other hand, one finds few if any citations to the *Code* (ANA, 2015) in works that analyze medicine and nursing from a theological perspective, such as O'Brien (2018), Doornbos et al. (2005), Lysaught, Kotva, Lammers, and Verhey (2012), or Thobaben (2009). We draw gratefully upon all these important works in what follows, but we attempt something they do not, namely, to determine what light the Bible sheds on contemporary nursing practice, as normed by the *Code*. See the Annotated Bibliography for a brief explanation of the relationship between those works and this one.

THE USES OF THIS BOOK: A WORD TO EDUCATORS

Here we wish to offer several suggestions for nursing educators who adopt this book for courses in nursing ethics. First, we encourage that it be used in tandem with two other books, namely, a critical, annotated edition of the Bible with the Apocrypha, and Marsha Fowler's (2015) *Guide to the Code of Ethics for Nurses with Interpretive Statements*, which includes the full text of the official *Code* (ANA, 2015) as an appendix. Our task in this book is to identify the connections between the main themes of our chosen biblical texts and of the *Code*, but students will profit greatly from drilling deeper into the primary sources for themselves. Second, we recommend that this book (along with the Bible and Fowler's *Guide*) be used during the first half of the course, and that other resources be used in the second half, especially those that analyze complex issues in contemporary health care or offer thought-provoking case studies in nursing ethics (e.g., Grace, 2018). Our students sometimes report that the material included in the present book seems a bit abstract *until* they apply it to their own practice or to hot-button issues in their field, at which point the framework provided here proves its worth. Third, we suggest that students prepare for the class session during which a given chapter in this book will be under discussion by writing out definitions of the Keywords and answering the Reading Comprehension questions provided at the end of each chapter. Fourth, we propose that in the days *after* a given chapter in this book has been discussed in class, the students be required to answer the Making Connections questions likewise provided at the end of each chapter. This will encourage them to apply the material covered here to their own practice even before moving to the case studies and current issues in the second half of the course. (Note: the Making Connections questions tend to work better with advanced practice nursing [APRN] students, who already have a rich fund of clinical experience under their belts, than with undergraduates, who are still mastering basic skills and concepts.) This learning activity is especially valuable if students have access to an online discussion board, where they can interact with each other's reflections. Examples of such discussion board interactions appear in the Clinical Voices sections toward the end of each chapter.

Figure 0.4. *Nursing postage stamp.* This US postage stamp was issued on December 28, 1961. For details on its historic significance, see Olin (2011, December 8). We display it here as a tribute both to the students in our classes, who have contributed so much to this book, and to the book's intended readers.

CLINICAL VOICES

As the reader begins to discover the connections between Christian Scripture and contemporary nursing, our ultimate hope is that these will be useful in a practical sense. Ideally, the nurse is able to integrate the profession's code of ethics with his personal values and beliefs to provide morally confident and competent patient care. Nurses from many backgrounds have found the discussions of connections described here to be useful on both personal and professional levels. They encountered a new way to wrestle with some of the difficult questions in practice. Each chapter includes some of their thoughts about integrating the strands and *Code* (ANA, 2015) with their individual approaches to practice. These experienced nurses—APRN students, who have deeply engaged in these discussions—have graciously given us permission to share their stories, thoughts and concerns here as a catalyst for discussions among other readers. Here are some of their initial thoughts about the framework of biblical strands connecting to professional nursing ethics:

Arely Garza: *Integrating strands*

> Nursing is a vocation. I have always felt caring for the sick is my calling. Even when considering other career options, they always felt wrong. Jesus cared for and healed the sick outside of work days, an act prohibited on the Sabbath. This demonstrates how nursing is more than a job. Nursing is stressful and often challenging both mentally and physically. My faith and sense of calling provides motivation to continue to care for others even through difficult times. My patient, an older gentleman with cancer, had a complex treatment plan. Over the multiple times I took care of him, my use of the four strands changed. At first, I emphasized the law strand, following policies and procedures to provide the safest care while he was in a critical state; then I became his advocate, committed to involve him in his own care. He had multiple doctors who didn't always communicate well with him. There was an instance where he and his family were frustrated with his care and confused as to what was happening. I pushed the residents to come speak to the family, which then became a care conference.

Cindy Mato: *Situational connections to faith*

> I have never thought much about my decision-making process related to nursing interactions from a spiritual standpoint. I can

honestly say that when I am caring for a difficult or angry patient, I rarely think of God or the Bible. Situations where I lean on God are often related to a critically ill patient—praying for them and asking God to grant me the skill, knowledge, and tools to help the dying patient. During further reflection, I believe my spiritual beliefs and nursing practice are intertwined when I am volunteering. I feel happy and close to God when I am participating in an activity that gives me a sense of purpose, such as volunteering. I can see how the four strands of Law, Holiness, Wisdom, and Prophecy are braided together during these times. I may be helping the oppressed (Prophecy) by using my nursing knowledge and skill (Wisdom) to do something that many others would not be willing to do (Holiness).

Inbok Wee: *Holistic care and collaboration*

The highlight of nursing is that we care for people with a holistic approach, not only for their physical needs but also for their emotional, mental, and social needs as a way to promote their well-being. I had a male patient admitted with malignant hypertensive urgency due to noncompliance of antihypertensive medications. There was not sufficient information about why and how long it had been since he had not taken the medications. One day after his symptoms were relieved, before treatment was completed, he wanted to go home. Once all the detailed information was given to the patient regarding his current condition, treatment, and the risks of incomplete treatment, he got upset and anxious. Later in the day, he opened up to me. He had recently divorced and lost a job, and stated he was depressed. I offered emotional support with therapeutic listening and coordinated with the provider and social worker to provide extensive support for follow-up care, charity medications, medical bills, and counseling. As a primary nurse, I promoted the patient's rights and health with compassion and respect by providing the patient with information and assertive communication regarding his condition, treatment, and risks. By notifying care team members and collaborating with them about my patient's emotional crisis and situation, I made a prompt decision and took accountability to provide optimal care for my patient's health.

Being a nurse, a member of the most trusted profession (Brenan, 2017), is very hard work. It is very much *heart* work, too. As nurses continue to pour themselves into caring for people who are at their most vulnerable, it is our hope that the connections between ethically strong nursing care and Christian Scripture provide a resource for thinking about practice and how nurses may approach the challenges that come on a daily, if not moment-by-moment, basis.

KEYWORDS

1. Canon

2. Holiness

3. Interpretive statement (of the ANA *Code*)

4. Law

5. Prophecy

6. Provision (of the ANA *Code*)

7. Strand (of biblical moral discourse)

8. Wisdom

READING COMPREHENSION

1. What is the aim of this book, and who are its intended readers?

2. How, in general terms, does the book propose to accomplish its aim?

3. What are the four strands of biblical moral discourse, and what are the specific provisions in the ANA *Code*, which this book will correlate with each strand?

4. Summarize the six "points of clarification" offered above.

5. Summarize the two "cautionary notes" offered above.

MAKING CONNECTIONS

1. Nursing is now widely recognized as one of the "professions," along with medicine, law, ordained ministry, etc. This book assumes, however, that, at least for those who self-identify as Christians, it is also a

"vocation," that is, a way of putting their faith into practice. How do you react to that assumption?

2. The ANA *Code* claims to be a "nonnegotiable" ethical guideline for nurses. How do you understand that claim? Have you ever been in a situation that required you to act in a way that was contrary either to the *Code* or to your own conscience? Explain.

3. What are your initial feelings about reading a book that relates Christian Scripture and theology to your chosen profession? Did this introduction address your concerns?

1

The Nurse as Citizen, Professional and Public Servant

The Legal Strand: "Keep the commandments . . . for your own well-being"

DEUT 10:13

Joe Jefferson works in the cardiac care unit of Good Samaritan Hospital. He graduated from nursing school with high honors a year ago and had no difficulty landing his dream job. The learning curve has been steep and the challenges great, but he has loved his work and is highly regarded by his colleagues and patients. One of Nurse Jefferson's favorite patients is Juana Suarez, who suffers from congestive heart failure and has been in and out of the hospital many times this year. Mrs. Suarez is a model patient: she eats a heart-healthy diet, exercises regularly, takes her meds on schedule, and maintains a cheerful disposition through thick and thin. But the end is now near, and she knows it. Nurse Jefferson walks into her room, and she smiles warmly at him, as she always does. Then she tells him, a bit shyly, that she has a special request. She wonders if she can spend what will probably be the last day of her earthly life with Beatriz, the toy poodle who has been her pride and joy for the past ten years. Her family wants to bring Beatriz into the hospital that afternoon and will stay in the room the whole time to assure that the dog is properly cared for. What should Joe say to this request—so reasonable and so touching, and yet so flatly contrary to the state health code and hospital policy?

20

If you had asked Joe yesterday to describe his role as a nurse, he might have said, "Well, as an American *citizen*, I am responsible for knowing and obeying the law, especially national, state and local healthcare law. As a *professional*, I am responsible for knowing and obeying the specific policies and procedures of Good Samaritan Hospital, and beyond that, for knowing and heeding the basic principles of bioethics and the ANA *Code of Ethics for Nurses*. As a *public servant*, I am responsible for meeting the physical and emotional needs of my patients and their families. And as a *Christian*, I am responsible for following Jesus—which for me means being a good citizen, a model professional and a faithful public servant, but which extends further and runs deeper than all of those other roles." That was yesterday's answer, when the specific responsibilities of his four roles seemed perfectly compatible—as, indeed, they usually are. But this is today, when "clinical judgment" and "patient care" seem to demand different answers to Mrs. Suarez's request (Benner, Tanner, & Chesla, 1996), and when the law of the land prohibits what the "law of Christ" seems to demand (Gal 6:2). It is one thing to advocate for "radical transformation" (Benner, Sutphen, Leonard, & Day, 2010) in healthcare practice and policy for the sake of a beloved patient, but quite another to pursue a course of action that might cost you your job, and indeed, might jeopardize the welfare of other patients on the unit.

The present chapter does not resolve Joe's dilemma. But it does explore the topic of law and its relevance for the practice of Christian nursing. It assumes that the respective responsibilities of citizenship, professionalism, public service and Christian discipleship are indeed generally in close alignment, as Joe has long believed, and leaves to subsequent chapters the question of how to handle the occasional tensions among them. It proceeds by distinguishing three types of law: *divine law, positive law* and *physical law*; by exploring the relationships among them; and by showing how each individually, and all three together, inform our understanding of the vocation of Christian nursing and account for the close intersectionality among the roles of citizen, professional, public servant and Christian disciple.

In section 1, we examine divine law as attested in Christian Scripture. First, we look at the Ten Commandments, which are foundational to the legal thinking of the Bible. Then we examine two other legal texts, Deuteronomy 10:12–21 and Luke 10:25–37, which clarify the *purpose* of divine law and reveal that God intends the law for our "well-being" (Deut 10:13). In section 2 we turn to positive law, which comprises the vast array of laws made by human beings to regulate their conduct and relationships.

We include in the category of positive law both civil laws, especially those pertaining to health care, and the rules, regulations, protocols and standard operating procedures of healthcare institutions. We show how Provisions 1–3 of the *Code* (ANA, 2015) provide the moral rationale for obedience to these positive laws. In section 3, we turn to physical law, which refers to the observable patterns and cycles in nature. We show how Florence Nightingale, the founder of modern nursing, applied the concept of the physical law to health care and nursing practice. Section 4 comprises several reflections by our students on the relationship between law and nursing. The chapter concludes with various teaching/learning helps (Sections 5–7).

LAW IN CHRISTIAN SCRIPTURE

In studying the Bible's concept of divine law, we must bear three things in mind. First, the terms for law in the Christian Scriptures (Hebrew = *torah*; Greek = *nomos*) have important connotations that are often missing in the English equivalent (Harrelson, 1962, p. 77). *Torah* (or *nomos*) can certainly refer to legislation in the narrow sense, that is, to the specific rules and regulations that govern God's people's public life. But *torah* is more than legislation; it is also instruction. When God commands, God teaches, and the sovereignty exercised by God as the sovereign Lawgiver is tempered by the warmth and loving-kindness displayed by a devoted parent to her children or a dedicated teacher to her pupils. Conversely, when God teaches, God commands, and God's instructions have the force of law. The biblical word for the relationship between God and God's people is "covenant" (Hebrew = *berith*; Greek = *diathēkē*), a word that represents a reciprocal bond of love, trust and commitment, but that always recalls God's role as the "senior partner." *Torah* thus represents the "terms" of the *berith* that God established with his people, and which God faithfully and mercifully continues to uphold, even when his people fail to do their part. Thus, the word *torah* is often used by Jews to refer to the *story* of the relationship between God and God's people, particularly that part of the story told in the first five books of the Bible. These books— Genesis, Exodus, Leviticus, Numbers and Deuteronomy, sometimes known collectively as the Pentateuch (Greek *pente* = "five" + *teuchos* = "scroll")— contain plenty of legislation, as we shall see. Yet that legislation is embedded in the story of the covenant relationship between God and God's people; and the purpose of that legislation is to keep the story going—that is, to keep the relationship intact. It is worth noting the highlights of the pentateuchal story:

- The creation of the world; the creation of humanity; the disobedience of humanity; divine punishments, punctuated by continued divine care (Gen 1:1—11:9).

- The establishment of God's covenant with Abraham and his descendants; their journey to and settlement of the "promised land" of Canaan, despite great hardship, fierce opposition and internal dissension (Gen 11:10—36:43).

- The decision by Abraham's descendants—known as "Hebrews" or "Israelites"—to leave Canaan in a time of famine and settle in Egypt (Gen 37:1—50:26).

- The enslavement of the Hebrews by the Egyptians, and their eventual deliverance by Moses (Exod 1:1—15:21).

- The wanderings of the Israelites in the wilderness of Sinai, sustained by God's provision, despite their doubts and dissatisfactions (Exod 15:22—18:27).

- God's delivery of the Ten Commandments and other legislation, through Moses, to the Israelites (Exod 19:1—31:18).

- God's faithfulness to the Israelites, and his continued care for their needs, despite their rebelliousness and repeated disobedience (Exod 32:1—40:38; Num 1:1—36:13).

- Further legislation, in anticipation of the establishment of a sovereign Israelite state in the land of Canaan (Lev 1:1—27:34; Deut 1:1—34:12).

To reiterate: the fact that Israel received its law as the crowning moment in a train of events in which God displayed his faithfulness to his people and his abiding care for their well-being, despite their frequent lapses and grumblings, decisively shaped how they came to understand the meaning of the law for their lives. It was not an expression of God's naked power and arbitrary will; it was an "instruction manual" for a way of life that promised blessing and security.[1]

1. Hauerwas and Willimon (1999) recount a charming rabbinic story that illustrates this: Someone asked "why, if the Ten Commandments are so important, God waited so long on the Exodus to give them to Israel. The rabbis answered, 'Suppose a man entered a city and said, "I shall rule over you." The inhabitants would say, "Who are you and what have you done for us?" What did the man do? He built a city wall, aqueducts, led them in battles. Then he declared, "I shall rule over you," and they gladly said "Yes!"' Similarly, God brought Israel out of Egypt, divided the Red Sea, provided food, then, late in the Exodus, God said, 'I shall rule over you,' and Israel answered, 'Yes indeed.'" (p. 17).

CHRISTIAN ETHICS AND NURSING PRACTICE

Second, modern secular people do not ordinarily think of law as a blessing or privilege. They may acknowledge that society cannot function without laws and believe that one measure of a just society is the equity with which its legal system apportions goods and services among its citizens, imposes civic obligations upon them (e.g., taxes and military service), adjudicates conflicts and prosecutes offenders. On this view, law is a necessary condition for establishing civil peace and maintaining order and prosperity, but it is hardly the object of anyone's joy or gratitude. Yet the Israelites thought differently—at least about *God's* law. They regarded it as a gracious divine gift and as a necessary condition for the eventual establishment of their nation-state—a story told in the books immediately following the Pentateuch (Joshua, Judges, 1–2 Samuel, and 1–2 Kings). Moreover, they understood obedience to *torah*, not as grudging compliance with the arbitrary will of an overlord, but as a way of life that assured their independence, blessedness and prosperity. Psalm 119 expresses the deep joy that God's people felt in God's law and is well worth reading at this point.

Third, when examining the actual legislation embedded in the early history of Israel, we discover two cross-cutting distinctions. The first is the distinction between "apodictic" laws and "casuistic" laws. Apodictic laws are unconditional and absolute, whereas casuistic laws are conditional and situation-specific (Matthews, 2000; Mendenhall, 1970a/1954). The second distinction is between "vertical" laws and "horizontal" laws. *Vertical* laws are those that govern Israel's relationship with God, whereas horizontal laws are those that govern relationships among God's people. The catch is that some apodictic laws are vertical, while others are horizontal; similarly, some casuistic laws are vertical and others horizontal. Table 1.1 illustrates how these distinctions interact and cites a specific biblical law that exemplifies each pairing. Any given law can be placed in one of the four boxes in this table. Yet whichever box it is placed in, it still possesses divine authority. (Note, however, that Christians hold that some Old Testament laws have been abrogated or significantly qualified with the coming of Christ or must be reinterpreted in light of the new covenant with God that he inaugurated.)

Table 1.1. Two Cross-Cutting Distinctions	
Apodictic Vertical (unconditional and God-directed): "You shall have no other gods before me" (Exod 20:3; Deut 5:7).	Apodictic Horizontal (unconditional and community-directed): "You shall not steal" (Exod 20:15; Deut 5:19).
Casuistic Vertical (situation-specific and God-directed): "If anyone secretly entices you . . . saying, 'Let us go worship other gods,' whom neither you nor your ancestors have known, . . . you must not yield to or heed any such persons" (Deut 13:6–8).	Casuistic Horizontal (situation-specific and community-directed): "If you go into your neighbor's vineyard, you may eat your fill of grapes, as many as you wish, but you shall not put any in a container" (Deut 23:24).

Let us now go a bit deeper into these two distinctions. The first, between apodictic and casuistic law, pertains to the *source* of their authority and the *reach* of their application. The word *apodictic* comes from the Greek word *apodeiknumi*, which means to declare, to reveal or to show forth. Thus, an apodictic law is one that is revealed by God to humanity and is meant to apply to all members of God's people, at all times, and in all situations. God is the sovereign Lord of Israel and issues certain laws that have universal and unconditional application. These are stated in the imperative mood: "Thou shalt do this" or "Thou shalt not do that." There are no ifs, ands or buts about them—no qualifiers, conditionals, exemptions or extenuations. The primary collection of apodictic laws in the Old Testament is the Ten Commandments or Decalogue, found in two slightly different versions (Exod 20:1–21; Deut 5:1–21) and quoted or referenced in numerous other places throughout the Bible (e.g., Exod 31:18; 34:1, 28; Lev 19:1–18; Deut 10:1–5; Matt 19:16–22; Mark 10:17–22; Luke 18:18–25; Rom 13:8–10).

To understand how an apodictic law works, consider the fifth commandment, which states, "Honor your father and mother" (Exod 20:12; Deut 5:16). This does not mean simply "Send flowers on Mother's Day" or "Throw a surprise party on their fiftieth anniversary." Flowers and surprise parties are great, but the duty to honor one's parents is in force for as long as they are alive. Similarly, the eighth commandment states, "You shall not steal" (Exod 20:15; Deut 5:10). In Victor Hugo's (1982) novel, *Les Misérables*, Jean Valjean is convicted of stealing a loaf of bread to save his starving family. That he was sentenced to hard labor was clearly unjust—not because his theft wasn't wrong but because the punishment was out of all proportion to the severity of the crime, and because the extenuating circumstances were not considered by the authorities. We are certainly meant to sympathize with Valjean against his nemesis, the police officer Javert, who represented a government that regarded property rights as more important than human lives. Yet the fact remains that Jean broke the eighth commandment. Apodictic laws are always and everywhere in force.

In contrast, casuistic laws are situation-specific. The word *casuistic* derives from the Latin word *casus*, meaning "case." Case laws reflect the long experience of God's people—their tried-and-true mores and social conventions and their accumulated wisdom about communal life. These laws often reflect very specific times, places, social circumstances and historical conditions. Moreover, they have a different form than apodictic laws. Whereas apodictic laws read, "Thou shalt do this" or "Thou shalt not do that," case laws read, "In such and such a situation, do thus and so," or "When this is so, do not do that." For example, consider Deuteronomy 23:24: "If you go into your neighbor's vineyard, you may eat your fill of grapes, as many as you wish, but you shall not put any in a container." Note three things about this law. First, it could not have been laid down when God's people were wandering nomads in the Sinai Desert. Nomads do not dress vineyards, and therefore do not need laws to regulate grape theft. Such a law presupposes the social and economic circumstances of a settled agricultural people—such as the Hebrews became after they reoccupied the promised land. Thus, as times change, case laws change. Second, this piece of case law is based on an apodictic law. It is a specification of the eighth commandment, which forbids stealing—in this case, taking away your neighbor's grapes in a basket. But it also says that someone who, while out hiking on a hot day, passes by a vineyard and plucks a handful of grapes for refreshment is not stealing at all. The hiker must respect the vintner's property, but the vintner must respect the hiker's life. For that, too, is protected by apodictic law, specifically the sixth commandment (Exod 20:13; Deut 5:17), which prohibits murder. Refusing to let a starving passerby have a few grapes would be tantamount to homicide. Case law applies common sense to human affairs, balancing people's competing claims and bringing the lofty general principles stated in apodictic laws down to ground level.

Or to return to our previous example, the plot of *Les Misérables* (Hugo, 1982) turns on the fact that although stealing is indisputably illegal, the circumstances of Valjean's actual theft were not considered at his trial, and thus the cruel enforcement of the law proved a greater injustice than the crime itself. We must bear a third point in mind, too. The fact that case law is situation-specific and reflects daily experience does not mean that it lacks divine authority. Rather, it means that God is concerned about the day-to-day particulars of our lives.

As we have noted, the weightiest collection of apodictic laws in the Bible is the Ten Commandments. These set forth the general principles on which all case laws are ultimately based. We are told that God inscribed the commandments on "two tables of stone" and ordered Moses to deliver them to the people waiting at the foot of Mount Sinai (Exod 31:18). Although the text does not specifically say this, ancient tradition has it that the first four commandments were inscribed on the first table, while the last six were inscribed on the second. This brings us back to the second distinction regarding divine law that we mentioned earlier, namely, the distinction between "vertical" or God-directed commandments, and "horizontal" or community-related commandments. Commandments one through four all pertain to the way God's people are to demonstrate their veneration to God himself, and commandments five through ten pertain to the way God's people are to demonstrate their respect for each other as members of God's covenant community.[2]

2. The Bible does not specifically number the Ten Commandments. Most religious groups accept the differentiation between the God-directed ("vertical") commandments of the first table and the community-directed ("horizontal") commandments of the second. But some groups (e.g., Catholics and Lutherans) conjoin what is shown in Table 1.2 as the first and second commandments and divide what is there shown as the tenth into two. This procedure puts *three* commandments on the first table and *seven* on the second (as illustrated in Philippe de Champaigne's painting below). We are following the numbering used by most Protestant (e.g., Calvin, 1960, pp. 376–417) and Eastern Orthodox Christians. Jews, for their part, regard the "prefatory" statement in the first commandment ("I am the LORD your God . . .") *as* the first commandment, fuse the prohibitions against "having other gods" and "making idols" into the second, and thereafter follow the same numbering used here.

First Table: "Vertical" Laws	Second Table: "Horizontal" Laws
(Exod 20:2–11; Deut 5:6–15)	(Exod 20:12–17; Deut 5:16–21)

Table 1.2. The Two Tables of the Law

First Table: "Vertical" Laws (Exod 20:2–11; Deut 5:6–15)	Second Table: "Horizontal" Laws (Exod 20:12–17; Deut 5:16–21)
1. I am the LORD your God, who brought you out of the land of Egypt, out of the house of slavery; you shall have no other gods before me.	5. Honor your father and your mother, so that your days may be long in the land that the LORD your God is giving you.
2. You shall not make for yourself an idol, whether in the form of anything that is in heaven above, or that is on the earth beneath, or that is in the water under the earth. . . .	6. You shall not murder.
	7. You shall not commit adultery.
	8. You shall not steal.
	9. You shall not bear false witness against your neighbor.
3. You shall not make wrongful use of the name of the LORD your God, for the LORD will not acquit anyone who misuses his name.	10. You shall not covet your neighbor's house; you shall not covet your neighbor's wife, or male or female slave, or ox, or donkey, or anything that belongs to your neighbor.
4. Remember the Sabbath day, and keep it holy. Six days you shall labor and do all your work. But the seventh day is a Sabbath to the LORD your God; you shall not do any work. . . .	

The story of the delivery of the divine law in Exodus 19–39 is exceptionally dramatic. It involves a theophany, a cataclysmic appearance of God himself. God not only reveals his *will* for his people through Moses at the summit of Mount Sinai. He reveals *himself* to them—in thunder and lightning and thick cloud, in fire and smoke, in a voice like a trumpet blast (Exod 19:16–20). Does this mean that God's majestic sovereignty is nothing more than naked, arbitrary power, or that God's law is an alien and arbitrary imposition upon people, who have no choice except to obey it? If that were so, God would be nothing more than a wilder and more brutal version of Pharaoh, a deity who takes sadistic delight in giving capricious orders to powerless slaves. But it is not so. Once again, we must consider the placement of this episode in the overall narrative structure of the Pentateuch. The delivery of the law on Mount Sinai is the culmination of Israel's liberation from bondage in Egypt and sets the stage for their new life as an independent nation in the promised land. The divine law is both Israel's charter of freedom and the "terms" of its relationship with the Lawgiver.

Figure 1.1. Phillipe de Champaigne, *Moses and the Ten Commandments* [oil on canvas]. (1648). 92 cm x 75 cm. The Hermitage, St. Petersburg, Russia

With this in mind, let us look at the Ten Commandments again. Table 1.3 shows the Ten Commandments, as delivered to Moses, on the left, and a "reframed" version on the right.[3]

3. The following discussion of the Ten Commandments draws freely from the following sources: Brueggemann (1994, pp. 839–52), Calvin (1960, pp. 376–417), Luther

Table 1.3. The Ten Commandments: Mosaic and Reframed

The Ten Commandments: Mosaic Version (Exod 20:2–17; Deut 5:6–21)	The Ten Commandments Reframed (Exod 20:12–17; Deut 5:16–21)
1. I am the LORD your God, who brought you out of the land of Egypt, out of the house of slavery; you shall have no other gods before me.	God has no rivals. Therefore, God's people can accept no other supreme authority over them, and must judge all human rulers, laws and institutions by the moral standards established by God, as stated by the other nine commandments.
2. You shall not make for yourself an idol, whether in the form of anything that is in heaven above, or that is on the earth beneath, or that is in the water under the earth. . . .	Nothing in creation can make God visible or comprehensible. Any religious practice or social custom that absolutizes the relative is self-delusory and/or oppressive.
3. You shall not make wrongful use of the name of the LORD your God, for the LORD will not acquit anyone who misuses his name.	God cannot be manipulated for human purposes or used for human ends. Any religious practice or social custom that relativizes the Absolute is, again, self-delusory or oppressive.
4. Remember the Sabbath and keep it holy. Six days you shall labor and do all your work. But the seventh day is a Sabbath to the LORD your God; you shall not do any work. . . .	God liberates us not only from tyrannical social and political systems but also from oppressive systems of economic production and from addictive patterns of consumption.
5. Honor your father and your mother, so that your days may be long in the land that the LORD your God is giving you.	God expects us to hold family relationships sacred and inviolable.
6. You shall not murder.	God expects us to hold human life sacred and inviolable.
7. You shall not commit adultery.	God expects us to hold the marriage bond sacred and inviolable.
8. You shall not steal.	God grants to us the right to provide for our own basic needs, and those of our family, and to contribute through our labor to the general prosperity of the community.

(1959, pp. 365–411), Hauerwas and Willimon (1999), and Mendenhall (1970a/1954, 1970b/1954).

9.	You shall not bear false witness against your neighbor.	God expects us to hold the truth sacred and inviolable. Our word should be our bond in legal testimonies, commercial transactions and interpersonal relationships.
10.	You shall not covet your neighbor's house; you shall not covet your neighbor's wife, or male or female slave, or ox, or donkey, or anything that belongs to your neighbor.	God expects us to respect the proper boundaries between what is ours and what belongs to others, and not to cherish fantasies of appropriating what does not belong to us.

The reframed version shows that each law aims either to prevent behavior that will in the long run be destructive to Israel's life-giving relationship with God or to mandate behavior that is needed for Israel's safety, security and prosperity. Thus, the first commandment affirms that before God was Israel's lawgiver, he was Israel's liberator. God had made Pharaoh's slaves his own children, and they would henceforth regard him—and no human ruler—as their true sovereign. God had thus reserved the right to stand in judgment of any human ruler who might oppress God's people or enact legislation at odds with the divine commandments (see 1 Sam 8:1–22; Dan 3:1–30; Amos 7:10–17; 2 Macc 7:1–42). The second commandment forbids idolatry—which is to say, it forbids treating any created thing as if it were of absolute value. The third forbids any wrongful use of God's Name: reframed, it prohibits us from treating the Absolute as a means to our ends, via magical incantations and superstitious ceremonies. The fourth, which requires people to set aside a day of rest and worship each week, prevents us from succumbing to the totalizing demands of political, military and economic systems, which would reduce us once again to peonage and wage slavery. A similar reframing can be done of the six commandments of the second table. These require the honoring of one's parents and prohibit murder, adultery, robbery, false witness and covetousness. Reframed—that is, expansively interpreted—they oblige every social, political, legal and economic system to promote the common good of its citizens, by affirming that things indispensable to human life and social stability must be held sacred and inviolable.

The moral law of God maps out the way of life for the people with whom God has established his everlasting covenant and states what the people must do to uphold their end of the relationship. They do so in the confident hope that God, in his faithfulness, will provide for their needs and protect their interests. Yet it is important to bear in mind that the relationship between God and Israel *is* a covenant, not merely a contract. That is, it is a reciprocal commitment of love and trust, not a quid pro quo arrangement that holds only as long as both parties find it advantageous (Mendenhall, 1970a, 1970b). Remembering the covenantal quality of the relationship is crucial, because it prevents God's people from an error that might follow from regarding the relationship merely as a contract. That error would be to obey the moral law from purely mercenary motives—or worse yet, to refrain from disobeying it for fear of punishment by the "senior partner"—or worst of all, to flagrantly disobey it out of the despairing or cynical belief that God had forgotten his people. When the people bear the true logic of covenant in mind, however, their obedience to the moral law is driven by joyful gratitude for what God has always done for them and may be trusted to continue doing for them. They regard the divine law as the *terms* of a relationship that God established with them out of love for them, out of his gracious desire to be in communion with them, and out of his parental concern for their flourishing. Consequently, they regard their own obedience to those terms as a grateful response to God's gracious initiative, not as an onerous burden.

Let us turn now to two scriptural texts that vividly illustrate these points. The first is Deuteronomy 10:12–21, which the NRSV titles "the essence of the law," and which one scholar describes as a "declaration of basic principle" (von Rad, 1966, p. 83).

> [12] *So now, O Israel, what does the LORD your God require of you?*
> *Only to fear the LORD your God, to walk in all his ways, to love him,*
> *to serve the LORD your God with all your heart and with all your*
> *soul,* [13] *and to keep the commandments of the LORD your God and*
> *his decrees that I am commanding you today, for your own well-*
> *being.* [14] *Although heaven and the heaven of heavens belong to the*
> *LORD your God, the earth with all that is in it,* [15] *yet the LORD set his*
> *heart in love on your ancestors alone and chose you, their descen-*
> *dants after them, out of all the peoples, as it is today.* [16] *Circumcise,*
> *then, the foreskin of your heart, and do not be stubborn any longer.*
> [17] *For the LORD your God is God of gods and Lord of lords, the great*
> *God, mighty and awesome, who is not partial and takes no bribe,*
> [18] *who executes justice for the orphan and the widow, and who loves*
> *the strangers, providing them food and clothing.* [19] *You shall also*
> *love the stranger, for you were strangers in the land of Egypt.* [20] *You*
> *shall fear the LORD your God; him alone you shall worship; to him*
> *you shall hold fast, and by his name you shall swear.* [21] *He is your*

praise; he is your God, who has done for you these great and awe-some things that your own eyes have seen. (Deut 10:12–21)

Three points about this passage stand out for our purposes. First, God's four requirements of his people—that they fear him, that they walk in his ways, that they love him, and that they serve him wholeheartedly—are linked as different aspects of an integral whole. Life in covenant with God involves much more than outward conformity with the Mosaic law. It also includes the humble veneration of God in his majestic holiness, as well as "a response of love and whole-hearted surrender" to him (von Rad, 1966, p. 83). The people's inward disposition must be congruent with their public performance. This point is underscored in verse 16, where circumcision, which had previously been construed as a physical sign of (a male's) membership in the covenant community, is reinterpreted to indicate a person's "commitment to God . . . and personal obedience to the commandments" (Clements, 2003, p. 260).

Second, God's people are to understand that what God requires of them is a faithful and grateful response to what God has been doing and is continuing to do for them. Divine grace is manifest to the enslaved as liberation, and to the liberated as legislation. And the appropriate response to liberation *and* legislation is worship and praise. We have already seen that people's inward disposition should be congruent with their public performance; now we see that this inward disposition is to include both reverent memory and joyful celebration.

Third, those members of the covenant community for whom God himself feels a particular concern, and whom God expects the community to protect and provide for, are those who are most vulnerable and most easily overlooked: orphans, widows and resident aliens (Clements, 1998, p. 369). The reason given for this expectation is that the covenant people today are one with their overworked, marginalized ancestors, whom God had redeemed from Egyptian servitude. Not only is God's law an expression of God's grace, but God's law stipulates that God's people be gracious—not by showing condescending pity to "the deserving poor," but rather by making just and humane provision for those at greatest risk of impoverishment, exploitation and debt slavery.

The second passage that we intend to examine for insight into the biblical conception of divine law is Luke 10:25–37. This passage includes Luke's version of "the love command," which is found in one form or another in all four gospels and in many other books of the New Testament (Furnish,

1972). It also includes the parable (or more precisely, "example story," per Furnish, 1972, p. 39; Fitzmyer, 1985, p. 883; Jeremias, 1966, p. 160) of the Good Samaritan, which is found only in the Gospel of Luke.

> [25] *Just then a lawyer stood up to test Jesus. "Teacher," he said, "what must I do to inherit eternal life?"* [26] *He said to him, "What is written in the law? What do you read there?"* [27] *He answered, "You shall love the Lord your God with all your heart, and with all your soul, and with all your strength, and with all your mind; and your neighbor as yourself."* [28] *And he said to him, "You have given the right answer; do this, and you will live."*
>
> [29] *But wanting to justify himself, he asked Jesus, "And who is my neighbor?"* [30] *Jesus replied, "A man was going down from Jerusalem to Jericho, and fell into the hands of robbers, who stripped him, beat him, and went away, leaving him half dead.* [31] *Now by chance a priest was going down that road; and when he saw him, he passed by on the other side.* [32] *So likewise a Levite, when he came to the place and saw him, passed by on the other side.* [33] *But a Samaritan while traveling came near him; and when he saw him, he was moved with pity.* [34] *He went to him and bandaged his wounds, having poured oil and wine on them. Then he put him on his own animal, brought him to an inn, and took care of him.* [35] *The next day he took out two denarii, gave them to the innkeeper, and said, 'Take care of him; and when I come back, I will repay you whatever more you spend.'* [36] *Which of these three, do you think, was a neighbor to the man who fell into the hands of the robbers?"* [37] *He said, "The one who showed him mercy." Jesus said to him, "Go and do likewise." (Luke 10:25–37)*

Four points about this passage are especially germane to our argument: First, Jesus' interlocutor is a "lawyer," that is, a rabbinic scholar trained in the interpretation of the Hebrew Bible and Jewish case law. This lawyer has come to "test" Jesus. Now the Greek verb used here (*ekpeirazō*) and its cognate (*peirazō*) mean both "to test" and "to tempt," and it is worth noting that these terms appear three times in Luke's version of the story of Jesus' temptation by the devil (Luke 4:2, 12, 13). So we can assume some degree of hostile intent toward Jesus on the part of the lawyer, though it is not clear whether the lawyer is trying to determine the extent of Jesus' *knowledge*—for he, the lawyer, is a pedigreed specialist in these matters, whereas Jesus is, from his point of view, an upstart layman from the back country (cf. Jeremias, 1966, p. 159)—or to expose any elements of *unorthodoxy* that may infect Jesus' message. In any case, Jesus avoids the trap, if it is a trap, by answering the lawyer's question, "What must I do to inherit eternal life?" with one of his own, "What is written in the law?" (vv. 25–26). Although Jesus has turned the tables, he has *not* changed the subject. To us it might look as if Jesus has induced the lawyer to give a "legal" answer to a "religious" question. But to understand this story properly, we must remember that for first-century Jews, "law" and "religion" were not separate domains. As we saw above, one stood in a right relationship with God *by* obeying the divine commandments. That is just what the lawyer affirms in his twofold summary of the 613 laws of the Hebrew Bible (Caird, 1972, p. 148). One attains "eternal life" by offering wholehearted love of God (Deut 6:5) and by loving one's neighbor as oneself (Lev 19:18). Jesus immediately confirms the correctness of this summary, adding that these formulas must be put into concrete action. Significantly, Jesus does *not* dispute the appropriateness of the lawyer's quest for eternal life or the legitimacy of self-love as such. Up to this point, the exchange between Jesus and the lawyer seems quite in line with what is said in Deuteronomy 10:13 about "keeping the commandments . . . for one's own well-being." Prudent self-interest as such is taken for granted, even though sincere love of God and neighbor are far more than prudent self-interest.

But, second, things take a turn for the worse when the lawyer asks a follow-up question: "And who is my neighbor?" (v. 29). The Greek term for neighbor, *plēsion*, literally means "one who is nearby." The issue here is clearly not geography, however; it is covenant kinship. The lawyer wants to know exactly who qualifies as his neighbor under the law and assumes that he bears no responsibility for anyone who does not. Jesus counters with the story of the traveler who fell among thieves, the priest and the Levite who passed him by, and the Samaritan who stopped to help. As many commentators have noted, this story amounts to a refusal to accept the religious validity of any attempt to set limits on the reach of neighbor-love. The *real* question is whether one acts *as* a neighbor to anyone who needs care. In the story, the one who acted as the true *plēsion*, the one who "came near," was the Samaritan, who might have appealed to his religion and ethnicity as grounds to "pass by." In shocking contrast, the two religious officials, who should have known that it was their duty to stop and help the injured traveler, rushed on.

Third, although Jews and Samaritans shared a common religious heritage and remained "neighbors" in the geographical sense, they were, by Jesus' time, bitter enemies, and generally had nothing to do with each other. For Jesus to answer a question posed by a Jewish lawyer, in the presence of a Jewish audience, with a tale in which a Samaritan was the hero and two Jewish religious officials were the villains was highly inflammatory. For the fundamental point of contention between Jews and Samaritans was over which people represented "the true Israel," the proper heirs of the Mosaic covenant. Jesus was suggesting to his fellow Jews that by obeying the divine requirement to "feed and clothe the stranger" (cf. Deut 10:18), the Samaritan showed himself to be not only "neighbor to the man" (v. 36) but "an Israelite indeed" (cf. John 1:47). Fidelity to the law is not a matter of ethnic purity.

Figure 1.2. Vincent van Gogh, *The Good Samaritan (after Delacroix)* [oil on canvas]. (1890). 73 cm x 60 cm. Rijksmuseum Kröller-Müller, Otterlo, Netherlands

Finally, the NRSV translation of Luke 10:33 says of the Samaritan that when he saw the man lying half dead in the ditch he was "moved with pity." The Greek verb here is *esplanchnisthē*, which is related to the noun *splanchnon*, meaning the vital organs or "innards." So the Lukan text literally states that the Samaritan's "guts churned" at the sight of the mugging victim's sufferings. Or as Eugene Peterson (2002) elegantly renders it, "his heart went out to him" (p. 1878). What the Samaritan had that the priest and the Levite lacked was what Paul calls *splanchna oiktirmou*, that is, "bowels of mercy" (Col 3:12; cf. Phil 2:1). In effect, Jesus was asking the lawyer, "Do you have

36

the guts to go beyond your little circle of legal obligation and tend to human need wherever you find it?"

Yet the problem lies not with the *law* as such but with *legalism*. A legalist is someone who scrupulously abides by the *wording* of the law while ignoring its *purpose*, namely, the protection of the rights and interests of the community. The legalist obeys the law to avoid trouble or to protect himself, without considering the needs of his neighbor. This, however, is to misunderstand the divine law, which is ordered toward human flourishing, and to forget that true obedience to the divine law is personal commitment to the neighbor's good. As we have seen, the Mosaic *torah*—or at least the summaries of it found in Deuteronomy 10:12–21 and Luke 10:25–27—seeks to overcome precisely the vicious tendencies to which legalism is prone. Let us now explore the relevance of all this for Christian nursing.

THE CODE OF ETHICS FOR NURSES, PROVISIONS 1–3

Whenever the *Code* (ANA, 2015) refers to legal matters at all, it refers not to *divine* law but to what we call *positive* law. This is law that has been "posited" by some constituted authority for the just and peaceful ordering of the lives of the people under its jurisdiction; for the establishment of their safety, security, liberty and prosperity; for the defense of their rights as human beings or citizens; and for the efficient and harmonious conduct of public business. Positive law operates at many levels: international, federal, state, county and municipal. For our purposes, the term will also include the rules, regulations, policies, protocols, mandates and standard operating procedures of any facility in which a nurse might work. Of course, "private" facilities such as hospitals, clinics, doctors' offices and nursing homes have no authority to pass "laws" in the strict sense, but they do operate under the jurisdiction of various governmental bodies, and such rules and regulations as they institute for their staff must accord with civil law. Any positive law (using that term in its broadest sense) that brings about an inequitable distribution of goods and services, or burdens and sacrifices, is by that very fact unjust. Accordingly, its revision or repeal is morally warranted, whether or not it is immediately politically feasible. The point here is that any positive law, to the extent that it is just, is congruent with divine law, as described above, precisely to the extent that it promotes general human flourishing.

References to positive law, and more specifically to the moral duty of nurses to contribute to society's efforts to promote human flourishing through legislation and various regulatory measures, though sprinkled throughout the *Code* (ANA, 2015), are found most pronouncedly in Provisions 1–3. It is to these three provisions that we now turn.

Provision 1 states, "The nurse practices with compassion and respect for the inherent dignity, worth, and unique attributes of every person" (ANA, 2015, p. 1). The "interpretive statements" for this provision emphasize that nurses "provide leadership in the development and implementation of changes in public and health policies" (p. 1); that they must "establish relationships of trust and provide nursing services according to need," regardless of the patient's nationality, gender or ethnic identity, primary language, religious affiliation, cultural background, socioeconomic status or health status (pp. 1–2); that they must recognize the patient's right to "self-determination" (pp. 2–3); and that they must "maintain professional, respectful, and caring relationships with colleagues" (p. 4). All this is in general accord with the principle of "equality before the law," which is fundamental to American jurisprudence. It is also, though less directly, in accord with the principle that all human beings are made in the image of God (Gen 1:26–27; 9:6; cf. Ps 8:5–6; Col 1:15; 3:10), which is fundamental to Christian medical ethics (see, e.g., Doornbos et al., 2005, pp. 29–30; Verhey, 2003, pp. 84–86; Reinders, 2008, pp. 227–275). More specifically, nurses are reminded that they "have an obligation to be familiar with and to understand the moral and legal rights of patients" in all cases (ANA, 2015, p. 2); that in cases of terminal illness they "must be knowledgeable about the benefits and limitations of various advance directive documents," which have quasi-binding legal force on healthcare providers, subject to "the rights of others, . . . the demands of law, . . . and the public's health" (p. 3); and that among the many roles that nurses play, there are several, including "administrator, educator, policy maker, researcher, and consultant," which go beyond bedside patient care and extend to the public welfare (p. 4). In short, Provision 1 stresses that nurses must pay close attention to the regulatory environment of contemporary health care, because their role in the system is both highly visible and profoundly influential on patient well-being.

Provision 2 states, "The nurse's primary commitment is to the patient, whether an individual, family, group, community or population" (ANA, 2015, p. 5). This provision makes somewhat less reference to legal issues than the previous one, at least directly. But after affirming that "the nurse's primary commitment is to the recipients of nursing and healthcare services," it acknowledges the moral complexities of many clinical situations, in which the claims of the various parties involved (patients, their families and employers, the medical staff, the hospital administration and the insurance company) can easily conflict, and in which the possibility of adversarial litigation may arise (pp. 5–6). To reduce the possibility of such conflicts, and to minimize the expense and rancor they can produce when they do arise, nurses, who are often caught in the middle of them, must practice the arts of collaboration and attend respectfully to all interests and points of view, while still upholding the distinctive perspective of their own profession (p. 6). Provision 2 closes with a discussion of the ways in which the deeply personal nature of nursing care can easily lead to "boundary violations" between the nurse and the patient or the patient's family. Scrupulous attention by the nurse to professional ethical standards and institutional policies is both morally obligatory and in the best interests of all parties.

Legal issues are central to Provision 3, which reads, "The nurse promotes, advocates for, and protects the rights, health, and safety of the patient" (ANA, 2015, p. 9). The opening section deals with the protection of the patient's rights of privacy and confidentiality, and although the Health Insurance Portability and Accountability Act of 1996 is not directly referenced, it is clearly in view, and the possibility that it will be violated (perhaps quite unintentionally) by the improper use of social media or the inappropriate handling of patient records and medical research data is noted (pp. 9–10). The following sections address the importance of protecting human participants in medical research (pp. 10–11), maintaining professional performance standards and deploying available review mechanisms (p. 11), and promoting patient safety in institutional settings (pp. 11–12). Presumably, proactive attention by nurses to these matters will reduce errors and near-misses, but the next two sections in Provision 3 deal with the nurse's responsibility to act in cases where he or she observes "questionable practice" or "impaired practice"—cases, that is, where patient health and safety are jeopardized and where professional malpractice litigation is likely (pp. 12–13).

In all this, we observe that the *Code* (ANA, 2015) is deeply sensitive to the legal aspects of modern health care, without lapsing into cramped legalism. It insists that ethically responsible nursing is far more than scrupulous adherence to the relevant civil laws and institutional policies. But it also affirms the significance of such adherence for nursing care, precisely because those laws and policies are intended to promote patient well-being.

Lewis M. Cohen (2011) offers an excellent example of the difference between lawfulness and legalism in nursing care in his riveting study of palliative medicine and euthanasia, *No Good Deed*. He tells of two devoted RNs, Amy Gleason and Kim Hoy, who were doing their utmost to provide humane end-of-life care to Rosemary Doherty, who was dying from renal failure and various comorbidities. But it seemed to Olga Vasquez, a nurse's aide on their unit, that Gleason and Hoy were cruelly denying Doherty much-needed oxygen and administering lethal doses of morphine to her. Now, Vasquez's limited nursing training, her narrow religious outlook, and perhaps her resentment at being treated as an underling in the hospital hierarchy all contributed to her misperception that Gleason and Hoy were actively trying to kill their patient, when it was their intention to relieve pain and provide comfort. Nor, indeed, did Vasquez follow the procedures outlined in the *Code* (ANA, 2015), Provision 3.5, for reporting "questionable practice" (p. 12). Yet perhaps Gleason and Hoy were a bit cavalier with respect to dosing procedures and collaborating with colleagues. To Vasquez, their procedural shortcuts were simply crimes. To Gleason and Hoy, Vasquez wasn't seeing the forest for the trees. In her obsession with following rules intended to preserve the patient's life, Vasquez couldn't see that in this case doing so was merely prolonging the patient's suffering.

FLORENCE NIGHTINGALE AND "THE LAW"

We come now to the third kind of law, physical law or the laws of nature. These include the law of gravity, the four laws of thermodynamics, the three laws of genetics, and so forth. These are the laws of "cause and effect" according to which natural phenomena behave, and it is the task of the natural sciences to discover and constantly refine these by observation and experiment. Early modern science was particularly enamored with the idea that nature operates according to such invariable "laws" and tends to be mechanistic and deterministic. Contemporary science, with its greater awareness of relativity, indeterminacy and randomness, generally construes the laws of nature as statistical probabilities, though it has not dispensed with the concept of law altogether. In either case, science presumes that natural phenomena follow regular patterns and predictable sequences. We expect ice on a mountaintop to melt when the temperature rises above 32°F and we expect the runoff to flow downhill—for such is the nature of water.

And although a spring thaw is spectacular from an aesthetic point of view, and even wondrous from a religious point of view, we do not regard the torrent and its effects as miraculous: nature is taking its course. It is the task of natural science to map that course.

Now, Christians regard "nature" as "creation," and therefore regard natural laws as the instrumentalities according to which God governs the "ordinary" course of events in the universe. In that sense, Christians—including those who are practitioners of natural science, insofar as they detect some divine purpose "behind" the phenomena they observe in nature—regard physical laws not only as explanatory principles but as the means by which God blesses his creatures and bends the course of events to his own benevolent purposes.[4] In this respect, if *only* in this respect, physical laws are crucially similar to divine and positive laws: they are beneficent. That is, they tend to the general good. Conversely, the fact that human beings can, and often do, disobey divine and positive laws, and sometimes ignore or try to circumvent the laws of nature, often leads to catastrophe. For example, addiction to opioids seems to violate divine law by impairing the health of the human body, God's temple (cf. 1 Cor 6:19),[5] and actions that might lead to opioid addiction (for example, advertisements by drug companies that inflate demand, or overprescription by healthcare providers) skirt or violate positive laws intended to protect public health. Let us now look at the use made by Florence Nightingale, the founder of modern nursing, of the concept of law, and all three of the varieties we have just described.

4. We are not asserting that one can simply "deduce" any divine purpose behind natural phenomena from an analysis of the phenomena themselves. Such an attempt would violate proper scientific method and constitute a lapse into deism. Rather, we are asserting that one who, through faith, has experienced the grace of God in the person of Jesus Christ, may find a divine purpose "within" natural phenomena (Newbigin, 1995, pp. 45–78).

5. But calling opioid addiction a violation of divine law does not authorize us to dismiss an opioid addict as a "sinner," regardless of how responsible he may be for abusing drugs or failing to seek treatment. Many other factors besides human "choice," such as a person's physiology and various social factors, contribute to his addiction. The point in calling anything that harms a person a violation of divine law is not to assign blame to another person in order to absolve ourselves of responsibility for his or her welfare. It is to remember that God himself has a deep stake in that person's welfare, and therefore that we do, too.

Figure 1.3. Jerry Barrett, *Florence Nightingale receiving the wounded at Scutari* [oil on canvas]. (Ca. 1856). 40.6 cm x 51 cm. National Portrait Gallery, London, England

Nightingale closely associated the moral law of God with the laws of nature, but she did not simplistically identify them, and from the resulting amalgam she derived her principles of nursing care (and of many other contemporary measures for human betterment and social reform). To illustrate how she joined divine and physical law, let us take note of several passages from her voluminous writings. In her unpublished essay "What Is Theology?," she refers to "the perfect plan" of a "perfect Creator," which consists both of the unchangeable "moral laws of nature" and the equally unchangeable "material [physical] laws" (Nightingale, 2002, p. 63). She goes on to assign "the almost utter failure of the most earnest Christian bodies in regenerating the world" to the unaccountable and deplorable fact that they generally ignore that plan (p. 63). In another unpublished essay, titled "Sympathy," she writes, "Sacred be that word 'right,' sacred the *law* which reveals to us its proper signification. *Law* we may think of as the conception of right in the mind of God and of the tendency to bring man to the same conception as God's. . . . If by God we mean the perfect Spirit of Wisdom and Benevolence, the thought and will of that Spirit would be law" (Nightingale, 2002, p. 109). Later in this essay she declares, "Every human feeling and action is a consequence of laws unalterable by man. Let me take for granted for the present that this is the case. We call these uniform relations 'laws of nature,' and thus we express the fact that they are as constant as if their constancy were the will of an *entity* called Nature, possessing power to realize her will that certain facts shall uniformly coexist with and follow certain other facts" (p. 110). Finally, in her *Notes on Nursing: What It Is and What It Is Not*, she comments in a footnote, "God lays down certain physical laws. Upon His carrying out such laws depends our responsibility (that much abused word), for how could we have any responsibility for actions, the results of which we could not foresee—which would be the case if the carrying out of His laws were *not* certain. Yet we seem to be continually expecting that He will work a miracle—i.e. break His own laws expressly to relieve us of responsibility" (Nightingale, 1992, p. 15).

From this amalgamation of moral and physical law, along with her extensive empirical knowledge of medical science and public health, Nightingale derived her principles of nursing. She articulated these with great precision, eloquence and authority, and enforced them with fierce determination in the hospitals under her supervision. Indeed, her early programmatic works, *Notes on Nursing* (1992; original work published 1859) and *Notes on Hospitals* (1863), are heavily prescriptive, and sometimes employ the concept of law to effect change in the healthcare practices of her day.[6] For example, in the former work she employs natural law language to chastise those who hold what she regards as the wholly unfounded "popular opinion" that there is no way to prevent children from contracting infectious diseases: ". . . the laws for preserving the health of houses which inculcate cleanliness, ventilation, white-washing, and other means . . . are *laws* . . ." (Nightingale, 1992, p. 20). She expects parents who obey those "laws" to improve the likelihood that their children will "escape altogether" the common "children's epidemics" of that time (p. 20).[7]

6. In the preface to her *Notes on Nursing*, she writes, "The following notes are by no means intended as a rule of thought by which nurses can teach themselves to nurse, still less as a manual to teach nurses to nurse. They are meant simply to give hints for thought to women who have personal charge of the health of others" (1992, p. 1). Despite this modest opening disclaimer, the book does not *read* like a collection of "helpful hints." It dispenses the best knowledge then available about personal and public health, corrects commonly held errors and prejudices, and gives elaborate instructions on sick room procedures. That does not make *Notes* a nursing "textbook," but rhetorically Nightingale cannot seem to help "laying down the law" for her readers.

7. Some of the "laws of health" that Nightingale enunciated with such certainty reflected her times but have not stood up under scrutiny. For example, she wrote *Notes on Nursing* and *Notes on Hospitals* in direct response to two public health crises through which England had recently passed: the London cholera epidemic of 1854 and the Crimean War of 1853–56. Her emphasis on the importance of ventilation in sick rooms reflects the miasma theory of disease to which she and many other medical authorities of that time subscribed, and which was widely—but, as we now know, mistakenly—used to

Nightingale's thought provides us with a convenient bridge between the Christian Scriptures and Provisions 1–3 of the *Code* (ANA, 2015), though we must modify and update her views at certain points. The Bible offers exceptionally rich reflections on God's moral law, stressing, as we have seen, both God's benevolent purposes in decreeing it and the well-being that God's people receive through obeying it. Of special concern to the Bible is the well-being of those who are incapable of providing for or defending themselves: the poor, the sick, the disabled, the indigent and "strangers" in the land, and the true measure of God's people's overall moral health is their attention to the rights and needs of these folks. The Bible, however, has nothing to say about the laws of nature, though its creation texts (Gen 1–3; Ps 8; Job 38–41; Col 1:15–23) do emphasize God's wisdom and providence. The *Code*, for its part, has much to say about positive law, that is, about civil laws relevant to health care and about the rules, regulations, protocols and operating procedures of specific healthcare facilities. And the overriding concern of the *Code*'s views on positive law is the health and safety of patients and the general public, though of course it makes no mention of God's moral law. Thus, both the Bible and the *Code* underscore the general principle that "the law is made for people, not people for law" (cf. Mark 2:27), though they mean somewhat different things by "law." Nightingale's reflections on physical law provide the linkage. She insists that the world is morally and providentially ordered, not merely naturalistically determined. There are, to be sure, laws of nature, or at least law-like patterns of events in the natural world, which we can determine through the procedures of science, and which ought to govern personal behavior and public policy. Physical laws cannot simply be equated with or deduced from the moral laws revealed in Scripture, but neither do they contradict them. Indeed, physical laws may even be considered the instrumentalities or "secondary causes" by which God wisely and benevolently governs his creation. When positive laws are in alignment with God's moral and physical laws, and when people obey all three types of laws, a community is likely to flourish. Conversely, when positive laws fail to heed God's moral or physical laws, or when people disobey divine laws and such positive laws as reflect the righteousness and wisdom of God, dire consequences are likely to follow. We need not regard the consequences of disobedience as direct "divine punishments," but we can at least affirm that

---

explain the cholera outbreak (Johnson, 2006, pp. 111–136). On the plus side, her emphasis on the importance of sanitation reflects the innovations she made in army hospitals during the recent war, which brought about the dramatic decrease in the death rate of wounded soldiers (Nightingale, 2010).

in a morally and providentially ordered creation, irresponsible behavior is ultimately self-defeating and self-destructive, while lawful behavior tends to promote the private and public good.

CLINICAL VOICES

The bridge between Christian Scripture and the *Code* (ANA, 2015) provides the nurse with a useful perspective to address the challenge of balancing laws and ethical principles in complex practice situations. This challenge is especially noticeable when nurses strive to advocate for their patients but encounter conflicts in fully speaking and acting in their patients' best interest. Nurses consistently hold patient advocacy in high esteem as a key professional value (Monroe, 2017). While the *Code* is clear on what the nurse ought to do for patient advocacy and promotion of health, it also articulates an expectation that the nurse support the patient's self-determination (Fowler, 2015). These principles may directly conflict with one another in some situations, and the nurse must determine which principle is the priority or if both can be reasonably, if not ideally, addressed. Situations involving conflicts between values create ethical dilemmas for the nurse. For example, when the nurse considers equitable health care just as important as the individual's autonomy and right to self-determination, but the patient makes unhealthy or unsafe decisions, the nurse may have difficulty choosing among available responses. Ethical dilemmas may present in myriad ways. It may be that a patient has little in the way of social or financial resources, which limits the ideal plan of care. If the patient has limited resources and chooses to avoid follow-up health care, the nurse must develop a plan that seeks needed resources but also respects the patient's reality and reduces the risk of harm. A patient may have mental health or addiction problems resulting in poor health. Perhaps the patient has a long history of unhealthy lifestyle choices that have taken their toll or maybe the patient has engaged in illegal behaviors resulting in the need for care.

Regardless of the circumstances that bring patients in for care, the nurse must address the immediate health needs. In the case of illegal behaviors necessitating nursing care, the nurse must also consider the potential for harm to the community at large, or even to others in the immediate healthcare environment. Poor health is often unrelated to patient choice at all, perhaps due to age, accident or "bad luck." Yet in situations where lifestyle choices influence health, nurses face challenges in determining how to deliver compassionate, respectful care, honoring human dignity while balancing the patient's right to self-determination. Nursing care becomes complicated in these situations. Is it more important to emphasize the patient's right to self-determination, even if the result is continued harm? Is there a way to acceptably compromise between patient preferences, protocols, laws, and health-promoting interventions? While compassionate, respectful nursing care always supports the principle of human dignity, striking a balance between advocacy for the patient and patient self-determination may be more difficult for the nurse to achieve. These nurses describe situations in which they encountered challenges balancing laws and ethical principles:

Jae Cho: *Balancing safety and dignity*

I took care of a patient who expressed suicidal thoughts in the emergency room. He was brought in by his family members, who were concerned about his well-being and safety. According to the Bible, his suicidal thoughts were against the divine law of the Decalogue: "You shall not murder" (Exodus 20:13). This divine law finds expression in the modern law that protects people from harm, including the harm they may do to themselves. The patient was cooperative with me initially, and he wished to keep his personal clothing. I let him do so but I had taken other things away per my hospital policy. Later, I heard a commotion and realized that the patient stormed out of the unit to smoke outside. This caused several staff, including me, to chase after him with a few security guards, bring him back to the unit, and take away every belonging. During more than twenty-four hours in the ER, our staff spent numerous hours to help him figure out the right person and the right place that could provide his needs. The patient was not happy about losing his rights and freedom, but the staff followed strict guidelines and rules to take care of him. I learned that there are complicated ethical and legal situations involved in taking care of suicidal patients. I thought I provided for the patient's dignity by letting him keep his own clothing. However, the patients' safety was a greater priority than one person's dignity in that case. I was able to reflect on how divine law, positive law, and the *Code* are related in terms of the biblical strand of law and what I need do to protect my patients' safety and others.

Anonymous: *Balancing freedom, attentive care, and natural law*

I will not forget V. I met her for the first time in an ICU room, and although her primary diagnosis was respiratory, a head-to-toe admission skin assessment confirmed she had unstageable bi-lateral ischial tuberosity wounds. They looked and smelled bad. I photographed, measured and dressed her wounds while she complained that she could not breathe with the head of her bed lowered down to position her for assessment and treatment. V. was a "frequent flyer" in the emergency room (ER). Homelessness, polysubstance abuse and noncompliance were included in her list of comorbidities. Outside of the hospital she had to position her body so that her chronic pain was tolerable and she could breathe; her wounds resulted from this. I created a plan that included chemical debridement with Dakin's solution and off-loading on an air fluidized mattress. The plan worked and soon the eschar turned into slough and then pale pink tissue surrounding her trochanters became visible. The consulting physician and I were considering our next steps when V. derailed our plans. She left the facility against medical advice because she wanted to smoke ciga-rettes. I was shocked that someone with her bones literally sticking out would consider leaving the hospital. V. returned three more times. She would leave, suffer from her inability to breathe, go to the ER, and get sent back to us. At the last admission she died of sepsis. The county came to investigate because they wanted to make sure that V.'s wounds were documented as present on admis-sion, and that our facility did not cause her wounds by negligent care, like failing to reposition her. I had good pictures and the investigators left satisfied with my answers. It is a story about the laws that govern nursing practice. Head-to-toe skin assessments on patient admission were hospital policy, as were regular pressure ulcer risk assessments. There are many rules and policies regard-ing wound photography, such as labeling the wound and properly storing the photographs to abide by patient privacy laws. Clear and precise documentation is a standard of practice. Elements of the *Code* such as right to self-determination, the nurse's relation-ship with patients, and respect for human dignity are also present in V.'s story. She was my neighbor. I tried my best to care for her even though she did not value the care and often saw it as an im-position and restriction of her freedom. I made the effort to form a therapeutic relationship with her and treat her wounds to the best of my ability every time she was admitted.

Anonymous: *Making exceptions to rules*

Patients often make choices that go against societal laws and even hospital policies. I respect their choice while trying to provide them education about the consequences of their choices. For example, we accepted a patient with end-stage heart failure who needed a continuous infusion of dobutamine at home to keep him alive. Our policy is that patients receiving inotropic medications must have a caregiver available at all times for patient safety and best outcomes. At first, we were going to decline accepting this patient on service without a caregiver, as this would be in violation of our policy if we did accept. However, after a long conversation with the patient, his family, physician, and our legal department, we agreed to accept the patient as long as he signed a waiver. We discussed all the risks with the patient, family, and physician. The patient not only verbalized understanding but also agreed to sign the waiver. We were able to successfully get him out of the hospital and home where he wanted to be. We were able to respect his autonomy even though it was at odds with our policy and procedures. I was able to advocate for the patient's wishes while protecting us legally.

Alix Lobaugh: *Experiencing compassion
and commitment as a family member*

A couple of weeks ago we had a family member undergo palliative care which led to a peaceful death in the hospital setting. Her nurses were lovely, guiding her through the process that would take place over the next two days and making sure that her family members had enough coffee to stay with her day and night until her last breath. The nurses emanated God's grace by lawfully following their hospital policy for comfort care and end-of-life care. The healthcare team respected the basic human rights of their patient. My family member was treated with compassion, as demonstrated by the discontinuation of routine nursing tasks that provoked pain, such as vital signs and turning in bed. The nursing team had compassion for us (as family members we had a tough time watching her suffer) and for their patient. The nurses and providers were determined to keep their patient's pain and anxiety under control. This determination was a demonstration of genuine commitment to their patient for a graceful transition at the end of her life. When she no longer had sound mental capacity near the end, the healthcare team listened to her power of attorney about what medical interventions to continue and which ones to stop. The collaboration of the nurse techs, nurses, physician assistant, and attending physician was smooth and evident. There was no hurry, no judgment— only empathy and compassion from each healthcare professional we encountered. We could tell in their eyes that they wanted what we wanted: a peaceful, comfortable death for our loved one.

Agata Millar: *Incongruencies and universal health care*

One of the main divine laws is to protect and provide for those who are the most vulnerable, and the *Code* calls nurses to provide care with compassion and respect to every person regardless of their ethnicity, cultural background, socioeconomic status, etc. These give clear messages to society and inform my role as a nurse and public servant. On the other hand, there are federal laws that don't necessarily align with the *Code* or divine laws. A great example of that is the American healthcare system, in which people from underserved and diverse populations often don't have equal access to care. Therefore, when a patient does not have insurance, it is very challenging to remain true to one's values of a compassionate public servant and a responsible citizen at the same time. It will become even more apparent in a nurse practitioner role when I am responsible for diagnosing and deciding patient treatment options. Even if I worked in a free clinic and was able to see patients who do not have insurance, I still would not be able to order all the testing and prescribe the medications as I would for an insured person. In some other countries, this disparity is less of an issue. In Poland, where I grew up, everybody had equal access to health care. Universal health care is an example of something that could close the gap between divine and positive laws. The Polish government openly refers to the Bible and Catholicism when creating laws, but that does not mean the American government would have to include religion in their policymaking. It means, however, that we need to ensure new regulations and policies originate from the needs of love and compassion versus the needs of order and prosperity.

Nicole Nguyen: *Compassion and incarceration*

There was a situation where I was at odds with the regulations of the healthcare facility and my duties to the patient. I was working at a long-term care facility and had an incarcerated patient. The patient was in handcuffs most of the time and constantly had guards at his bedside. I was instructed to go and perform my nursing duties but was not allowed to talk to the patient or provide any additional care. I looked at him as a patient, not an inmate. Although I was not allowed to, I talked to and cared for him as if he was any other of my patients. At times I was spoken to by guards; other times the guards did not interfere. If I did not provide him care, I would have felt that I was going against the *Code*. I would not be showing compassion and protecting the patient. During that instance, I felt that duty and obligation to him were more significant than the law and rules in place.

Donna Kang: *Intentions of the heart*

There are many times when I know that I make nursing care to be more about getting things done than being there for my patients. If my job is to care for and help my patients, then meeting only their physical needs is not enough; but oftentimes, we just get too busy to be present for our patients. I have concluded that busyness is not what causes me to become task-oriented or legalistic in the way I try to get things done. It is a matter of attitude—usually when I try to control things to go my way or for my convenience. I had a patient who was extremely particular about the way things were done for her. Even though she only required one person to assist her to the bedside commode, she always wanted two females to help. Having a male tech, it was taxing on me to find someone else who was available. The patient also had to have her room arranged a certain way, and it would require extra time and extreme patience to get everything right the way she wanted. I grew impatient with her and abruptly left the room after a stream of incessant requests. I felt guilty when, after my shift was over, the patient gave me a bouquet of flowers from her room and thanked me for the way I cared for her. In my heart, I knew that there were moments when I did not treat her well. Although I fulfilled the legal aspect of being a "good neighbor," I knew I could have done better. No matter how busy things get or the challenges I face, I want to bring intention to the way I love and serve people, and to put that above the things I need to get done. The patient as the care recipient is of primary interest, and not the self. Although the patient may not even be aware, or outwardly nobody would know the difference, I believe that God cares not only about our behaviors but also about the intentions of our hearts.

Nurses hone their skills with practice and experience, merging the concrete knowledge of laws, policies, protocols and the *Code* with the nuanced problems and complicated lives of patients in their care. Despite the nurse's professionalism, best planning and highest-quality care, the long-term well-being of the patient may at times be beyond the nurse's sphere of influence; patients may continue to lack resources or make choices resulting in harm to themselves or others. While ideal solutions may not be realistic or achievable given the complexities of patients' lives, the strand of law in Christian Scripture in tandem with principles from the *Code* provides valuable perspective for nurses to develop the best available plan for patient care.

KEYWORDS

1. Apodictic (or unconditional) laws

2. Casuistic (or situation-specific) laws

3. Covenant

4. Divine (or moral) laws

5. Horizontal (or community-related) laws

6. Physical (or natural) laws

7. Positive law

8. Vertical (or God-directed) laws

READING COMPREHENSION

1. What is the difference between a "contract" and a "covenant," and why is the difference important for understanding divine law?

2. What is the difference between "lawfulness" and "legalism," and why is the difference important for understanding divine law?

3. Summarize the three key points made about Deuteronomy 10:12–21.

4. Summarize the four key points made about Luke 10:25–37.

5. Summarize the contents of Provisions 1–3 of the ANA *Code*.

6. Summarize Florence Nightingale's understanding of law and explain why it provides a bridge between the Christian Scriptures and Provisions 1–3 of the ANA *Code*.

MAKING CONNECTIONS

1. How does the account of divine law, positive law, and the laws of nature in this chapter shape your understanding as a professional, a public servant, and a citizen of this or some other country?

2. Have you ever faced a situation in which your duties to a patient were at odds with the law of the land or the regulations of the health-care facility in which you were working? How did you handle that situation?

3. Have you ever faced a situation in which one of your patients was breaking a divine law, a positive law and/or a "law of nature" (in Nightingale's sense of the term), such that the health or well-being of that patient or other persons was jeopardized? How did you handle that situation?

4. Study Philippe de Champaigne's painting *Moses and the Ten Commandments*, shown on p. 29 above. How does de Champaigne depict the relationship between God's *law* and Israel's *lawgiver*? What do Moses' posture, dress and facial expression suggest? What does the rod he is holding represent (see Exod 7:1–24; 14:16; 17:1–13)? Note that the two stone tables of the law are angled, almost like an open book: what might de Champaigne be suggesting by rendering them that way? Now let the picture speak to you as a nurse. Does your experience of how the law (in all three of its forms) functions in your professional life square with what de Champaige seems to be saying about the authority of the divine law in the common life of God's people? If not, why not?

5. Study Vincent van Gogh's painting *The Good Samaritan*, shown on p. 36 above. Which moment in Jesus' parable of the Good Samaritan (Luke 10:25–37) does Van Gogh capture? How does he position the four characters relative to each other on the canvas to communicate the message of Jesus' story? How are colors and brushstrokes used to indicate the physical energy and moral determination of the Samaritan, the helplessness and suffering of the victim, and the indifference of the priest and the Levite? Now let the picture speak to you as a nurse. Have you ever gone home after a shift feeling like any of the characters in the story, as Van Gogh has captured it? The victim? The priest or Levite? The Samaritan? The thieves (not shown

in the picture)? The donkey? Share your reflections with a classmate or colleague.

6. Study Jerry Barrett's painting *Florence Nightingale Receiving the Wounded at Scutari*, shown on p. 42 above. Nightingale is clearly the "commanding" figure in this crowded scene. How does Barrett achieve that affect artistically? How does the kind of "command" that she exercises differ from that exercised by the military officers who populate the picture? Now let the picture speak to you as a nurse. How often do you experience the mixture of tranquility and determination that Barrett's Nightingale exudes here in your own busy, sometimes frantic, clinical work? What helps a skilled point-of-care or advanced practice nurse to achieve that frame of mind?

7. Read the Clinical Voices on pp. 45–51 above. Do any of them seem to "speak" to you, conjuring up memories, reflections, hopes, or fears related to your own practice? Explain.

2

The Nurse as Healing Presence

The Holiness Strand: "Be holy, for I am holy."

LEV 19:2; CF. MATT 5:48; 1 PET 1:16

Nursing students are often asked, "Why did you decide to go into nursing?" We have found that most students answer in words that convey the idea of *caring for others*. It is common to hear, "I really care about people and want to help them," or "I'm good in the sciences, and I really want to do something where I'm taking care of others." These are important foundational desires and go hand in hand with the idea of bringing oneself into the patient-care relationship and building trust. The aim of bringing healing to people in need is not unique to Christian nurses. As a rule, nurses must not only care for and about their patients but must also develop a trusting relationship with patients so they *can* optimally help—and people do trust nurses! Nurses have a reputation for promoting the good of others. When polls rank public trust in a variety of professional roles, nursing is consistently at the top, widely perceived as most honest and ethical (Brenan, 2017).

While we can and should celebrate a reputation of trustworthiness and caring, experienced nurses understand that there are complexities that defy simple definitions of these concepts and how a nurse embodies them varies according to context. Care and trust in the clinical environment can be very complicated and messy to achieve, both literally and figuratively. People may not always appear to want a nurse's help, which can frustrate the nurse's best efforts and highest ethical standards. In fact, while new nurses come out of their educational experiences well-versed in the ways nurses *ought* to function according to the profession's ethical standards, there is evidence that the realities and complexities of clinical work take a toll on this idealism between two and ten years of experience (Monroe, 2017). Some patients may do or say things that make it very difficult for the nurse. Patients sometimes are people who have committed horrible crimes, such as the 19-year-old Boston marathon bomber who ended up requiring intensive care in the same hospital caring for the victims (Kowalczyk, 2013). Sometimes the patients are hard to like—they throw feces across the room, call the nurse racist names, refuse care by the nurse because of gender, or have families who are disruptive with each other or the staff. One of our students, Sandra Bell, gave a poignant example of the challenges nurses often face and of how she effectively responded: "I recall a patient who was extremely rude and threw several items at me in her room. Despite her negative attitude and actions, as a nurse I was determined to persevere and find some way to deliver the needed care and help to improve her situation. I took the approach of 'killing her with kindness,' and it worked. From my desire to do good despite adversity, by shift end, I had established trust and was able to work effectively with this patient over several days to her discharge."

Compounding these situations may be issues in the work environment that cause moral distress for the nurse; the nurse knows the morally right action to take but is unable to do so (Jameton, 1993). Perhaps a child is dying and the parents insist on continuing his painful, invasive treatments, desperately clinging to hope for a cure. Maybe an opioid-addicted patient has undergone painful surgery but has providers who hesitate to write effective pain-management orders. The idea of the nurse being a "healing presence" can at times seem unattainable, and the ideals of caring and trust may be elusive; however, there are ways to integrate professional nursing values and complex clinical care with one's own moral values. Nurses who find themselves in these situations must not go it alone; these are the times to seek collaboration from the healthcare team, support from coworkers and administrators, and insight from ethics consult resources. The intersection of Christian ethics and professional nursing values can also provide the nurse with guidance to reconcile moral values with clinical work.

Christian Scripture provides insight on the trust and caring central to nursing through the pursuit of caregiving virtues. The *Code* (2015) calls for nurses to take care of themselves and to work with others to address challenging patient and work environment situations. The *Code* is clear that a nurse's character and personal integrity are important to professional bearing, and for the Christian nurse this means understanding how to integrate faith and work. While trustworthy, compassionate care of patients is critically important, the classic example from the airline industry points out that this cannot be valued above prudent self-care—the nurse must take care of herself in order to care well for others, "putting on her own oxygen mask" before helping others to do the same, lest she pass out—or burn out. There is evidence that experienced nurses have figured out how to persist beyond the challenges of reconciling personal and professional values they embraced as new nurses (Monroe, 2017). They may have found ways to better care for themselves by debriefing a stressful code with the team, calling the ethics consultant, going hiking on their days off, or gathering with friends over a shared meal and laughter. With a strong understanding of how the *Code* and Christian Scripture enhance each other, the nurse may truly become a "healing presence" to others. Together, caregiving virtues and professional values can help the nurse determine what is reasonable, moral, and wise to do, both for self and patient care.

Our procedure in this chapter will be as follows: In section 1 we examine the biblical concept of "holiness"—the kind of holiness proper to God alone, and the related but distinct kind to which God's people should aspire. We focus on two key biblical passages, Leviticus 19:1–18 and Matthew 5:17–30, 43–48. The first includes the morally daunting verse, "Be holy, as [God is] holy" (Lev 19:2), and the second includes the parallel and equally daunting admonition, "Be perfect, as your heavenly Father is perfect" (Matt 5:48). These passages, and their respective theme verses, assert that the holiness of God's people consists in the imitation of the holiness of God, to the extent that that is possible under the conditions of human finitude and fallenness. In section 2, we look at Provisions 5–6 of the *Code* (ANA, 2015). Provision 5 emphasizes the importance for nurses of self-respect and self-care, "wholeness of character and integrity," and continuing personal and professional growth (p. 19). Provision 6 underscores the nurse's duty to work with fellow nurses and healthcare professionals to establish a clinical environment that is "conducive to safe, quality health care" (p. 23). In section 3, we show the linkage between the scriptural concept of holiness and the concept of moral virtue, as developed by the moral philosophers of classical antiquity and their heirs in early and medieval Christianity. Of special interest to us are what we call the "care-giving virtues," namely, those qualities of character needed by persons who are entrusted with the physical, emotional and spiritual healing of the sick, the injured and the disabled. The "clinical voices" included in section 4 relate what we have learned about "holiness" and "virtue" to bedside nursing practice. Sections 5–7 contain the usual teaching/learning helps.

It is worth recalling here the distinction we drew in the introduction between *conduct*-focused and *character*-focused ethics. We noted that the legal and prophetic strands of biblical moral discourse concentrate on human *conduct*—on what people *do*, on how their actions, relationships and institutions are best to be governed. Accordingly, the chapters of this book devoted to those strands, namely chapters 1 and 4, along with the provisions in the *Code* (ANA, 2015) that correspond to them, examine the laws, policies, protocols and procedures that regulate a Christian nurse's personal life and professional practice. By contrast, the holiness and wisdom strands focus on human *character*—on who people *are*, on how they attain moral maturity. Accordingly, the present chapter and the following one study these two strands, together with their corresponding provisions in the *Code*. We inquire into the virtues and values, the motives and dispositions, the habits and skills that mark a Christian nurse's personal and professional identity.

HOLINESS IN CHRISTIAN SCRIPTURE

In his classic study *The Idea of the Holy*, Rudolf Otto (1950) differentiates two main senses in which religious people (and scholars of religion) use the term *holiness*. The first pertains to what he calls the "non-rational" or "suprarational" factor in the idea of the divine, and the second to the "rational" or "ethical" factor (pp. 1–4). In earlier works, Otto had exhaustively investigated the rational factor; in *The Idea of the Holy* he concentrates on the non-rational, which he regards as the older of the two, and which he finds in many "primitive" religions across the world, including that of the ancient Hebrews. In the present chapter, we are primarily concerned with what Otto regards as the second, derivative sense of the term, and specifically with how it is used in the Christian Scriptures. Yet a few preliminary words of explanation about the first sense are in order here, for as we shall see, the first was modified, but by no means forgotten, as biblical religion evolved.

Otto (1950) described the non-rational factor in humanity's experience of divinity as a *mysterium tremendum et fascinans*, a mystery which causes a person both to tremble with dread and to gaze in wonder and adoration. The divine is felt to be "numinous," "awe-inspiring," "overpowering," untameably "energetic," and "wholly other" than the world human beings ordinarily inhabit (pp. 12–30). Yet it is also "fascinating" or enchanting in its unearthly beauty (pp. 31–40). When people experience the "numinosity" of the Holy—its frightful but alluring mysteriousness—their response is to tremble, not only with fear, as at something dangerous, but also with love, as at something ineffable but alluring. In the story of the burning bush, God informs Moses that he is treading on "holy ground" and bids him to remove his sandals. In humble reverence, Moses promptly does so—but then, in fascination, he approaches (Exod 3:1–12). Kenneth Grahame (1961) captures the double-sidedness of the Holy in its primal sense in his delightful children's novel *The Wind and the Willows*. At one point, Mole and Rat set out to find a missing young otter. They journey to a "holy place," where they find the lad in the protective embrace of a numinous being, who is clearly the pagan god Pan. In a whisper, Mole asks Rat if he is afraid. "'Afraid,' murmured the Rat, his eyes shining with unutterable love. 'Afraid! Of *Him*? O never, never! And yet—and yet—O, Mole, I am afraid!'" (p. 136).[1]

As Israel's relationship with God deepened with the passing years, a new way of thinking about his "holiness" began to emerge, without, however, fully displacing the earlier one. More and more, holiness came to refer to God's moral goodness—and, by extension, to the moral goodness which God demanded of his covenant people. People continued to experience powerful religious emotions in the presence of God. Yet these emotions—still present as contrasting pairs—now had an ethical element that had previously been absent or latent. God was still "tremendous," but the shudder of awe in his presence was now accompanied by a pang of guilt over one's unworthiness to draw near to him. God was still "fascinating," but one's fascination with the divine mystery was gradually turning into adoration of God's transcendent goodness. For example, in Isaiah's temple vision (Isa 6:1–13), the prophet is overwhelmed by God's majesty and suddenly conscious that he is "a man of

1. It should be mentioned that in some biblical stories, the presence of the Holy induces great "terror" but little discernible "fascination." In 1 Samuel 4:1—6:18, the Philistines capture the ark of the covenant from the Israelites, but its presence in their midst wreaks havoc. Later, in 2 Samuel 6:6–11, after the ark has been safely returned to Israel and is being brought into Jerusalem amidst great festal joy, an oxcart driver is struck dead when he simply tries to prevent his cargo from tipping. In chapter 1 above, we saw that the covenant between God and God's people was "a reciprocal bond of love, trust and commitment," in which, however, God always remained the "senior partner." Absent that bond, God's majesty and authority are terrifying—and the terror can be deadly.

unclean lips, [living] among a people of unclean lips" (v. 5). Yet immediately thereafter, he is purified of his guilt by the seraph, and then commissioned to preach. Similarly, in the Gospel story of the miraculous catch of fish (Luke 5:1–11), Peter is both astounded by Jesus' wonderworking power and yet ashamed to stand in his presence: "Go away from me, Lord, for I am a sinful man!" (v. 8). Jesus consoles him: "Do not be afraid; from now on you will be catching people" (v. 10). In both cases, a sense of guilt is added to a person's primal religious terror, while a sense of moral purpose is added to his primal fascination. People continue to experience God as "the Wholly Other" but increasingly understand God also as the "Highest Good."

Figure 2.1. Raphael, *The miraculous draught of fishes* [tempera on paper, mounted on canvas]. (1515). 360 cm x 440 cm. Victoria and Albert Museum, London, England

Accordingly, the relationship between God and God's people is now mediated by a formal covenant: laws are promulgated, promises exchanged. The Israelites have become a "holy people," in that they must reflect in their common life the moral excellence of the Deity who has called them into partnership with himself. Their formal approach to God now takes place on designated "holy days" (festivals), in specially consecrated "holy places" (the tabernacle, the temple, etc.), and in accordance with prescribed "holy ceremonies" (liturgies). Biblical religion has become "rationalized," to use Otto's (1950) term. It has become "ethical monotheism."[2] Yet as we shall see, the holiness of God's people is not merely a matter of outward conformity to God's law. Rather, it is a matter of imitating God's character. We saw in chapter 1 that even the legal material in the Bible must not be understood "legalistically," merely as a set of arbitrary rules and regulations, imposed from on high, to be obeyed mechanically or cringingly. For the law is correlative to human nature, capable of adaptation to changing circumstances, and oriented toward human flourishing. Yet the legal material focuses on human *conduct*, on what people are commanded to *do*. In the holiness material, attention begins to shift to human *character*, on who people are supposed to be, that is, on their virtues, intentions, motives and dispositions. One early Christian theologian summarized the distinction thus: "Fulfilling a commandment is one thing, and virtue another, although each promotes the other. Fulfilling a commandment means doing what we are enjoined to do; but virtue is to do it in a manner that conforms to the truth" (Mark the Ascetic, 1979, p. 123).

We must not press this point too far, however, for two reasons. First, legal material is everywhere in evidence in the Bible's holiness texts. Indeed, these texts constantly underscore the abiding authority of the law, even though they shift the emphasis from people's moral obligation to obey God's law to the new identity they acquire by covenantal partnership with him. Second, the distinctions between "doing" and "being," and between "conduct" and "character," are somewhat artificial. We only know *who* a person is by reference to what she *does*, and when a person sets out to cultivate a particular character trait, she first identifies those types of conduct that are thought to display it, and then practices them diligently and deliberately until they become "second nature" to her, habitual and fully internalized. Still, these distinctions are useful, and indeed unavoidable. For a person's conduct is not always congruent with her character. When someone whom we take to be morally mature and well-intentioned does something foolish

---

2. But Otto (1950) shows that the belief in God's numinosity is present throughout the Old and New Testaments, and is never fully eclipsed by the growing emphasis on God's ethical character and covenantal love (pp. 72-93). Muilenburg (1962) agrees and shows that the many-sided biblical concept of "holiness" involves both rational (i.e., "ethical") and non-rational (i.e., "numinous") factors. Finally, C. S. Lewis (1962, pp. 13-23) differentiates our ancestors' experiences of the numinous from their sense of ethical obligation and credits the Jews for discovering that these constitute distinct aspects of the experience of a single divine reality.

or immoral, we wonder, "What's gotten into her?" as if she were under the control of some alien force. Or we say of her, "She's not herself today," as if she had somehow become someone else. On the other hand, when someone whom we know to be selfish or thoughtless does something admirable, we suspect hypocrisy. The holiness strand of biblical moral discourse adds to the legal strand this heightened attention to moral *agency*. It emphasizes that a person's actions must reflect her "heart." It affirms that social justice and harmony are determined not only by the equity of a nation's laws and the stability of its institutions but also by the godliness of its citizens—their moral maturity, their religious devotion. Let us now examine two holiness texts that illustrate this.

Our first text is from the book of Leviticus. This great compilation of Israelite law has two main parts. The first part comprises chapters 1–16 (plus chapter 27 as a kind of appendix). It focuses on "priestly" matters: sacrifices, ordination rites, ritual cleanliness and so forth. The second part, which comprises chapters 17–26, is known to scholars as the Holiness Code and focuses on "ethical" matters.[3] The centerpiece of the Holiness Code is our selected passage, Leviticus 19:1–18, in which, according to John Hayes (2003), "the ethical teachings of the [Old Testament] find their apex" (p. 173).

> [1] *The* LORD *spoke to Moses, saying:* [2] *Speak to all the congregation of the people of Israel and say to them: You shall be holy, for I the* LORD *your God am holy.* [3] *You shall each revere your mother and father, and you shall keep my sabbaths: I am the* LORD *your God.* [4] *Do not turn to idols or make cast images for yourselves: I am the* LORD *your God.*
>
> [5] *When you offer a sacrifice of well-being to the* LORD, *offer it in such a way that it is acceptable in your behalf.* [6] *It shall be eaten on the same day you offer it, or on the next day; and anything left over until the third day shall be consumed in fire.* [7] *If it is eaten at all on the third day, it is an abomination; it will not be acceptable.* [8] *All who eat it shall be subject to punishment, because they have profaned what is holy to the* LORD; *and any such person shall be cut off from the people.*

3. As noted in the introduction, there are no complete *books* in the Old Testament that represent the holiness strand. In this respect, Strand 2 differs from Strands 1, 3 and 4, all of which have entire books devoted to them, and indeed, entire canonical units ("The Law," "the Writings" and "the Prophets," respectively). Some scholars believe that the Holiness Code was originally a standalone work, which later editors subsequently inserted into the book of Leviticus, so that it now forms part of the Mosaic Law (our Strand 1).

⁹ When you reap the harvest of your land, you shall not reap to the very edges of your field, or gather the gleanings of your harvest. ¹⁰ You shall not strip your vineyard bare, or gather the fallen grapes of your vineyard; you shall leave them for the poor and the alien: I am the LORD your God.

¹¹ You shall not steal; you shall not deal falsely; and you shall not lie to one another. ¹² And you shall not swear falsely by my name, profaning the name of your God: I am the LORD.

¹³ You shall not defraud your neighbor; you shall not steal; and you shall not keep for yourself the wages of a laborer until morning. ¹⁴ You shall not revile the deaf or put a stumbling block before the blind; you shall fear your God: I am the LORD.

¹⁵ You shall not render an unjust judgment; you shall not be partial to the poor or defer to the great: with justice you shall judge your neighbor. ¹⁶ You shall not go around as a slanderer among your people, and you shall not profit by the blood of your neighbor: I am the LORD.

¹⁷ You shall not hate in your heart anyone of your kin; you shall reprove your neighbor, or you will incur guilt yourself. ¹⁸ You shall not take vengeance or bear a grudge against any of your people, but you shall love your neighbor as yourself: I am the LORD. (Lev 19:1–18)

Two points about this passage bear mentioning for our purposes. First, nine of the Ten Commandments are cited in it, though in scrambled order, and the missing one, the seventh, is cited later in the following chapter (20:10). Yet as Walter Kaiser Jr., (1994) points out, Leviticus 19 is not simply a "revision of the Decalogue" but "a further reinforcement and a practical illustration of it" (p. 1131). This "reinforcement" is achieved by the repetition of the formula "I am the LORD" or "I am the LORD your God" after nearly every admonition. What does this incessant reminder add to each bit of legislation? Not simply that it enjoys divine authorization, for that was established at the outset: "The LORD spoke to Moses, saying..." (v. 1). Rather, the formula adds the assurance that when God's people do God's will, they are reflecting God's own holiness—not his numinosity, of course, for that is unique to him, but his moral goodness. They are acting *as* his "holy people." Verse 2 states this expressly: "You shall be holy, for I the LORD your God am holy." Hayes (2003) comments, "'Holiness' is understood as more than just ethical excellence; it is behavior that imitates God's behavior, the so-called *imitatio Dei*" (p. 173). In view of what we have said above, we might reformulate Hayes' point thus: The holiness of God's people is more than outward conformity to divine law. It is their sincere attempt to model their own character and conduct on the character of their God, as revealed to them by the "mighty works" he has performed on their behalf over the years in faithfulness to his covenant promises (2 Chr 17:13; Ps 145:4; Sir 18:4; 2 Esd 9:6).

Second, although many of the laws contained in Leviticus 19:1–18 echo those in the Decalogue, others do not, and of those that do not, many pertain to the protection of the vulnerable or the maintenance of precious, fragile social relationships. One must leave a portion of one's grain and grapes unharvested, so that "the poor and the alien" may glean enough for their basic needs (vv. 9–10; cf. Ruth 2:1–23). One must avoid fraudulent business dealings and promptly pay day laborers their wages (v. 13). One must show special concern to the disabled (v. 14),[4] avoid deferring to the rich and powerful during court proceedings and avoid showing uncritical partiality to the poor. Finally, one must eschew "slander against one's people," profiting from violence against one's neighbor, "hatred" toward one's kinfolk (i.e., malicious plotting, per Hayes, 2003, p. 174), turning a blind eye to the crimes of fellow citizens, and vengefulness and grudge-holding against fellow Israelites. God's holiness (*qua* moral goodness) is displayed in his special concern for the weak and the defenseless: the same must be true of his holy people. Summing up the entire passage is a verse that we encountered in chapter 1: "You shall love your neighbor as yourself" (v. 18). This underscores the point that outward conduct and inward motivation must be congruent.

Our second holiness text is Matthew 5:17–30 and 43–48, portions of Jesus' Sermon on the Mount. Like Leviticus 19:1–18, these verses refer directly to the Ten Commandments but warn repeatedly against a "behaviorist" or "legalistic" interpretation of them. Jesus endorses the validity of the Mosaic law (Matt 5:17–20), but he insists that true obedience extends beyond outward conformity to the letter and includes the heartfelt embrace of its purpose, its "spirit."

> [17] *"Do not think that I have come to abolish the law or the prophets; I have come not to abolish but to fulfill.* [18] *For truly I tell you, until heaven and earth pass away, not one letter, not one stroke of a letter, will pass from the law until all is accomplished.* [19] *Therefore, whoever breaks one of the least of these commandments, and teaches others to do the same, will be called least in the kingdom of heaven; but whoever does them and teaches them will be called great in the kingdom*

---

4. Although the disabled are here guaranteed protection from cruelty and mockery, later in the Holiness Code they are disqualified from priestly service, because their "blemish" is believed to "profane [God's] sanctuaries" (Lev 21:16–24).

of heaven. ²⁰ For I tell you, unless your righteousness exceeds that of the scribes and Pharisees, you will never enter the kingdom of heaven.

²¹ "You have heard that it was said to those of ancient times, 'You shall not murder'; and 'whoever murders shall be liable to judgment.' ²² But I say to you that if you are angry with a brother or sister, you will be liable to judgment; and if you insult a brother or sister, you will be liable to the council; and if you say, 'You fool,' you will be liable to the hell of fire. ²³ So when you are offering your gift at the altar, if you remember that your brother or sister has something against you, ²⁴ leave your gift there before the altar and go; first be reconciled to your brother or sister, and then come and offer your gift. ²⁵ Come to terms quickly with your accuser while you are on the way to court with him, or your accuser may hand you over to the judge, and the judge to the guard, and you will be thrown into prison. ²⁶ Truly I tell you, you will never get out until you have paid the last penny.

²⁷ "You have heard that it was said, 'You shall not commit adultery.' ²⁸ But I say to you that everyone who looks at a woman with lust has already committed adultery with her in his heart. ²⁹ If your right eye causes you to sin, tear it out and throw it away; it is better for you to lose one of your members than for your whole body to be thrown into hell. ³⁰ And if your right hand causes you to sin, cut it off and throw it away; it is better for you to lose one of your members than for your whole body to go into hell. . . .

⁴³ "You have heard that it was said, 'You shall love your neighbor and hate your enemy.' ⁴⁴ But I say to you, Love your enemies and pray for those who persecute you, ⁴⁵ so that you may be children of your Father in heaven; for he makes his sun rise on the evil and on the good, and sends rain on the righteous and on the unrighteous. ⁴⁶ For if you love those who love you, what reward do you have? Do not even the tax collectors do the same? ⁴⁷ And if you greet only your brothers and sisters, what more are you doing than others? Do not even the Gentiles do the same? ⁴⁸ Be perfect, therefore, as your heavenly Father is perfect. (Matt 5:17–30, 43–48)

Two points about this passage stand out: First, we note that Jesus is speaking, in his own name, with nothing short of divine authority (Meier, 1979, pp. 62–66, 240–244). Our passage is a portion of a longer block of text (Matt 5:17–48), which contains six "antitheses," on the topics of anger (vv. 21–26), adultery (vv. 27–30), divorce (vv. 31–32), oaths (vv. 33–37), retaliation (vv. 38–42) and love for enemies (vv. 43–48), respectively. In each antithesis, an Old Testament commandment is quoted or summarized

("You have heard that it was said . . ."), after which Jesus either extends the scope of its application or altogether replaces it with new legislation ("but I say to you . . ."). Regarding anger and adultery, Jesus reaffirms the Mosaic commandment but insists that his disciples renounce the dispositions from which they arise—anger and lust, respectively. Regarding divorce, oath-taking and retaliation, Jesus regards the Mosaic commandment as unduly permissive and requires his disciples to renounce these practices altogether. Regarding the treatment of neighbors and enemies, Jesus rejects the conventional idea that neighbors should be "loved" and enemies "hated" and insists instead that all persons must be loved impartially. The very fact that Jesus *can* extend, interiorize, intensify or radically modify a Mosaic law indicates that he possesses divine *authority*, not merely divine *authorization*, to do so. Moses was "authorized" to speak on God's behalf by virtue of the *office* to which God had assigned him (Lev 19:1). But Jesus' "authority" to teach and heal, which is stressed repeatedly in Matthew's Gospel (7:29; 9:2–8; 10:1; 21:23–27; 28:18), is intrinsic to his *person* as the Son of God (8:29; 14:33; 16:16) and the Son of Man (8:20; 9:6; 10:23).[5]

Second, if the key verse in our passage from Leviticus 19 was, "You shall be holy, for I the LORD your God am holy," the key verse in our passage from Matthew 5 is, "Be perfect, therefore, as your heavenly Father is perfect." The latter is clearly an allusion to the former, and it, too, asserts the *imitatio Dei* principle. That is, Jesus' disciples are to cultivate those moral qualities that mirror the moral qualities of God—though naturally under the conditions of human finitude. Moses prohibits murder (Exod 20:13; Deut 5:17; Lev 19:16), but Jesus prohibits even vengefulness and vicious talk (Matt 5:21–26), for God is merciful to "the righteous and the unrighteous" alike (Matt 5:45). Moses forbids adultery (Exod 20:14; Deut 5:18), but Jesus forbids any sexual objectification of others (Matt 5:27–30), for all human beings, "male and female," are made in God's image (Gen 1:27). Moses commands us to love our neighbors as ourselves (Lev 19:18), but Jesus commands us to love not only those who are naturally inclined to love us in return but also our enemies and persecutors (Matt 5:43–47), for God "desires everyone to be saved and to

---

5. The christological titles "Son of God" and "Son of Man," as used in Matthew and elsewhere in the NT, do not bear quite the same meaning as they took on in later Christian doctrine, where they signify his divine and human natures, respectively. Yet Matthew does use these titles to affirm Jesus' unique filial relationship with the Father and his divine mission as humanity's savior, such that his authority greatly exceeded that of "the law and the prophets" (Matt 7:12; 11:13; 12:40–41; 17:3–4; 22:40), the sages (Matt 12:42) and the temple (Matt 12:6).

come to the knowledge of the truth" (1 Tim 2:4). Moses demands congruence between the outward observance of the law and the inward motivation of the heart. Jesus concurs but goes a step further by opposing people's tendency to do as little as necessary in the moral domain and pushing them to do as much as humanly possible. This applies not only to our responsibility to extend neighbor-love to anyone who needs assistance or support but also to our responsibility to examine our own hearts, so that our motivations, intentions, desires and appetites are clarified and purified. *That* is what it means for a disciple of Jesus to imitate the moral perfection of God.

Figure 2.2. Rembrandt van Rijn, *Christ preaching and healing the sick* (or *The hundred guilder print*) [etching]. (1649). 278 mm x 388 mm. Rijksmuseum, Amsterdam, Netherlands

Even if the attainment of "holiness" or "perfection" is assumed to be morally possible, we might still ask whether the attempt to achieve it is emotionally *healthy*. Jewish and Christian history is replete with examples of people who, in attempting to meet this challenge, tortured themselves, and everyone around them, with their picayune scrupulosity and narrow-minded religious zeal.[6] Steele once had a counseling session with a middle-aged SPU

6. John Wesley (1985), the founder of Methodism, the religious tradition to which our university belongs, quite explicitly states that "Christian perfection . . . and holiness . . . are two names for the same thing" (p. 104). Other functional synonyms include

student who remarked, "When I was younger, I was an awful perfectionist, but I've improved a lot since then." If she had only spoken those words with a self-ironic twinkle in her eye, they would have been words of wisdom, indeed! Alas, she spoke them with a straight face and evident pride in her imagined accomplishment, never realizing that they reflected the continuing presence of the very malady she was boasting of having conquered.

We shall return to this delicate issue in chapter 5, when we show how the interweaving of the four strands of biblical moral discourse serves to correct the aberrations and exaggerations to which any one of them, taken by itself, is prone. Here we shall only say that the quest for the kind of perfection that Jesus calls for involves not worrying too much about whether one has attained it, or how far short of it one remains. Theologically, perfection is a flying goal—a moral *horizon*, not a moral *destination*. The quest for it is serious business—which requires a keen sense of humor. It involves deep reflection and fierce intentionality—as well as blithe self-forgetfulness and joyous spontaneity. To pursue the "righteousness that exceeds that of the scribes and Pharisees," one must abstain from checking how far ahead one is of the scribes and Pharisees (or how far behind) and avoid the moral scorekeeping they sometimes indulged in (Matt 23:1–36). The aim should not be to congratulate oneself for surpassing others; it should be to transcend oneself by serving others.[7]

What does all this have to do with Christian nursing? We address that question in section 3 below, after first examining Provisions 5 and 6 of the *Code* (ANA, 2015).

"full salvation" and "entire sanctification." Wesley was fully committed to the principle that Christians should understand themselves to be "going on to perfection," but he also recognized that the misinterpretation of that principle could lead to spiritual pride and various behavioral aberrations.

7. The following story from the Desert Fathers chillingly illustrates the importance of discretion and humility in the pursuit of holiness: Three younger monks visited an elder and began bragging to him of their accomplishments: "'Father, I have committed the Old and New Testaments to memory.' And the old man answered and said, 'Thou hast filled the air with words.' And the second asked him saying, 'I have written the Old and New Testaments with my own hand.' But he said to him, 'And thou hast filled the windows [i.e., window-sills, which were used as bookcases in monastic cells] with manuscripts.' And the third said, 'The grass grows on my hearthstone.' And the old man answered and said, 'And thou hast driven hospitality from thee.'" (Waddell, 1998, p. 111)

THE CODE OF ETHICS FOR NURSES, PROVISIONS 5-6

The *Code* (ANA, 2015) does not use such theological terms as *holiness* or *perfection*. Yet Provisions 5 and 6 emphasize "wholeness of character" (p. 19, p. 20) and "virtue" (pp. 23–24), which parallel some of the root concerns of the holiness strand of biblical moral discourse. The following statement is particularly noteworthy in view of what we said above about the differences in emphasis between the legal and holiness strands: "Virtues focus on what is *good* and *bad* in regard to whom we are to *be* as moral persons; obligations focus on what is *right* and *wrong* or what we are *to do* as moral agents" (p. 23). For this reason, we have paired these two provisions in the *Code* with our two representative holiness texts, though we should not push the parallels too far, for there are some major differences between the biblical concept of holiness and the treatment given in the *Code* to "wholeness of character."

Figure 2.3. *Walt Whitman with his Nurse Warren Fritzenger, on the wharf, probably near his Mickle Street House in Camden, NJ.* (1890).

Provision 5 states, "The nurse owes the same duties to self as to others, including the responsibility to promote health and safety, preserve wholeness of character and integrity, maintain competence, and continue personal and professional growth" (ANA, 2015, p. 19). The first interpretive statement of Provision 5 concerns "Duties to Self and Others" (p. 19). The stress laid here on duties to *self* is striking and reflects important changes both in American society and in the nursing profession that have been taking place since the 1960s. The situation before that time was something like this: First, most nurses were women. There were some exceptions, but not many. This demographic fact fed the common assumption that nursing was "women's work." Second, most physicians were men. True, women had begun entering the profession as early as the late 1800s, but it was still generally assumed that medicine was "men's work." Third, it was the duty of nurses to carry out the directions of physicians. Nursing was regarded as a noble career and an admired service to humanity, but it did not possess the prestige of a "profession" in its own right, or at least not one on par with medicine, law, engineering, the ordained ministry, or the university professoriate.[8] And fourth, it was also the duty of nurses to be models of self-sacrificial devotion to their patients, to perform their responsibilities in a spirit of tireless, cheerful "selflessness." The upshot was that the relationships between nurses and physicians, and between nurses and patients, usually mirrored the stereotypical gender roles and prevailing power arrangements of the wider society.

Thankfully, both demographic facts and social attitudes have been changing. Men are entering the field of nursing, and women the field medicine, in greater and greater numbers. The assumption that women should be subservient to men, whether in the home or the workplace, is widely challenged. Furthermore, nursing is now recognized as a scientific discipline and a full-fledged profession. Licensure requires increasingly rigorous academic training; demanding standards of ethical conduct and professional performance are in place; and the distinctive nursing voice is now heard in the planning and delivery of patient care and in the administration and management of healthcare institutions. Moreover, it has become clear that "selflessness" as a nursing ideal was often used to disguise the fatigue, resentment and burnout that nurses were experiencing on the job. Provision 5.1 in the *Code* (ANA, 2015) both reflects and commends these changes. It insists that nurses have an ethical duty

8. For example, in his study of the plight of "professionals" in contemporary society, William May (2001) devotes chapters to doctors, lawyers, engineers, corporate executives, politicians, media professionals and celebrities, ministers and university professors, but does not once mention nurses. Yet May was a pioneer in medical ethics!

to care properly for themselves in all aspects of their personal and professional lives. Conversely, the *Code* expects healthcare institutions to respect the personal needs of nurses, to provide them with opportunities for professional development and career advancement, and to acknowledge their distinctive contributions to health care at every level. (See especially Provisions 6.3 and 7.1.)

The next interpretive statement, "Promotion of Personal Health, Safety, and Well-Being" (ANA, 2015, p. 19), takes up the same theme. It underscores that living a healthy and balanced life, with due attention to diet, exercise, rest, family life and personal relationships, is something the nurse must "model" personally, as well as advocate for patients and others. There is little in the Holiness Code of Leviticus or in Jesus' Sermon on the Mount to match this stress on prudent self-care, although the biblical Wisdom literature (Strand 3) contains a good deal of it, and we might well have treated Provisions 5.1 and 5.2 in the following chapter instead of here. Yet we have not done so, for we agree with the *Code*'s insistence that self-care is a virtue. Indeed, *not* to construe self-care as a virtue in the strictest sense might suggest that it is a sign of selfishness, or at best a sign of enlightened self-interest.[9] That would perpetuate the idea that nurses and other persons in the helping professions should "burn out before they rust out." Self-giving service to others is the glory of nursing, but self-immolation is folly and very poor stewardship of one's gifts and graces.

If the inclusion of Provisions 5.1 and 5.2 (ANA, 2015) in a chapter on Christian holiness requires some justification, the inclusion of Provisions 5.3 and 5.4 does not. Titled "Preservation of Wholeness of Character" and "Preservation of Integrity," these fit perfectly with the theme of holiness. The former addresses the nurse's role in fostering "a community of moral

9. The distinction between "holiness" and "wisdom," and the parallel distinction between "virtue" and "enlightened self-interest" should not be overdrawn, however. A holy person may sometimes act in obedience to God, even when doing so is contrary to his temporal interests. And as various ancient moralists insisted, virtue is its own reward, and is not practiced rightly if it is practiced for the sake of personal gain. Yet holiness and virtue are both generally ordered to human flourishing, and those who practice them will generally benefit both themselves and others. Conversely, although "wisdom" occasionally seems to mean little more than "shrewdness," it usually refers to the kind of impulse control, emotional balance and general maturity, which come from wide experience and sustained reflection, and which deserve moral approval. The prologue to the book of Proverbs indicates that the work offers "instruction in wise dealing, righteousness, justice and equity" (Proverbs 1:3), with no suggestion that "wise dealing" is a non-moral category, in contrast to the other three items on the list. Thomas Aquinas regards prudence itself as a virtue, and indeed, as "the mother" of all the others (Pieper, 1966, p. 3).

discourse." The "community" in view here is the specific healthcare facility in which a nurse works, one likely to be fraught with morally complex and ambiguous situations, which the nurse should *be* free, and *feel* free, to speak into from her distinctive professional perspective. Once again, the *Code* reminds its readers that "authentic expression of one's own moral point of view is a duty to self" (p. 20), as if they might suppose that keeping silent were the moral default mode. But Provision 5.3 quickly shifts to the nurse's responsibility to facilitate the involvement by others, especially patients, in healthcare decisions, noting that that those with social power must guard against coercing, manipulating or exerting undue influence on the needy and helpless. Provision 5.4 addresses situations in which nurses are pressured into acting illegally, immorally or unprofessionally, or are subjected to threats or abuse. Nurses are also reminded that maintaining their integrity under such circumstances is a "self-regarding duty" (p. 20). Provision 5.4 acknowledges the need for patience, negotiation and compromise in morally complex or emotionally fraught circumstances, but in the end it stoutly affirms the principles of "whistle-blowing" and conscientious objection.

Provisions 5.5 ("Maintenance of Competence and Continuation of Professional Growth") and 5.6 ("Continuation of Personal Growth") guard against stagnation and inertia (ANA, 2015). Insofar as nursing is a science and a profession, it is always developing new methodologies, discovering new truth, and devising new strategies for human betterment, and nurses are obliged to keep abreast of their discipline (p. 22). But one of the glories of nursing has always been its refusal to separate science from art, knowledge from wisdom, or best professional practice from wholesome personal conduct. The *Code* affirms that nursing care "addresses the whole person as an integrated being" (p. 22) and insists that nurses apply this principle both to their patients and also to themselves.

Provision 6 states, "The nurse, through individual and collective effort, establishes, maintains, and improves the ethical environment of the work setting and conditions of employment that are conducive to safe, quality health care" (ANA, 2015, p. 23). In this provision, the resonances between the *Code* and the holiness strand of biblical moral discourse become strikingly evident. If Provision 5, in its constant stress on self-regarding duties, has a decidedly "wisdom" ring to it, Provision 6 hammers home the importance of moral virtue. Of course, there are no references here to "holiness" or "Christian perfection" as such, but the intention is to delineate the characteristics of the "morally 'good nurse'" ("The Environment and Moral

Virtue," p. 23), as well as the characteristics of a professional environment which promotes virtue in its employees ("The Environment and Ethical Obligation," pp. 23–24). A mark of moral goodness in individuals is their commitment to building "morally good environments." Conversely, a mark of moral goodness in an institution is its commitment to fostering virtue in its employees. Yet the moral goodness of an institution is always more than its own self-perpetuation or the well-being of its employees. It must exist *for* something; it needs a purpose, a mission. A healthcare facility, for example, exists to promote the well-being of its patients and their families. It shows its own moral legitimacy, and fosters virtue in its employees, precisely by its conscientious attention to the needs of those it exists to serve—and not by preoccupation to its balance sheet or public image. On the other hand, no healthcare facility can claim moral legitimacy if it appeals to "the needs of its patients" in order to justify the mistreatment or exploitation of its employees or causes its employees moral harm by expecting them to violate the ethical standards of their respective professions or to give sub-optimal care to patients. These points are emphasized in Provision 6.3, "Responsibility for the Healthcare Environment" (pp. 24–25). All this is very much in line with Leviticus 19 and Matthew 5, which constantly stress that the test of moral excellence is one's responsiveness to the neighbor's need.

MORAL VIRTUE AND CAREGIVING

A Christian nurse will see in the *Code*'s (ANA, 2015) call for "wholeness of character and integrity" a secular analog to the Bible's call for "holiness." Of course, the *Code* makes no mention of the God-relationship, which is fundamental to the biblical concept of holiness. The *Code* assumes, quite rightly, that a nurse can attain "wholeness of character and integrity" without being "religious" in any overt way. (Alas, the reverse is also true: one can be "religious" without displaying moral character or integrity.) But people who espouse the Christian faith, and who aspire to be truly "holy" in the rich biblical sense of that term, will not only engage faithfully in the various prescribed liturgical and devotional practices of their church; they will assiduously cultivate the four "cardinal" and the three "charismatic" moral virtues briefly described below. And Christian nurses who wish to put their personal religious convictions and values into practice in their professional work will also cultivate the six "caregiving" virtues, which are discussed at somewhat greater length in what follows. These three classes of virtues, and the specific virtues in each class, are shown in Table 2.1 below.

Table 2.1. A Catalogue of Virtues		
Cardinal Virtues	Charismatic Virtues	Caregiving Virtues
1. Prudence	1. Faith	1. Veracity
2. Temperance	2. Hope	2. Attentiveness
3. Courage	3. Love	3. Patience
4. Justice		4. Generosity of spirit
		5. Compassion
		6. Reverence for life

From a Christian perspective, the practice of the virtues is synonymous with the *imitatio Dei* principle discussed above. Although our holiness texts from Leviticus or Matthew do not explicitly name or define these virtues, the cardinal and charismatic virtues specify various elements of the character of a person who is living by the spirit of the Levitical Holiness Code and Jesus' Sermon on the Mount, and the caregiving virtues name the qualities of a person who is putting that spirit into practice in the activities specific to the healing of the sick, the injured, the disabled and the dying.[10]

Ancient moral philosophy identified four "cardinal" virtues: prudence, temperance, courage and justice (Pieper, 1966). The English word *cardinal* comes from the Latin *cardo*, meaning "hinge," and the idea was that a good life hinged on the cultivation of all four. Conversely, a life lacking one or more of these was deemed morally askew. Each of these virtues represented a suitable response to a major moral challenge that every human being faces. Prudence or practical wisdom is the capacity to assess people and situations accurately, lubricating social relationships with guileless charm,

---

10. To say that one who aspires to "imitate God" must practice the virtues is not to say that God possesses virtues that one can imitate, or at least that God possesses them in the same way that human beings do (or should). For example, God does not need prudence, because, being all-wise and all-powerful, God does not have to deliberate over how to achieve his ends. But a godly person does need prudence, which is the habit of eagerly seeking to know what an all-wise, all-powerful God wants of her, and then acting accordingly—always recognizing that her powers of discernment are limited and that her obedience is imperfect. Christians, of course, practice the *imitation of God* by way of the *imitation of Christ* and have in Jesus of Nazareth a human exemplar of the virtues on whom to pattern their lives. That renders "Christian perfection" easier to *picture*, though no easier to *achieve*.

avoiding conflicts and "scenes" whenever possible, and handling those that arise with finesse and aplomb. Temperance is the capacity to enjoy life's pleasures with moderation and in accordance with social norms, not renouncing pleasures out of shame, disgust or self-righteous pride but taking them with moderation and thereby avoiding the consequences of unbridled excess. Courage is the capacity to face life's dangers with equanimity and resolution, not courting trouble or harm by recklessness, but not shrinking from one's duty because of the risks involved. Finally, justice is the capacity to analyze what each person in each situation is due, along with the determination to render each person his or her due to the fullest extent possible. The ancient philosophers identified many other virtues but regarded these four as morally indispensable for all persons in all circumstances—the essential groundwork of a praiseworthy character. Indeed, they regarded them as a "unity," with each depending on and contributing to the proper practice of the other three.

To the four cardinal virtues identified in antiquity, early and medieval Christian theologians added the triad of "charismatic" virtues mentioned by St. Paul: faith, hope and love (1 Cor 13:13; Col 1:5; 1 Thess 1:3; 5:8; Pieper, 1997). A "charism" is a gift, and these three virtues were thought to be gifts given by the Holy Spirit to all Christians in some measure. Yet they also require deliberate cultivation and intentional practice by the recipients. Faith is trust in God's providential ordering of creation, together with confidence in the sufficiency of God's provision for all one's needs, physical and spiritual. Hope is the assurance that the future, like the past and the present, is under the secure control of a gracious God. Love is responsiveness to the needs of others, respect for the rights of others, sorrow over the troubles of others, joy in the joys of others—all offered in gratitude for God's reconciling love for us. Many other distinctively Christian virtues are named in the New Testament (see, e.g., Gal 5:22–25; Eph 4:1–3; Jas 3:17; 2 Pet 1:5–7), but Christian theologians have generally understood the others as modalities, specifications or expressions of faith, hope or love. Moreover, just as the ancient philosophers had taught that the cardinal virtues were a dynamic unity, so Christian theologians regard the cardinal virtues *plus* the charismatic virtues as an integral whole, collectively constitutive of a "holy" life (Augustine, 1887a, especially chapters 3–8; Augustine, 1887b, especially chapter 15). Through baptism, one becomes a member of the body of Christ; through the practice of the virtues, under the guidance and

by empowerment of the Holy Spirit, one makes one's sacramental membership in Christ an existential reality.

We have repeatedly asserted that the virtues must be "cultivated." How
does one do that? The ancient Greek philosopher Aristotle (1998) answered
that to acquire a specific *virtue*, one must consistently and deliberately act
in ways that society regards as expressive of that virtue. It may be that such
actions are contrary to one's natural inclinations, at least at first, and that
painful deliberation, forceful self-talk and the support of friends may be
required. An alcoholic who wishes to become "temperate," for example,
may require constant encouragement from a diligent sponsor, a faithful fel-
lowship of other recovering addicts, and all the complicated apparatus of a
detox facility and a twelve-step program. Yet if things go well, the constant
performance of "temperate" actions will eventually render those actions
less onerous, less in need of white-knuckled determination. At that point,
when virtuous action has finally become "second nature," something one
performs with a kind of effortless promptitude, one possesses the virtue
itself (pp. 28–29). In short, one must act virtuously in order to attain virtue,
but once one attains virtue, one acts virtuously. Although this sounds sus-
piciously like circular reasoning, in actual practice, the process of acquir-
ing a virtue is more like a helix. One makes genuine progress over time by
deliberate, and deliberately repetitive, activity, whereby one's character is
slowly but steadily transformed.

The cardinal and charismatic virtues are fundamental to the Christian
moral life, and all the other virtues are variant forms of one or more of
these seven. Yet a Christian's specific life circumstances and distinctive professional obligations will determine how the seven are adapted, combined
and concretely expressed. The six virtues that we discuss below—veracity,
attentiveness, patience, generosity of spirit, compassion and reverence for
life—are those which the challenges of tending the sick, the injured, the
disabled and the dying call forth in the caregiver. They have their own
names, characteristics and morphologies, and for purposes of classification
and analysis it is handy to call them, collectively, the "caregiving virtues."
We assert that all six are manifestations or blends of one or more of the
cardinal and charismatic virtues, but we make no claim that these six represent an exhaustive list of the specific virtues needed by caregivers. We
contend only that Christians who dedicate their lives to nursing those who
are unwell need at least these six "additional" virtues and that the diligent
cultivation of these virtues is an expression both of Christian holiness and

of that "wholeness of character and integrity" called for by the *Code* (ANA, 2015). Collectively, these six virtues enable a nurse to be a "healing presence" to her patients. The steady practice of these virtues, day in and day out, in various clinical situations, is a key factor in rendering the nurse trustworthy to patients, thereby predisposing them to gain maximal benefit from her healing ministrations.

Before describing the caregiving virtues one by one, however, it is important to introduce a distinction that will significantly shape how we understand their clinical function, and that will also shape how we understand the clinical function of the problem-solving, decision-making and human relations skills described in the next chapter. This is the distinction between two kinds of human troubles, namely, "difficulties" and "problems." William F. May (1991) tells the following story about T. S. Eliot, who was delivering a lecture on some serious issue in American life:

> At the close of [the] lecture . . . an undergraduate arose to ask him urgently, "Mr. Eliot, what are we going to do about the problem you have discussed?" Eliot replied, in effect, "You have asked the wrong question. You must understand that we face two types of [troubles] in life. One kind of [trouble] provokes the question, 'What are we going to do about it?' The other kind poses the subtler question, 'How do we behave towards it?' The first type of [trouble] demands relatively technical, pragmatic, and tactical responses that will eliminate the [trouble]; the second poses deeper challenges which no specific policy, strategy, or behavior can dissolve. The [trouble] will persist. It requires behavior that sensitively, decorously, and appropriately fits the perduring challenge" (pp. 3–4).[11]

For clarity's sake, we call troubles of the first type "problems," and troubles of the second type "difficulties." "Problems" are troubles that demand solutions and call for the acquisition of the knowledge and skills necessary to imagine, design and implement those solutions. In contrast, "difficulties" are troubles built into the human condition itself, such as our susceptibility to disease, injury and disablement; the decline in our bodily and mental faculties as we age; and the inevitability of death. Difficulties call for a very different kind of response than problems do, namely, the

11. For the sake of clarity, given the distinction we are drawing between "problems" and "difficulties," we have substituted the word "trouble" wherever the word "problem" stands in May's (1991) text. The distinction between "problems" and "difficulties" is borrowed from Watzlawick, Weakland, and Fisch (1974, pp. 38–39).

cultivation of the virtues necessary to face and endure them (Steele, 2018, pp. 26–28; Steele, 2018, May).

We stated above that the second and third strands of biblical moral discourse, holiness and wisdom, both focus on human *character*. The former, which is the topic of the present chapter, pertains to one's moral virtues and life values; the latter, to which we turn in the next chapter, pertains to one's personal habits and professional skills. The distinction between problems and difficulties is correlative—and highly relevant to our account of nursing ethics. Nurses are all too well acquainted with both, insofar as these relate to people's physical and mental health. They dedicate themselves to helping people (1) to avoid or delay the occurrence of both problems and difficulties, through education and anticipatory guidance; (2) to *solve* such *problems* as arise, whenever possible; (3) to *face* such *difficulties* as arise, when these prove unavoidable and incurable; and (4) to *reduce the severity* of such problems and difficulties as arise, whenever *that* is possible. The caregiving virtues are those aspects of a nurse's character that constitute his "healing presence" in the face of life's intractable difficulties; the problem-solving, decision-making and human-relations skills are those aspects of a nurse's character that constitute his "savvy" in the face of health problems that are avoidable or susceptible to effective management and eventual resolution. It may not always be obvious which kind of trouble a given patient is facing. For example, a persistent cough may seem, at first, to be a solvable problem, but turn out to be the first symptom of an incurable throat cancer—as grim a difficulty as one can face. Conversely, some difficulties, themselves permanent and unsolvable, may entail problems that can be solved, thus alleviating the felt severity of the specific difficulties that cause them. A spinal cord injury, for instance, may prevent a person from ever walking again, but a wheelchair may restore some measure of mobility. Effective nursing care requires that one be able both to identify and solve problems and to care for people in their tragic difficulties, and therefore they need both holiness and wisdom, that is, both the caregiving virtues to which we now turn, and the clinical and interpersonal skills discussed in chapter 3 below.

We turn now to the six caregiving virtues mentioned above. The first is *veracity* or truthfulness (Bok, 1999). This virtue entails both the practice of telling the truth and the skill of telling it in such a way that one's hearers can understand and benefit from the truth that is told to them. For nurses, this requires a deep understanding of the etiology, symptomatology, prognosis and plan of care for the patient's medical condition, as well as a deep respect for the patient as a human being in the concrete particulars of her personal situation (frame of mind, educational level, family dynamic, finances, etc.).[12] It is possible to communicate "information" accurately—but in a way that is hurtful, overwhelming or confusing to one's listener. It is equally possible, in the name of sensitivity to one's listener, to give too little information, or to state the facts in a way that minimizes or obscures their seriousness and implications. Neither approach to the truth is properly "truthful," in the richest sense of the word, and listeners who catch healthcare providers either distorting the facts or conveying them in a way that is brusque, coldly "clinical" or inattentive to the human realities at play are apt to lose trust in the provider or the system.

Steele recalls a particularly vivid example of clinical veracity. He was looking at a CT scan of his daughter's brain tumor with a pediatric neurosurgeon. "You see that squiggly line there," said the doctor. "That's the mid-basilar artery. If I nick that sucker, it's curtains." No doubt this was an accurate statement, but its crude brutality hardly inspired trust in a frightened father. Yet in that case, the physician's truthfulness—that is, his deep humanity, and not simply his "scrupulous honesty"—was vindicated by what he said next: "I've done this kind of surgery before, but not often. Last time I blinded the patient. The mother was ecstatic that I had saved her daughter's life, but I was devastated because I couldn't save her vision. I advise you to take your daughter to someone who specializes in treating this kind of tumor." He did not want his prospective patient's father to trust him, because he did not fully trust himself in this case.

Veracity is closely akin to the cardinal virtue of prudence, for both entail not only deep respect for the "plain facts" of a given situation (in this case, the diagnosis of the disease and the likely effectiveness and possible side effects of the proposed treatment) but also for its psychosocial context and personal ramifications. In the modern healthcare context, however, veracity has a slightly more "scientific" ring than prudence often does, but that only increases the importance of the element of tact and sensitivity in communication. Veracity also partakes of the cardinal virtue of justice. When healthcare providers present the relevant medical facts of their situation, use

12. This point is forcefully stressed by Dietrich Bonhoeffer (1975), who writes that "'telling the truth' . . . is not solely a matter of moral character [i.e., scrupulous honesty]; it is also a matter of correct appreciation of real situations and of serious reflection upon them. The more complex the actual situations of a [person's] life, the more responsible and the more difficult will be his task of 'telling the truth'" (p. 364).

understandable language, explain the risks and benefits of alternative treatment options, and offer frequent opportunities for question-and-answer, the patient and his family are in the best position to make wise medical decisions and to participate actively in the chosen plan of care. Yet truthfulness is not simply a matter of *telling* the truth skillfully and tactfully. It is also a matter of *protecting* the truth vigilantly. This involves, first, protecting patients' *privacy*, that is, helping them to control who has access to their persons, to their property, to their decisions and their reasons for making those decisions and to information about them. It involves, second, protecting patients' *confidentiality*, that is, helping to assure that information about patients is available only to those who have a clearly defined "need to know" (Bok, 1982, pp. 116–35; Beauchamp & Childress, 2013, pp. 311–24). To summarize, veracity involves stating the facts, painful as they may sometimes be for the patient to hear, in ways that the patient can understand; maintaining confidentiality; and protecting the patient's privacy. This caregiving virtue is crucial for all healthcare workers, but especially for nurses, because of how much time they spend in their patients' company. Nurses are skilled in judging how well their patients are processing information and in offering hope, encouragement and realism in facing whatever lies ahead.

The second of the caregiving virtues is *attentiveness*.[13] This is the practice of showing to another person that his immediate needs and feelings are at that moment one's greatest concern and that attending to his immediate needs and feelings is one's joy and a privilege. It is crucial not to provide "care" in a way that feels coldly impersonal, suggests that doing so is a burden or a hassle, or conveys the impression that the caregiver desperately needs to be needed. In such cases, the caregiver may be "paying attention" to her work, but she is not "being attentive" to the patient—and the patient can usually tell the difference! True attentiveness is "the habit of communicating through the gentleness of one's eyes and the restfulness of one's body language that one takes genuine pleasure in being in the company of another" (Steele, 2010, pp. 31–33), and making a human connection in the process of meeting a need, providing a service or doing a kindness. Attentiveness is a

---

13. The following discussion of attentiveness, patience, generosity of spirit, compassion and reverence for life draws heavily on two of Steele's earlier publications, as cited in the appropriate places below. Those essays pertained to the care given to persons with disabilities by parents, friends, personal attendants, etc. We subscribe to the basic definitions Steele gives to the virtues under consideration here, but we have recast his discussion to make it specifically relevant to *nursing* care and to the care of patients with *any* medical condition, not just disability.

blend of prudence, justice, faith and love. To be attentive, one must be prudent, because genuine helpfulness (as opposed to mere busyness) requires a realistic assessment of the other's true needs and a degree of resourcefulness in figuring out how best to meet them. One must be just, always seeking to render the other his due. One must be faithful, demonstrating a seriousness of commitment to the other person, which the other can rely on without question, and which the other does not feel the need to earn or deserve. And one needs love to keep in check one's ego investment in the relationship with the other person, while investing in the other's betterment. Nurses require this virtue because they must efficiently execute a patient's plan of care without giving the impression that the efficient performance of one's professional duties is more important than displaying a genuine interest in the "the patient as person" (Ramsey, 2002; cf. Mohrmann, 2005, pp. 85–141; Schiedermayer, 1994; Tournier, 1960, pp. 121–36.)

Figure 2.4. Jean-Baptiste-Siméon Chardin, *The attentive nurse* [oil on canvas]. (1747). 46 cm x 37 cm. National Gallery of Art, Washington, DC

Patience is the third caregiving virtue. It is "closely related to attentiveness, yet distinct from it. The distinction lies partly in the time horizon within which the two virtues are practiced and partly in how they are practiced. Attentiveness is being fully present to a person in the moment of direct, face-to-face encounter. It is the willingness to clear one's schedule and free one's mind from personal agendas, in order to make a deep human connection with another person. Patience, in contrast, is the firm resolution to be concretely helpful in improving the health, comfort and/or general welfare of the other person . . . over an extended period of time, and to assist him or her in facing the challenges and difficulties of his or her situation, however long it takes, and whether or not a complete and permanent cure or recovery is possible" (Steele, 2010, p. 35). Patience combines the virtues of temperance, hope, and faith. It requires temperance, for it obliges the caregiver to set aside her own aims and interests in order to attend to the needs of the other—and perhaps to do so many times each day, day in and day out, for as long as it takes the patient to heal. The nurse's immediate aims may be short-term goals involving brief patient encounters, as in day surgery or urgent care interactions; yet for patients, these interactions may be critical moments for their long-term well-being. In these situations, patience may manifest in thorough handoffs between nurses and careful discharge teaching, with the knowledge that these efforts help the patient move incrementally toward healing or quality of life. Patience requires faith, for it refuses to abandon the sufferer to his plight. And it requires hope, for it involves the caregiver's renunciation of any need to have her efforts get quick results. That a nurse requires this virtue seems self-evident, partly because the time it takes a patient to heal cannot always be predicted with precision, and partly because the nurse's act of communicating hope to the patient is itself a key factor in the patient's healing process.[14]

The fourth caregiving virtue is *generosity of spirit*. This involves both open-handed bounteousness—that is, the willingness to give gladly of one's own time, energy, wisdom or possessions to another—and courteous receptivity, that is, the willingness to accept words or tokens of thanks from another with grace and modesty. "The reason for this is that generosity springs from the conviction that the true value of any gift is determined, not by the monetary worth of the gift, but by the intrinsic dignity of the persons involved in the exchange, and by the incalculable moral and spiritual significance of their relationship" (Steele, 2010, p. 37). Generosity of spirit thus blends the cardinal virtue of temperance with the charismatic virtue of hope. Temperance is the mastery of our selfish desires and carnal appetites, enabling us to forgo what we want in favor of what others need, and conversely, to take genuine delight in the gifts and kindnesses of others.

14. For a thorough discussion of the virtue of patience in medical care, see the section on "Waiting" in Mohrmann (2005), pp. 143–206. For a moving example of caregiving over the long haul, both by the primary care physician and by the patient's family, see Schiedermayer (1994), pp. 23–35.

Hope comes into play by orienting both parties to this blessed reciprocity toward the future. Accordingly, generosity of spirit is a critical virtue for nurses, as it brings a much-needed note of joy into the somber ordeal through which their patients are often passing. It can also reduce the inherent lopsidedness of the power relations in the nurse-patient relationship, where the former can so easily be only the "giver" and "doer," and the latter only the passive recipient (Doornbos et al., 2005; Fadiman, 2012).

Figure 2.5. *A flower for nurse. French baby at the American Red Cross nursing home near Paris.* (1918).

Compassion, the fifth of the caregiving virtues, is the disposition to identify oneself so closely with suffering people that their sufferings become one's own. The immediate aim of compassion is ordinarily to *relieve* the sufferings of others, perhaps through concrete acts of caring service or public advocacy. Yet truly compassionate people do not make the likelihood that the sufferings of others can be relieved a condition of identifying with their plight, for if that were so, they might consider themselves absolved of all further responsibility to the sufferers if no improvement in their situation were possible. That is precisely what compassionate people do *not* do, because the aim of compassion—as the very etymology of the word suggests—is to "suffer with" others, so that the sufferers do not suffer alone. Thus, compassionate people relieve the alienation and loneliness which suffering induces, even if they cannot relieve the suffering itself. Compassion, then, is a blend of the charismatic virtue of love and the cardinal virtues of courage and prudence. Through love, one concerns oneself with the neighbor's need; through courage, one willingly endures vicarious pain and makes personal sacrifices that he might have avoided; through prudence, one discerns the concrete interventions, if any, that are best suited to lessen the neighbor's sufferings. We note, accordingly, that of the six caregiving virtues listed here, compassion has the highest content of raw emotion (Steele, 2000). Because of it, one suffers *with* another, *for* another, and sometimes *from* another. Indeed, we could speak of it as a "virtuous emotion" (Harak, 1993; Roberts, 2007). That nurses must cultivate it in order to be effective in their work is obvious. But practicing it day in and day out can take its toll in fatigue, resentment and burnout, and precautions must be taken to avoid them.[15]

If the fifth caregiving virtue, compassion, is the most heavily laden with emotion, the sixth, *reverence for life*, is the most deeply grounded in specific doctrinal content. It is not simply a way of behaving toward others or identifying with their sufferings. It is a way of construing their personhood. It springs from the biblical testimony that human beings are made in the image of God (Gen 1:26–27; 9:6–7; cf. Ps 8:5). Earlier in this chapter, we examined the biblical concept of holiness. We saw that God's holiness has two elements, numinosity and moral excellence, and that the former was gradually muted in the religious consciousness of Judaism and Christianity, though never fully eclipsed, as the latter assumed greater and greater importance. We saw, too, that God's people become holy by imitating the holiness of God—but that such imitation primarily has God's moral excellence in view, rather than God's numinosity. We stand by that analysis. But the claim that human beings are icons of God suggests that a touch of divine numinosity clings to them after all. Accordingly, they are not only worthy of respect as rational beings and autonomous moral agents; they should also be treated with a sense of wonder and gratitude, as "earthly manifestations of a transcendent and divine Reality" (Steele, 2010, pp. 40–42). Moreover,

---

15. Here is another story from the Desert Fathers: "A brother asked one of the elders, saying: There are two brothers, of whom one remains praying in his cell, fasting six days at a time and doing a great deal of penance. The other one takes care of the sick. Which one's work is more pleasing to God? The elder replied: If that brother who fasts six days at a time were to hang himself up by the nose, he could not equal the one who takes care of the sick" (Merton, 1970, pp. 59–60). Although we agree that genuine compassion for the sick and injured is a holy calling, we reiterate that the prudent caregiver must always balance self-sacrifice with self-care.

if we ask which of the cardinal and/or charismatic virtues constitute reverence for life, we are inclined to answer, all of them! Prudence bids us to honor their uniqueness and complexity. Courage requires us to protect them from all harm, even at great cost to ourselves, for they are creatures of infinite dignity and worth. Temperance induces us to deliver them from such temptations as might lead them to tarnish the divine image they bear. Justice demands that we scrupulously give each person her due, knowing that she is "Christ incognito" (cf. Matt 25:31–46). Faith teaches us to honor all persons as beloved children of God. Hope teaches us to bear in mind their eternal destiny, while caring for their temporal needs and wants. Love teaches us to do unto them as we would be done by (Matt 7:12), and indeed, to do unto them as Christ has already done unto us (John 15:12). Mary O'Brien (2018) beautifully captures the significance that reverence for life has for nursing practice when she describes the care of patients and their families as entering upon "holy ground" (p. 7). Like Moses approaching the burning bush with a mixture of awe and fascination, nurses rightly approach those entrusted to them with a deep veneration for their infinite value as bearers of the divine image and a kind of joyful enchantment over the profound mystery of their human personhood.

CLINICAL VOICES

We have discussed how the *Code* (ANA, 2015) and Christian Scripture enhance each other and how they suggest the nurse may truly become a healing presence to others. It may seem daunting to aspire to holiness as a nurse. However, when reframed into caregiving virtues, the nurse may be able to see more clearly how holiness relates to being an excellent nurse of outstanding character and heart. The experienced nurses here discuss challenges and ways in which holiness and caregiving virtues promoted excellence, both in the workplace and in pivotal moments of caring for vulnerable patients:

Cory Klein: *Leadership in caregiving*

I was lucky enough to have an amazing role model in my very first nursing job. She was a charge nurse who had charisma, grace, intelligence, and patience to make every single person who spoke to her feel important and heard. From settling a difficult family dispute (which often arises in oncology and end-of-life care), to mediating care and advocating for patients amongst a collaborative medical team, to creating a culture of mutual respect and caring on our floor, she managed everything effortlessly. In the year that followed, I recognized that most everyone on the unit tried to do the same, which helped create a culture of warmth, unity, and excellence on our floor. I realized that this nurse embodies all the "caregiver virtues." To be a leader, the most important thing is to take the time to truly listen and then act with grace and love. While perfection is an unattainable and daunting task, her attributes certainly demonstrated the ability of embodiment of caregiver virtues and collaborating to move a whole unit forward towards "moral maturity."

Kara Kozemzak: *Attentiveness and professional boundaries*

Attentiveness allows for accurate assessment of patients' physical and mental well-being, fosters a trusting nurse-patient relationship, and establishes a respectful work environment. There have been times where I have been so caught up with juggling tasks that I haven't been mentally present in a patient room. I had a nonverbal patient who was restless, and rather than taking the time with him to be attentive and thoroughly investigate the source of his discomfort, I assumed his positioning was the reason for his restlessness; I repositioned him and rushed on to the next patient awaiting me. When he continued to be restless, I found that his IV had infiltrated. Had I been attentive, I could have caught that early and eased his discomfort immediately. Other times when I have taken a moment outside a patient room to collect myself and put other worries aside, I have been able to connect with my patients in a meaningful way and assess them thoroughly, catching things I otherwise wouldn't have. Although there are clear benefits to attentiveness, it is time-consuming and difficult to incorporate into nursing practice. There are times when attentiveness towards one patient delays care to another or causes professional boundaries to be crossed. I have cared for many patients who take my attentive approach as permission to share extremely personal information or use me as their primary emotional support. Not only is this time-consuming, preventing me from providing quality care to my other patients, but it has placed me in an unhealthy role. I have also experienced negative effects while showing attentiveness to coworkers, who have taken the opportunity to gossip or put me in a therapist role, distracting me from my work.

Mimie Bagalwa: *Leading with compassion and justice*

I remembered one of my previous managers for his courage in saving lives and attentiveness to not only patients, but staff also, especially minorities. He knew what to say when, and how to tell the right words to a grieving or discontented staff or family member. To staff members with complaints about others, the manager would seek to hear the other person's story. Aware of an individual's emotional state, he would talk to and encourage staff, demonstrating the essence of understanding coworkers and the importance of putting personal differences aside for the patient's sake. He genuinely cared about what staff went through and heard what the other person "really" said or meant. During high census seasons, he would report to work very early to help on the floor. On numerous occasions, he would engage in code blue events and offer to start an IV. He would come to work at 0300 as a resource, to help staff with any patient-care-related activity for any team member lagging behind in charting. He so genuinely cared about subordinates' professional and personal growth that he initiated an on-site part-time BSN evening class session. Under his leadership, more minorities got hired, persuaded towards leadership responsibilities such as charge nurse, and he stood up for those he felt were not treated fairly. As an act of justice, the manager would provide an opportunity to each applicant and those he managed. For example, a new hire into the residency struggled with different aspects of providing care and struggled with communicating with families. Most nursing staff rallied against the new hire and wanted him relieved of his duties. As a manager who believed in equal opportunities for every race, he referred the new hire for extra communication skills and leadership courses. I still cherish his passion for believing in each subordinate's growth, and justice for those who are not quick to speak for themselves.

Flannery Moran: *Generosity of spirit*

B. E. was a quiet, patient, and incredibly sweet man who suffered with Parkinson's. He no longer walked, barely spoke more than a few words in a whisper, and his main expression was through his eyes. But he taught me an incredible amount about holiness—whether it was reaching from his wheelchair to the next to help an elderly female resident turn the page of a book when she couldn't remember how, or straightening another resident's beads so she felt put-together, or sitting near enough the nurses' station to offer a warm smile or hug whenever staff or visitors passed. I cared for

B. E. for four and a half years before graduating RN school and moving jobs. Six months later he passed away peacefully. The last time I saw him, his last words to me were more than I'd heard him say in years: "Please take care of yourself, dear friend." He'd always asked me whether I'd had lunch yet, before I'd fed him his, and in this way and a million others that I later recalled, he made sure that I gave thought to how well I was caring for myself, in the midst of caring for others. He made me a better nurse and a kinder human—specifically, I learned that generosity of spirit is simple to offer, and priceless to receive.

Alix Lobaugh: *Connecting during crisis*

We had a patient that was very well versed with the healthcare system, as she'd had more than ten abdominal surgeries. She gave birth to twins pretty early in her gestation and after a day or two one of the babies died. She also had history of fetal demise: one miscarriage and another preterm baby that died. When I met this family, emotions were high and their grief was manifesting in aggression toward the nursing staff. They were interrogating each: how many years of experience in NICU they had, if they were familiar with the type of respiratory support their child was using and if they were specialized in caring for extremely preterm infants. I quickly recognized their emotional status and exhaustion and sat down with them to discuss their sweet baby's care. What did they want that night to look like? What particular things can you share with me that will help hands-on care go smoothly? What do you want to do during cluster care? Can I give you any information about your baby's care to help you through this process? I had ten other things I had to do right then but I took the time and was patient as I listened to their wants and needs and how I could help them care and learn about their baby. I was attentive to the needs that no one else was tending to; other providers were so focused on the critical status of the patient, which was significant, but we would not get anywhere if we could not establish rapport with these parents. Being patient and truly present in that moment can be so difficult and requires practice and reflection.

Anonymous: *Reverence for the life of the "noncompliant" patient*

Working in the busy hospital setting, I did not feel like I could be as attentive as I needed to be with patients and felt I was not doing the job that I needed to do. This left me feeling burned out and unsatisfied with my profession. However, after being given the opportunity to meet patients in their homes where I could be more attentive to their needs, this satisfaction blossomed. I was proud to be called a nurse as I was able to feel like I was not just "doing my job" but actually making a difference in my patients' lives. I remember a diabetic elder that I cared for who was a referral to our agency for uncontrolled diabetes with multiple ER visits and hospital admissions for both hypo- and hyperglycemic episodes. She had been labeled "noncompliant." The referral source wanted our agency to help with diabetic and medication management. I went into her home with these preconceived ideas of noncompliance, but what I found out from being attentive to this patient is that she didn't understand her medications, didn't have the resources for a diabetic diet, and had multiple family members taking advantage of her. By sitting down, listening to her and what her needs and goals were, we were able to come up with a plan of action in a way that was acceptable to her and her situation. Ultimately, this improved her health and quality of life.

Jen Mac: *Attentive listening or task completion*

I cared for a patient who had a one-on-one sitter for a suicide attempt by drug overdose. It was a busy day on the unit, so I hadn't seen her much throughout the day. The sitter, and other nurses previously caring for this patient, had told me they tried but failed to convince her to take a shower. Her unpleasant odor was evident, and it was an issue beckoning to be addressed. My primary intent to convince this patient to perform self-care quickly turned into an hour-long conversation. She described her relationship with a man and how its resolution left her with deep void. As I listened, I saw tears in her eyes and felt them forming in mine. Eventually, I was pulled away to tend to another task, but I remember while I was in that room it was as if time had slowed down. I don't remember giving her any advice. I mostly listened, and I can't recall if she had showered or whether I even asked. I recognize caring for others doesn't always translate into being attentive. As a provider, if I'm not careful I will find myself wrapped up in the monotonous, seemingly never-ending task of completing orders, charting, and paperwork instead of pursuing depth in relationships with those I'm caring for. "Holiness" implies we are called by God to be all we can be, and while I understand we are not the sum of our actions, they often are indicators of what we regard as important. In encounters with those who are in pain, I hope to be a provider who "suffers with" patients, and in turn renders healing presence even when I don't have all the answers.

Julia Bell: *Self-care innovations*

When I started my nursing career, I struggled a lot with self-care. I worked in a long-term acute care hospital where every patient is ICU level, and I normally had 5–6 total care patients in 12-hour shifts. I felt too exhausted by the end of my shift, morally and physically, and thought about quitting nursing. However, I understood very quickly: if I do not care for myself, nobody will, and my condition is not safe for my patients. I talked to my manager and told her that I refused to take such an assignment anymore. I found a few research articles about the staff-patient ratio negatively and severely affecting patient outcomes. I was fighting for myself and my patients. A tired and burned-out nurse is a great opportunity for deadly mistakes. Administration accommodated my complaints to some degree but did not solve the issue, so I developed some strategies to take care of myself while taking care of my patients. Every time I filled a patient's cup with water, I hydrated myself. Every time I took them to the toilet, I used the bathroom as well. I learned to say no and keep my boundaries to prevent myself from being overused. My patients appreciated the changes too. Many of them told me that I became more attentive and caring, less task-oriented, and was not preoccupied by my agenda. I really felt better and provided better care for my patients.

KEYWORDS

1. Attentiveness

2. Character

3. Compassion

4. Difficulties

5. Generosity of spirit

6. Holiness

7. *imitatio Dei*

8. Moral distress

9. Patience

10. Perfection

11. Problems

12. Reverence for life

13. Veracity (truthfulness)

14. Virtue

15. Wholeness

READING COMPREHENSION

1. Summarize the two key points made in the discussion of Leviticus 19:1–18.

2. Summarize the three key points made in the discussion of Matthew 5:17–30, 43–48.

3. What is Jesus signifying by his repeated statement "You have heard that it was said . . . but I say to you . . ."?

4. Explain the statement "Theologically, perfection is a flying goal—a moral horizon, not a moral destination." What moral and spiritual error is that statement meant to correct?

5. Summarize the content of Provision 5 of the ANA *Code*.

6. Summarize the content of Provision 6 of the ANA *Code*.

7. Name the four cardinal virtues and give a brief definition of each.

8. Name the three charismatic virtues and give a brief definition of each.

9. Name the six caregiving virtues and give a brief definition of each.

10. Explain why the authors regard the caregiving virtues as "manifestations or blends of one or more of the cardinal and charismatic virtues."

MAKING CONNECTIONS

1. Choose one of the six caregiving virtues described in this chapter and discuss its relevance for the specific kind of clinical work you are currently doing or intend to do in the future.

2. Are there any other caregiving virtues, aside from the six discussed in this chapter, which you regard as indispensable for nursing practice? What are they? How would you describe them? Which of the cardinal and/or charismatic virtues do they reflect?

3. Think of a nurse who serves as a role model for you. Which of the cardinal, charismatic and/or caregiving virtues does that person display in her personal and professional life? Give examples.

4. Study Rembrandt's etching *Christ Preaching and Healing the Sick*, shown on p. 66 above. Notice several things: (1) Light radiates from Christ in all directions. (2) The people standing to Christ's right, who are listening to his preaching, are so "bathed" by the "light" of his words that their bodies look washed out. (3) The people standing to Christ's left, who have come for healing, are in various postures of helplessness or supplication. Their figures are more shadowed than those on Christ's right, symbolizing their illnesses and injuries. They are not *yet* healed, but are *just about to be*, and Christ's "light" is *already* shining upon them. Now consider nursing care as a Christian vocation (cf. Mohrmann, 1995), that is, as a reflection and extension of Christ's own ministry of teaching and healing. What thoughts and emotions does this way of considering your work stir up in you?

5. The photograph of the great American poet Walt Whitman and his nurse, Warren Fritzenger, shown on p. 68 above, was taken in 1890, about two years before the poet's death. It is noteworthy that Walt Whitman not only *had* a male nurse at a time when nursing was regarded as "women's work" but that he himself had *been* a nurse in a battlefield hospital during the Civil War. You may want to read his moving poem "The Wound-Dresser," in the Drum-Taps section of *Leaves of Grass* (1881–82, available online at https://whitmanarchive. org/published/LG/1881/poems/169). In this poem he describes his wartime experiences of caregiving. What stereotypes of the nursing profession do the photo and the poem challenge?

6. Study Jean-Baptiste-Siméon Chardin's painting *The Attentive Nurse*, shown on p. 80 above. What symbols of attentiveness (and perhaps other caregiving virtues) are shown in the picture? Does the painting reinforce or challenge the stereotypes of nursing mentioned in the previous question? How?

7. The American Red Cross photograph titled "A Flower for Nurse," shown on p. 82 above, was taken in June 1918 in Paris, some five months *before* the armistice that ended World War I. Let the picture—and its historical context—speak to you as a nurse. What does the picture communicate about the ethics of caregiving and the moral character of caregivers in a time of international catastrophe and unparalleled human suffering?

8. Read the Clinical Voices on pp. 84–89 above. Do any of them seem to "speak" to you, conjuring up memories, reflections, hopes or fears related to your own practice?

3

The Nurse as Savvy Problem-Solver

The Wisdom Strand: "God's works will never be finished; and from him health spreads over all the earth"

SIR 38:8B

Whether or not you often pray, there is a good chance you have encountered situations where the answer was not obvious, the best thing to do was unclear, and you hoped for the wisdom to decide or respond well. Nursing is full of these kinds of situations, often on a daily or hourly basis. A nurse's moral maturity requires an awareness that interpersonal interactions affect decisions in these situations—"microethical" decisions made moment by moment that matter to the well-being of patients (Benner et al., 2010; Truog et al., 2015). It also requires the nurse to develop skills in emotional intelligence, that is, to perceive, use, understand, and manage emotions in ways that promote problem-solving necessary for wise and compassionate care (Mayer, Salovey, & Caruso, 2008).

A pediatric nurse friend illustrated these attributes when he described a situation that puzzled nursing staff (J. Mitre, personal communication, October 24, 2011). Jim was the rounding psychiatric nurse consultant, and unit nurses approached him to discuss their challenges in caring for a seriously ill child. The family had flown in from Alaska, and the care team was having a difficult time communicating with the adults. This family belonged to a coastal tribe in southeast Alaska, and while there did not seem to be an obvious barrier or particular point of disagreement, the nurses had a sense that all was not well in the interactions. The family seemed to go on heightened alert when anyone entered the room and appeared tense despite nurses' efforts to explain their actions and support the family's preferences. As Jim entered the room, he found that the team was already talking to the family, so he introduced himself and quietly stood back. He observed as a medical resident tried to engage the child in conversation by marveling over a hand-carved wooden model on the bedside table. It was a miniature fishing camp complete with a tiny carved canoe. The physician picked the canoe up to look more closely at it, commenting on how cute the toy was. Jim saw the parents freeze as the physician turned it over in his hands and dropped it back into the model. The parents' reactions were barely noticeable, but after the team left, Jim sat down to have a conversation with them about how the hospitalization was going and asked if they would tell him about the model. He listened calmly and asked open-ended questions. The parents indicated that their shaman—a holy man specializing in healing and divination—had sent this model with them, and the canoe signified the life of their child. The model was spiritually significant to the family, and they treated the canoe with reverence, as their child's life was sacred. The family was in a foreign place, the healthcare culture was new to them, and they were overwhelmed with worry for their child. The model had been touched and moved regularly as team members came and went with information, meal trays, and other materials. The family was afraid to speak up about it, and no one had asked. While this conversation did not cure the child's illness, Jim's astute observations and skillful attention to the family's emotional state yielded powerful changes in the child's care; with his input, nurses facilitated a protected location in the room for the model and communicated its sacred nature to the rest of the care team. The family became less guarded, more interactive with caregivers, and more able to focus on treatments for their child's disease.

As in Jim's savvy care, nurses do their work at the intersections of people's lives—those places where mind, body, and spirit come together—and nurses have the responsibility and opportunity to provide uniquely tailored, holistic care (ANA, 2015; O'Brien, 2018). This position carries great responsibility and high expectations, requiring the nurse to be not only compassionate but also knowledgeable and wise. That is the theme of the present chapter, which deals with the third of the four strands of biblical moral discourse—the "wisdom" strand—and with Provisions 4 and 7 of the *Code* (ANA, 2015).

We argue that the wisdom literature plays much the same function in Christian Scripture as these two provisions play in the *Code* (ANA, 2015), underscoring the importance of practical wisdom and sound judgment for a personally satisfying and morally mature life and for effective nursing care. Of course, differences abound. The Bible is testimony to the living God, whereas the *Code* is nontheistic. Moreover, the Bible serves as the ultimate moral authority for all Christians, whereas the *Code* claims only to be the ethical standard for practitioners of a single profession. Nevertheless, we see parallels between the biblical wisdom material and Provisions 4 and 7 of the *Code*. Stated simply, it is this: to live a good life, one must possess insight into how the world works, finesse in handling people, astuteness in analyzing problems and resourcefulness in solving them, and a high level of mastery over one's own impulses and emotions. For the Christian, these aspects of practical wisdom are relevant to most areas of life; for the Christian nurse, they are relevant to the challenges that arise in clinical, administrative and research settings. As we have said, the wisdom and holiness strands pertain heavily to human *character* (in contrast to the legal and prophetic strands, which pertain largely to *conduct*). We contend that people whose character is deemed admirable generally have a healthy measure of both wisdom (or "know-how," or "savvy") and holiness (or "virtue"). Indeed, one of the cardinal virtues we mentioned in chapter 2, prudence, can involve a high degree of enlightened self-interest, and in that respect can also be considered a mark of wisdom: that is, it straddles both Strands 2 and 3. Nevertheless, wisdom can be distinguished from holiness, at least insofar as a person who has an abundance of one and a shortage of the other is in for trouble. One thinks of Prince Myshkin, the protagonist of Dostoyevsky's (2010) novel *The Idiot*, as an example of radiant virtue without common sense, and of Iago, the antagonist of Shakespeare's (2016) tragedy *Othello*, as an example of unprincipled shrewdness. The moral ideal is to blend goodness and practicality. In its delineation of practicality—that is, of savviness and skill—the biblical wisdom literature insists that it serve the same end as law, holiness and prophecy, namely, the good of one's neighbors and community, and repeatedly points out that worldly wisdom apart from that end is great foolishness after all.

In section 1 of this chapter, we discuss three general characteristics of the biblical concept of wisdom: its *moral prudentialism* ("When we do good, we do well"), its *theological optimism* ("God rewards our obedience to his moral law with health and prosperity") and its *pedagogical empiricism* ("We learn about God's moral order, and thus learn how to do well in life, from personal experience"). Then we look at two wisdom texts that illustrate these characteristics: Sirach 38:1–15, which praises physicians as divinely appointed agents of health, and James 5:13–18, which touches on the relationship between prayer and health. In section 2, we look at Provisions 4 and 7 of the *Code* (ANA, 2015). Provision 4 discusses the nurse's decision-making authority and areas of accountability and responsibility in patient care. Provision 7 describes the nurse's expected contributions to research, to the development, maintenance and implementation of professional practice standards, to the development of nursing and health policy, to the advancement of the profession and to the shaping of public health policy. Section 3 explores the linkage between the biblical notion of wisdom and contemporary health science and section 4 illustrates this linkage with several "clinical voices." The chapter concludes with the usual end matter (sections 5–7).

WISDOM IN CHRISTIAN SCRIPTURE[1]

The biblical wisdom literature is exceptionally diverse in both literary style and religious content. It includes the following works, listed here in canonical order—in the Old Testament: Job; Psalms 1, 34, 37, 73, 92, 112, 127, 128, and 133; Proverbs; Ecclesiastes; and the Song of Solomon; in the Old Testament Apocrypha: the Wisdom of Solomon and Sirach (a.k.a. Ecclesiasticus); in the New Testament: the letter of James. The authors of these diverse writings are known as the "sages" or wise men and women of Israel. The surviving writings of the earliest sages, collected in the book of Proverbs, are marked by three core convictions, which are especially important for our purposes and may be termed "moral prudentialism," "theological optimism," and "pedagogical empiricism."[2]

The first core conviction of the early biblical wisdom literature is moral prudentialism, which holds that God's universe is morally ordered, such

---

1. The following discussion distills material from Steele (2013), a series of nine lectures prepared for *Lectio: Guided Bible Reading*, a collection of open-source Bible studies produced by the Center for Biblical and Theological Education (CBTE) at Seattle Pacific University. The CBTE website includes both audio recordings and printed texts. All *Lectio* series are intended for use in adult church school classes, and each lecture is posted as a "weekly" installment. Accordingly, any in-text citation to one of these lectures will identify it by week number rather than page number.

2. Later sages, such as the authors of Job and Ecclesiastes, subject these convictions to severe criticism. Still later wisdom writers, such as Sirach and James, reassert them in a chastened and nuanced form.

that good actions generally have favorable consequences, while bad actions generally have unfavorable ones. Here, "good" means "in accordance with God's law" and "bad" means "contrary to God's law." The beginning of wisdom, and a point on which all further progress in wisdom depends, is recognizing that the law of cause and effect operates in human affairs. Consider, for example, this verse: "The fear of the LORD is the beginning of knowledge; fools despise wisdom and instruction" (Prov 1:7; cf. Prov 4:7; 9:10; Ps 111:10; Sir 1:14). Why should the *fear* of God be the proper starting point in the quest for wisdom? Now, the "fear of God" does not mean cringing terror at what will happen if a vindictive deity catches us messing up. Rather, it means the veneration of God, the healthy respect for God's sovereignty. That understanding of the fear of the Lord provides a valuable corrective to a false view of God and to the obsessive moralism which that error can trigger. However, this corrective should not tempt us to overlook the moral seriousness of the human condition reflected in Proverbs 1:7. When we read that "the fear of God is the beginning of knowledge [or wisdom]," we learn that following God's wise and righteous laws is likely to bring happiness and well-being, while breaking God's laws is likely to mean breaking yourself against them. We are being told, in short, that if we do good, we will do well; but if we do wrong, we will do badly. The linkage between wisdom and law is obvious (Steele, 2013, Week 2).

The moral prudentialism of the early sages is closely connected with a second conviction, namely, their theological optimism. The sages of Israel possessed deep faith in the sovereignty and righteousness of God. They believed that God has revealed what he expects of us and has promised to reward our best efforts to comply with his expectations. Now, it is cheering to believe that God's world is rationally ordered and justly governed, but it is also sobering to consider how much rides on our individual and corporate willingness to follow the rules according to which divine providence operates. The optimism of the sages is not "Pollyanna" sentimentality. They did not suppose that all people were basically good, or that things always worked out for the best. People must *become* good—or else! And becoming good takes a lot more time and effort than many people are willing to invest. The stakes are high and the consequences of failure are potentially dire. Nor did the sages imagine that human beings possessed, or ever would possess, the know-how to build a heaven on earth. Thus, although the sages were theological optimists, they were not utopian idealists. They believed in God, not in humanity. True, the God in whom they believed was intimately involved in human affairs and could be trusted to do *his* part in keeping the world running properly. The problem is that people cannot be *trusted* to do their part. They must be *trained* to do their part by wise instruction from their sagely elders and ultimately from God himself (Steele, 2013, Week 3).

A third conviction of the early sages is that young people attain the array of life skills that constitute wisdom either through deep reflection on their own experiences or through paying careful attention to their more experienced elders. In that sense they were pedagogical empiricists. The word *empirical* comes from the Greek word *empeiria*, meaning "experience," and an empirical method of instruction is one in which pupils are taught by their elders to keep their eyes and ears open to the world, to observe the relations between cause and effect, to discern the patterns and regularities in nature and human relations. Frederick Gaiser (2010) goes so far as to suggest that this method is "a precursor of scientific method" (p. 119). The sages introduced their charges to that great fund of human experience that is enshrined in the wisdom literature itself and also taught them to reflect deeply on their own experience of life's trials and tribulations, its joys and blessings. The method is neatly summarized in Proverbs 4:7–8: "The beginning of wisdom is this: Get wisdom, and whatever else you get, get insight. Prize her highly, and she will exalt you; she will honor you if you embrace her." In the previous chapter we discussed Aristotle's (1998) theory of virtue acquisition, whereby one's frequent and deliberate performance of the *actions* that express a given virtue gradually transform one's *character* and *motivation*. Proverbs 4:7–8 says something similar about the acquisition of *wisdom*. The first step in attaining wisdom is realizing that there is nothing more important in life *than* attaining it, and that it will take you much work over many years before you *do* attain it. Yet it takes at least a rudimentary measure of wisdom even to know that you need to begin the journey. The "fool" does not simply lack wisdom; he lacks even the desire for it and refuses to learn from his elders or from his own experience (Prov 15:5; 18:2). All that said, the sages of Israel did not suppose that the attainment of wisdom was *solely* the result of instruction or personal reflection, even if they insisted that the attainment of wisdom was impossible without them. Something else was necessary, and that was opening oneself to *divine* Wisdom, to illumination by God himself. On this point, see Proverbs 1:20–33 and 8:1—9:36; Job 28:1–28; Wisdom of Solomon 6:1—9:18; Sirach 1:1–20 and 24:1–34 (Steele, 2013, Weeks 4, 8).

Let us now examine two texts that exemplify these features of the wisdom tradition with reference to health and the care of the sick. The first is

Sirach 38:1–15, a tribute to "the physician" (*iatros*)—that is, to one who is engaged professionally in healing the sick and the injured—and secondarily, to "the pharmacist" (*myrepsos*; literally, a "myrrh-boiler" or perfumer), that is, to one who makes potions and salves from medicinal plants. No mention is made here of nurses, for that profession as we know it today did not exist in the ancient world. Nevertheless, this passage sheds much light on how health care was understood in biblical times, and thus on how Christian Scripture might inform contemporary Christian nursing practice.

> [1] *Honor physicians for their services,*
>> *for the Lord created them;*
>
> [2] *for their gift of healing comes from the Most High,*
>> *and they are rewarded by the king.*
>
> [3] *The skill of physicians makes them distinguished,*
>> *and in the presence of the great they are admired.*
>
> [4] *The Lord created medicines out of the earth,*
>> *and the sensible will not despise them.*
>
> [5] *Was not water made sweet with a tree*
>> *in order that its power might be known?*
>
> [6] *And he gave skill to human beings*
>> *that he might be glorified in his marvelous works.*
>
> [7] *By them the physician heals and takes away pain;*
>> [8] *the pharmacist makes a mixture from them.*
> *God's works will never be finished;*
>> *and from him health spreads over all the earth.*
>
> [9] *My child, when you are ill, do not delay,*
>> *but pray to the Lord, and he will heal you.*
>
> [10] *Give up your faults and direct your hands rightly,*
>> *and cleanse your heart from all sin.*
>
> [11] *Offer a sweet-smelling sacrifice, and a memorial portion of choice flour,*
>> *and pour oil on your offering, as much as you can afford.*
>
> [12] *Then give the physician his place, for the Lord created him;*
>> *do not let him leave you, for you need him.*
>
> [13] *There may come a time when recovery lies in the hands of physicians,*
>> [14] *for they too pray to the Lord*
> *that he grant them success in diagnosis*
>> *and in healing, for the sake of preserving life.*

> [15] *He who sins against his Maker,*
>   *will be defiant toward the physician.* (Sir 38:1–15)

The book of Sirach was originally composed in Hebrew by Jesus ben Sirach, a Palestinian Jew, sometime between 195 and 180 BCE. It was translated into Greek by the author's grandson in 117 BCE, some years after the latter had migrated into Egypt (Crenshaw, 1997, pp. 610–611). The setting of the book is important to note, for our passage reflects the ambivalence of Hellenistic Jews toward physicians. Jews had traditionally been quite suspicious of doctors (2 Chron 16:12; Job 13:4; Tob 2:10; Sir 10:10; cf. Mark 5:26; Luke 8:43). They believed that illness was divine punishment for sin (Deut 28:58–61), that healing depended on repentance (Ps 38), and that God was the only true healer (Exod 15:26; Ps 30; 116; Crenshaw, 1997, pp. 807–8; von Rad, 1972, pp. 134–36). In ancient Egypt and throughout the Hellenistic world, however, medicine had a long and distinguished history. As an Alexandrian Jew, Sirach reflects both traditions and tries to mediate between them, in what to modern readers looks very much like an early attempt to reconcile "science" and "religion." As an heir to the prudentialism and optimism of the Hebrew wisdom tradition, he assumes that God rewards wise and righteous conduct with health and prosperity and punishes foolishness and sin with illness and misfortune. Accordingly, he advises those who are in poor health to "give up their faults," "cleanse their hearts," and offer prayers and sacrifices to God. Yet Hippocratic medicine and Aristotelian science had by then spread throughout the Mediterranean world, and Sirach not only recognizes that doctors have achieved a high level of social status, but believes they deserve it because of their great skill (*epistēmē*, literally "knowledge"). Indeed, he urges his readers—who presumably needed the urging—to "honor" physicians (v. 1) and to take advantage of their services (vv. 12–13). We might have expected Sirach, who is also the heir to the "empiricism" of the Hebrew wisdom tradition, to give more credit to doctors themselves for learning from careful observation and long practice. He presumably intended that, though he does not make it explicit. Instead, he piously emphasizes divine providence, both in creating plants with medicinal properties (vv. 4–5) and in granting to doctors and pharmacists (vv. 6–8, 12–14) their therapeutic knowledge.

For our purposes, three points about this passage stand out. First, for Sirach, the practice of medicine has two distinct but closely related objectives: the glorification of God (v. 6) and the preservation of life (v. 14). By way of the healing arts, God is doing God's own never-ending works and spreading health "over all the earth" (v. 8). The word translated here as "health" (*shalom* in the Hebrew original, and *eirēnē* in the Greek version) refers to the state of wholeness and wellness that God intends for his creation, and the phrase "over all the earth," or more literally, "upon the face of the earth," seems to echo the creation story in Genesis 1:29 and 2:6. In short, those dedicated to the healing arts—and there seems no good reason not to include nurses here—are doing God's work in the world, using skills and tools that God has provided for the purpose. This stands in sharp and welcome contrast to the negative picture of doctors that was widespread among ancient Jews and points the way to the more positive view that we begin to see in the New Testament (Matt 9:12; Mark 2:17; Luke 5:31; Col 4:14).

Second, we must be very cautious in using Sirach's advice to the sick. It is one thing to encourage persons who are suffering from injury or disease to ask God for healing and to incorporate religious practices into their course of treatment. It is quite another thing to tell them that their predicament is a divinely wrought punishment for their sins. The maxim "If you do good, you will do well; if you do bad, you will do badly" is good advice, providing it is understood to mean that in a morally ordered universe, virtue generally pays off in the long run. But the inference that people who are *not* doing well have been behaving badly, and have therefore brought misfortunes upon themselves, is cruel and manipulative. Job rebukes his three visitors as "miserable comforters" (Job 16:2) for explaining his terrible sufferings as consequences of sins that he "must" have committed. Similarly, Jesus rejects the notion that great personal misfortune is a sign of deep moral failure (Luke 13:1–5; John 9:3).

Third, Sirach emphasizes that it is not only those who need healing who should commend themselves to God. Those who practice the healing arts likewise "pray to the Lord that he grant them success in diagnosis and in healing, for the sake of preserving life" (v. 14; Gaiser, 2010, pp. 123–25). As noted above, Sirach sees no dichotomy between religion and science. Just as the patient is expected both to pray to God for healing and to honor the physician as the agent of God's *shalom/eirēnē*, so too the physician— and presumably also the pharmacist and today's nurse—are expected both to *use* their specialized knowledge for the well-being of their patients and to remember the ultimate source of that knowledge. And as Gaiser rightly notes, for Sirach the sequence is crucial (p. 122). Patients must first pray to God, repent of sin and give sacrifice (vv. 9–11); only *then* may they seek medical services (v. 11). Similarly, physicians must first pray to God for "success in diagnosis and in healing" (v. 14), and only *then* can they attend to their patients rightly. For patients, to seek God's help as a last resort when medicine fails is an act of superstition and desperation; to seek God's help through the agency of medicine, pharmacology and nursing is an act of faith. For healthcare professionals, to jump immediately to therapeutic practice without first remembering the source of medical knowledge and skill is arrogance; rather, one is to engage in therapeutic practice as an expression of one's religious devotion.

Our second text is from the letter of James, which is the closest thing to a piece of wisdom literature in the New Testament. Stylistically, James is very different from the wisdom writings in the Old Testament and the Apocrypha. Those writings contain a wide variety of literary forms: maxims, riddles, blessings, curses, prayers, hymns, dialogues, exhortations, love songs, an autobiographical monologue, songs of praise for Israel's heroes and poetic recitals of Israel's history—but no letters. James, in contrast, is clearly a letter. Or at least it has traditionally been regarded as one, though it lacks some of the typical elements of other New Testament letters. Whatever its literary form, James consists almost entirely of moral instruction, and for that reason can be placed within the biblical wisdom tradition (Johnson, 1998, p. 178; Riesner, 2001, p. 1255)—though the influence of the prophetic tradition is noticeable as well (D. Nienhuis, personal communication, July 9, 2018). James repeatedly emphasizes that readers should seek wisdom from God (1:5; 3:13–17); and many of the topics it addresses, such as keeping one's temper (1:19–21), avoiding favoritism toward the rich (2:1–13) and taming one's tongue (3:1–12) have parallels in the OT wisdom writings. Moreover, its famous (or infamous) affirmation that faith without works is dead (2:14–26), which is clearly intended as a corrective to a hyper-Pauline emphasis on salvation by faith alone (Nienhuis, 2007; Wall, 1997, pp. 3–4), is thematically analogous to the moral prudentialism of Israelite wisdom. Those who walk the righteous talk, not those who merely talk the righteous talk, receive the Lord's favor. Accordingly, we may expect to find wisdom motifs when we examine what James has to say about sickness and health in 5:13–18:

> *¹³ Are any among you suffering? They should pray. Are any cheerful? They should sing songs of praise. ¹⁴ Are any among you sick? They should call for the elders of the church and have them pray over them, anointing them with oil in the name of the Lord. ¹⁵ The prayer of faith will save the sick, and the Lord will raise them up; and anyone who has committed sins will be forgiven. ¹⁶ Therefore confess your sins to one another, and pray for one another, so that*

you may be healed. The prayer of the righteous is powerful and ef-
fective. [17] Elijah was a human being like us, and he prayed fervently
that it might not rain, and for three years and six months it did not
rain on the earth. [18] Then he prayed again, and the heaven gave rain
and the earth yielded its harvest. (Jas 5:13–18)

Several things about this passage catch our eye. First, like Sirach
38:1–15, James affirms that God hears the prayers of the faithful, heals their
illnesses, and forgives their sins. These are standard biblical affirmations,
which are characteristic of the wisdom writings but commonly found in
other books, too. Second, and again like Sirach, James exhorts those who
seek healing from God to engage in certain religious exercises, although
the specific exercises recommended in the two texts differ somewhat. Sirach, addressing a Hellenistic Jewish readership, proposes a "sweet-smelling
sacrifice, and a memorial portion of choice flour," moistened with an abundance of oil (Sir 38:11), before consulting a physician.[3] In contrast, James,
addressing the Christian communities of the late first century, instructs
the "elders of the church" to visit the sick person, anoint him or her with
oil, and offer "the prayer of faith." James emphasizes the church's solidarity
with the sick person (Johnson, 1998, p. 222) but makes no mention of the
involvement of medical personnel in the cure.

Third, both Sirach and James see a close relationship between illness
and sin but they do not explain exactly what that relationship is. They
agree that repentance for sin should be part of the regimen of treatment for illness
but do not state in so many words that illness is a divine punishment for sin.
As we have noted, wisdom prudentialism can easily lead to that assumption.
Neither Sirach nor James makes that mistake, though both come dangerously
close to it. Yet in resolving not to "guilt-trip" the sick, we should not overlook the deep spiritual and psychological wisdom of these two texts, which
foreshadow modern developments in psychosomatic medicine (cf. Riesner,
2001, p. 1262). For at just this point, wisdom empiricism has a key role to
play. Anyone who has long experience tending the sick knows that they often
feel the need to make meaning of their sufferings. Moreover, sick people who
also happen to be religious are likely to understand their sufferings as divine

---

3. Sirach's instructions recall the directions given in Lev 3:1–17 and 7:11–18 for making a "sacrifice of the offering of well-being" (or "peace offering"). These passages from
Leviticus, however, presume that the person making the sacrifice will secure the services
of a priest, and require that the offering itself include both a slaughtered animal and
unleavened cakes, whereas Sirach makes no mention either of clerical involvement or of
an animal victim.

punishments, or at least to seek relief from their sufferings by invoking divine mercy. Although it is not for "elders of the church," much less for today's nurses and other medical personnel, to agree blithely with the idea that objective guilt is the cause of anyone's illness, it *is* prudent of them to consider the possibility that one aspect of a sick person's sufferings might be a sense of estrangement from God. Accordingly, prayers of supplication, rituals of healing, and assurances of divine pardon all have a role to play in the plan of care. Sick persons may also feel estranged from their faith community. James is particularly alert to this danger. Whereas Sirach 38:1–15 is addressed to "my child," and all its imperative verbs are second-person *singulars*, James 5:13–18 is addressed to the entire congregation, and the verbs in all its imperative and interrogative sentences are second-person *plurals*. James stresses community solidarity—in sickness and in health, in guilt and in penitence: "Confess your sins to one another, and pray for one another, so that you [pl.] may be healed" (Johnson, 1998, p. 322; Wall, 1997, pp. 262–67).

Figure 3.1. Albrecht Dürer, *St. Peter and St. John healing a cripple at the gate of the temple* [engraving]. (1513). 118 mm x 74 mm. Metropolitan Museum of Art, New York, NY

Finally, Sirach and James both reveal a strain of wisdom optimism. Again, this is not the "cock-eyed optimism" of those who assume that things always turn out for the best; it is the theological optimism of those who believe, as one wisdom psalm puts it, that God is "near to the broken-hearted, and saves the crushed in spirit" (Ps 34:18). Both insist that God's providence is oriented toward health and blessing and that the prayer of faith is efficacious. Faith is not magic, of course, and trust in God is not presumption that God will come when whistled for. Yet the optimist knows by experience that confidence in God's grace helps to mobilize the sick person's physical and psychological resources and thus predisposes her to receive the grace that God offers.

THE CODE OF ETHICS FOR NURSES, PROVISIONS 4 & 7

We turn now to Provisions 4 and 7 in the *Code* (ANA, 2015), which seem to have close parallels to the concerns displayed in the wisdom strand of biblical moral discourse. Provision 4 states, "The nurse has authority, accountability, and responsibility for nursing practice; makes decisions; and takes action consistent with the obligation to promote health and to provide optimal care" (p. 4). Four interpretive statements flesh this out. Provision 4.1 ("Authority, Accountability, and Responsibility"), Provision 4.2 ("Accountability for Nursing Judgments, Decisions and Actions") and Provision 4.3 ("Responsibility for Nursing Judgments, Decisions and Actions") note the variety of duties that may fall to a nurse, depending on the context in which he works, and exhort the nurse to accept responsibility for the performance of these duties. This performance obviously involves compliance with the relevant laws and regulations (see chapter 1 above); beyond that, it involves "the exercise of judgment in accepting responsibilities, seeking consultation, and assigning activities to others who provide nursing care" (p. 15).

This emphasis on "the exercise of judgment" corrects the notion that a nurse's *responsibility* extends no further than her *accountability* (ANA, 2015). True, nurses are individually accountable *for* their actions and *to* their superiors in the institutional hierarchy: they must diligently obey the law, faithfully carry out the terms of their job description, carefully keep within their defined scope of practice, and scrupulously follow the orders of doctors and administrators. Although passing the buck and blaming patient care errors on "system or technology failure" (p. 16) are unacceptable, nurses have a responsibility to participate in organizational efforts to address systemic issues that may create potential for human error. Because responsibility for unit operations and patient care is often distributed among all the members of the unit staff, nurses must actively participate in the decision-making procedures, risk assessment protocols, committee assignments and review mechanisms of their unit or facility. Provision 4.4 ("Assignment and Delegation of Nursing Activities or Tasks") presses these points still further (p. 17). It recognizes that as nurses advance in their career, they assume greater and greater responsibilities as supervisors, administrators, managers, classroom educators and clinical preceptors. This means that they must be vigilant in determining the competency and reliability of those to whom they delegate various tasks and assume responsibility for assessing the performance of those to whom those tasks are delegated.

Figure 3.2. Pietro Longhi, *The apothecary* [oil on canvas]. (Ca. 1752). 59 cm x 48 cm. Gallerie dell'Accademia, Venice, Italy

Provision 7 states, "The nurse, in all roles and settings, advances the profession through research and scholarly inquiry, professional standards development, and the generation of both nursing and health policy" (ANA, 2015, p. 27). This provision addresses the professionalization of nursing from another angle. Patient care is based on an expanding body of clinical and scientific knowledge, and nurses are responsible for contributing to it "through research and scholarly inquiry" (pp. 27–28), "through developing, maintaining and implementing professional practice standards" (p. 28), and "through nursing and health policy development" (pp. 28–29). A central theme to all these interpretive statements is that nursing knowledge is never "knowledge for knowledge's sake." It is always knowledge for the patient's sake. This means, first, that in research involving human subjects, the rights and needs of individual patients are of primary importance, whereas efficient data collection is strictly subordinate. It means, second, that the guiding purpose of nursing research and health policy development must always be the improvement of patient care and public health.

WISDOM AND HEALTH SCIENCE

At a deep level, the parallels between the biblical wisdom literature in general and Provisions 4 and 7 of the ANA (2015) *Code of Ethics* are significant, although we acknowledge at the outset that the dominant concerns of the specific wisdom texts that we examined in section 1 differ somewhat from the central themes of these two provisions. In the previous chapter, we differentiated between "difficulties" and "problems." We then argued that nurses must cultivate the caregiving virtues in order to help their patients face the intractable difficulties of illness, injury, disability, aging and mortality. Collectively, the caregiving virtues constitute the nurse's "healing presence," a quality of character that is crucial in all Christian healthcare delivery, but especially in situations where "healing" cannot eventuate in a full and permanent cure. Here we argue that nurses must also cultivate an array of decision-making, problem-solving and human relations skills in order to help their patients face various healthcare problems, such as curable diseases, treatable symptoms, and the solvable aspects of life's major difficulties. Collectively, we term these skills "practical wisdom," which is crucial to effective nursing care, especially in situations where a well-timed intervention can bring a patient comfort and consolation. Of course, both "presence" and "practicality" are needful, and in the case of a morally and spiritually mature Christian nurse, they are so beautifully integrated that one could scarcely say which of the nurse's actions display the one and which display the other, for *all* of her actions display *both*. Nevertheless, the conceptual distinction is useful, for the nurse is constantly presented with situations in which a patient with a difficulty must be attentively, patiently, generously, compassionately and reverently—in short, healingly—cared for, even if the difficulty is permanent and severe. The nurse is also constantly presented with situations in which patient problems can be fixed, if only the nurse possesses enough experience, ingenuity, creativity, resourcefulness, emotional intelligence and "savvy."

Figure 3.3. Nikolai Aleksandrovich Yaroshenko, *Sister of mercy* [oil on cardboard]. (1886). State Art Museum, Ivanovo, Russia

Much of the biblical wisdom literature offers guidance in situations of this latter sort—situations calling for sound judgments and practical solutions.[4] So, too, Provision 4 of the ANA (2015) *Code* addresses "nursing judgments, decisions, and actions" (p. 15) and the "assignment and

---

4. As we indicated in footnote 2 above, however, the books of Job and Ecclesiastes launch sharp critiques of the moral prudentialism and theological optimism of the earlier sages. They did so precisely by focusing attention on life's intractable *difficulties* (e.g., lingering illness, approaching death, the fear that a lifetime of toil has been meaningless, etc.), whereas the book of Proverbs tends to focus on avoiding or correcting life's *problems*.

delegation of nursing activities or tasks" (p. 17), while Provision 7 centers on the "advancement of the profession" (p. 27). Let us look at two parallels.

First, both the wisdom literature and the *Code* (ANA, 2015) recognize that effective problem-solving requires sensitivity to the moral context of the problem. A proposed "solution" to a problem that fails to take into account either the cultural and/or institutional setting in which the problem has arisen or the values, beliefs, personal goals, cultural norms and lifestyle of those involved is likely to confuse or offend the very people it is intended to help, and to make the situation worse. For the wisdom literature, this context is the moral order of the universe, as mapped by divine law. For the *Code*, it is the environment of the specific healthcare facility in which a given nurse works and the lifestyle of a given patient and his family. The Hebrew sages, for their part, taught that human beings generally flourish if they live in accordance with the just laws of God and the state, but also that human wisdom is more than obedience to the law: it is lawfulness joined with flexibility, creativity, insight and decisiveness.

Consider a homespun analogy: Law is to life what the rulebook is to the game of baseball, while wisdom is to life what a champion team displays in playing the game. The team must follow the rules, but winning the game is more than following rules: it takes shrewd strategy on the part of the manager and skillful play by the athletes. Just as a champion baseball team's tactics will be adapted to the immediate situation on the field, so wisdom in life requires both unswerving loyalty to godly values and keen sensitivity to the demands and opportunities of one's immediate context. Similarly, Provision 4 of the *Code* (ANA, 2015) construes the moral context of a nurse's work to be framed by civil laws, by the policies and regulations of the facility in which he works (hospital, clinic, laboratory, classroom, etc.), and by the ethical norms of the *Code* itself. At the same time, the *Code* recognizes that nursing decisions require critical evaluations of other persons, on-the-spot assessments of unique situations, judgment calls on matters of procedure, and a great deal of improvisation. Anne Fadiman's 2012 book *The Spirit Catches You and You Fall Down* is a heartbreaking account of the tragedy that ensues when healthcare personnel, who are scrupulously obeying all the laws, following "proper" medical procedure, and using the "best" available techniques of Western medicine, fail to understand the language and culture of their patient and her family. Savvy problem-solving requires attunement both to the moral ethos of the wider culture (or of each of the multiple commingling cultures) in which a given problem is set and to the morally significant aspects of that problem, in its specificity and uniqueness.

Second, both the wisdom literature of the Bible and the *Code* (ANA, 2015) espouse "empiricism" as a key to savvy problem-solving, though in somewhat different ways. The pedagogy of the sages of Scripture was rooted in their theology. They believed that in a morally ordered and providentially governed universe, wisdom is achieved by paying close attention to natural phenomena, human interactions and one's own daily experience; by assimilating the inherited insights of one's tradition; and by engaging in animated conversation with wise elders. To be sure, God's universe is full of wonders, and human life is complex and shot through with ambiguities and perplexities. Intellectual humility is no less important for the attainment of wisdom than intellectual curiosity, and the more we learn, the more we realize how little we really know. Nevertheless, the more we learn, the less likely we are to blunder badly, and in the end, personal experience and formal instruction pay off. In contrast, the empiricism of the *Code* reflects the assumptions of medical science and the canons of Western academia: Nursing practice relies upon a "developing body of knowledge," (p. 28), no less than upon "nursing's ethical commitments," and that body of knowledge is achieved through "research and scholarly inquiry" (p. 27). Put sharply, the empiricism of the wisdom literature aims at helping people solve the problems of daily living, whereas the empiricism of the *Code* aims at training nurses in preventive health care, in the healing arts, and in solving the myriad of problems that arise from illness, injury and disability.

Figure 3.4. *Gold key to door of nurses memorial building, Florence Nightingale School, Bordeaux, France.* (1922). **American National Red Cross Photograph Collection**

CLINICAL VOICES

As savvy nurses responsible to care for body, mind and spirit, we carefully consider the various impacts on a patient's well-being and decide which actions on our part must take priority. The scope of nursing care is broad and a nurse's time is limited, which means nurses must develop the skills to be both efficient and effective. These skills pertain not only to knowing and understanding physiological impacts, but also to holistic consideration of other influences on the patient, care environment and nurse himself as he applies clinical reasoning (Benner et al., 2010). Jesus, too, referenced the critical combination of caring and intellect when he sent his disciples into the community to be healers of people suffering from sickness and disease: he advised them to be both wise and innocent as they went about their work of healing (Matt 10:1–16). Nurses need this combination of wisdom and compassion as we strive to consider all aspects of others' lives in our approach to care (ANA, 2015). These nurses describe how they applied skillful problem-solving in a variety of situations to address their patients' care needs in a holistic manner:

Toe Zaw: *Assuming positive intent*

Some of our mainstream cultural beliefs (e.g., pulling oneself up by one's bootstraps, being independent, choices have con-sequences) factor into our biases and how we care for patients. Some of these beliefs are ingrained in us even before entering the field of nursing, and it took a while for me to change some of my perceptions. I realized in caring for patients with certain chronic diseases (e.g., diabetes, hypertension, chronic obstructive pulmonary disease), one could argue that their current state of health was in part due to the decisions they had made. However, we treat them with respect, demonstrate understanding of the disease process, provide encouragement, and educate on disease management. This contrasts with individuals who suffer from addiction: we tend to blame them for bad lifestyle choices, for being mentally weak, for being difficult/noncompliant with plan of care, and for feeling that we are a means to an end (to get more prescriptions for opiates and benzos). These stigmas and gener-alizations are unfairly placed upon them, negatively affecting the care they receive. A tool I have found useful to help overcome my own biases is to "assume positive intent" until more facts are known when in difficult situations.

Alix Lobaugh: *Silent prayer*

In my practice, I have not openly prayed with my patients. I have had parents pray over their infant, and many times during their emotional, loving prayer I find myself wiping tears from my eyes before they lift their heads from the infant's Isolette. I silently say amen and have a full heart for their prayer. Recently, I have taken a silent practice in which I do all my safety checks after handoff report and stop to look at the patient I am responsible for during the next twelve hours. I lay my hand near them or gently on their abdomen (only if stable and I am going to be doing hands-on care very shortly) to pray for an uneventful, safe shift ahead. I take that moment to be present and focus my heart on them. I pray for their health and for their future. I do not share this practice with my coworkers or patients' families; it is for me and my faith alone. The reason I keep this practice of prayer to myself is that I do not wish to offend. I welcome all faiths and take great care to respect each and every patient no matter the differences that may exist. I do not need to share my own beliefs to be able to provide high-quality, safe, effective care. If a parent ever asked me to pray aloud for their infant, I would happily do so. If they asked me to join them in prayer, I would.

Kelsey Johnson: *Applying the maxim*

Within my current clinical setting, there is relevance when considering the maxim "If you do good, you will do well, but if you do bad, you will do badly." Using this rule of conduct can be beneficial when interacting with particular patients. While this is not always appropriate to say to everyone, when timely stated, this maxim can leverage patients into refocusing their behavior on our unit. While our hospital often feels like a revolving door, there is a unique community that forms between our involuntarily admitted patients and our staff. Court is a large component of our discharge process and remains a focal point for many who are anxious to leave. I have found myself providing similar statements of that maxim to support and guide patients' behaviors and expectations. I recently informed a patient that judges, attorneys, and public defenders are examining documentation and scrutinizing medication compliance, patterns of behavior, and involvement in care. If, for example, this individual was throwing tables and chairs while shouting profanity at others, my staff and I would be transparent that this will reflect "badly" both here and outside of the hospital walls. Through this honest approach with patients, we are sharing in a small way how "doing good" can reflect as "doing well," particularly in regard to the nature of the court system. I have seen small improvements of how individuals change the way they speak or interact within our unique community to ultimately "do well" throughout their hospitalization and hopefully after discharge.

Stacy Henderson: *Prayer as patient care*

I had the privilege of closely caring for a patient in her last days of life and she asked me to pray with her while I was giving care. Her providers informed her she did not have much time left on this earth: her prognosis was "months or less." Although she had beaten cancer in the past and could feel that her body was ill, she was stunned to hear this news. This prognosis, or "difficulty," was a situation which only presented one outcome—death. In my last visit with her, she asked if everyone in the room would join her in a prayer. I did not hesitate to engage in this religious activity. First, my involvement in this interaction was simple. All I needed to do was hold the hands of my patient and her daughter while my patient said a prayer. Second, I could see that this prayer was important to her and I was not going to deprive her of the things she truly desired in her final days on this earth. Finally, I believe a "healing presence" filled the room to a degree where my patient was consoled. Three weeks later, I received a phone call from her daughter, who confirmed her death earlier that morning. She was rightfully sad but also grateful that her mother was no longer suffering from the cancer that was taking over her body. She also thanked me for the care I provided to her mother.

Melissa Frondozo: *Respecting patient choices*

A patient was admitted for infection and had a history of being bipolar, verbally abusive to staff, and noncompliant with care. I was trying to get the patient to agree to an assessment and stoma change with the doctors. I have learned that maintaining a nonjudgmental attitude and being respectful and kind helps when making a plan to provide optimal care that he would agree with. In the end, we agreed to a plan, and after coordinating a specific time to meet with the doctors, he left the unit, did not come back for a few hours, and missed the opportunity to confer with the doctors. Although this particular situation did not go as planned, I still felt that I did all that I could as this patient's nurse. First and foremost, I remained true to virtues (being kind, respectful, and understanding) that I believe are essential to align with my faith in God, and therefore made me content with my interaction with this patient. Additionally, I used my nursing knowledge of bipolar disorder and experience in dealing with difficult patients to be respectful and focus on one issue during an interaction. I avoided conflict and confrontation by maintaining a nonjudgmental attitude and honoring the humanity of my patient. In the end, sometimes, we just have to respect that it is ultimately their decision.

KEYWORDS

1. Accountability

2. Difficulties

3. Moral prudentialism

4. Nursing savvy

5. Pedagogical empiricism

6. Problems

7. Responsibility

8. Theological optimism

READING COMPREHENSION

1. Summarize the two key points made in the discussion of Sirach 38:1–15.

2. Summarize the four key points made in the discussion of James 5:13–18.

3. Summarize the contents of Provisions 4 and 7 of the ANA *Code*.

4. Explain the difference between "difficulties" and "problems." Explain why the cultivation of the caregiving virtues, as described in the previous chapter, enables a nurse to attend to a patient's difficulties, and why the cultivation of practical wisdom, as described in the present chapter, enables a nurse to attend to a patient's problems.

MAKING CONNECTIONS

1. Describe a clinical situation in which you and/or the care team to which you belonged had to make a "judgment call," that is, in which your course of action was not determined by the law of the land, or by the policies of the facility in which you worked, or by standard medical protocol. To whom were you accountable, and for what? Was responsibility for that course of action shared by anybody else? On what basis, and by what means were decisions made? What was the outcome for the patient and the care team?

2. Consider the prudentialist maxim "If you do good, you will do well, but if you do bad, you will do badly." What relevance, if any, might this maxim have in counseling patients or supervising colleagues? Under what circumstances might you invoke it? Under what circumstances would you *not* invoke it?

3. The foregoing discussion of the theological optimism of Strand 3 distinguishes it from "Pollyanna sentimentality" and "utopian idealism." Let us suppose that a Christian nurse understands the distinction and shares the Bible's kind of optimism. How would such optimism shape the nurse's approach to patient care, her interactions with colleagues, and other aspects of her professional work?

4. Both Sirach 38:1–15 and James 5:13–18 counsel the sick to pray for healing and to engage in other religious rituals. Presumably most patients who wish to do so at all would do so privately, or with their families, or with a pastor or chaplain or designated members of a congregational care team. But are there ever circumstances in which a nurse might appropriately pray for or with a patient and/or the patient's family, or officiate at bedside religious ceremonies? If not, why not? If so, what might those circumstances be, and what ethical considerations should the nurse bear in mind in proceeding?

5. Study Albrecht Dürer's engraving "Saint Peter and Saint John healing a Cripple at the Gate of the Temple," shown on p. 104 above. The picture illustrates a story told in Acts 3:1–26 (which you might benefit from reading). The care demonstrated in the story by the two apostles toward the disabled man foreshadows the later Christian practice of having congregational elders visit, anoint and pray over the sick (per James 5:13–18). But why the look of suspicion and disapproval on

the faces of the onlookers? Perhaps they hold the belief that illness, injury, and disability are divine punishments for sin, and therefore object to the fact that the apostles did not make the healing conditional upon the man's "repentance" (cf. John 5:1–18). And doesn't a variant form of that ancient belief persist today in the tendency of some people to advocate that medical treatment be given only to those who can "afford" it and withheld from people who don't "deserve" it (e.g., smokers and substance abusers)? How should nurses respond to this attitude when they encounter it in others—or detect it in themselves?

6. Study Pietro Longhi's satirical painting *The Apothecary*, shown on p. 106 above. What do the poses, actions, and facial expressions of the six characters, as well as the furnishings of the room, suggest about what a patient in the eighteenth century who had to consult such a "professional" for relief must have experienced? (It may be grimly illuminating to consider (1) that the old-fashioned term *apothecary* comes from the Greek word *apothēkē*, meaning "barn" or "storehouse"; (2) that the Greek word used in Sirach 38:8 for pharmacist is *myrepsos*, which literally means a myrrh-boiler or perfumer; and (3) that the Greek word *pharmakos*, from which we get our word *pharmacist*, has the connotation of a poisoner or magician!) Granting that the science of pharmacology has come a long way since Longhi's time, might contemporary hospital patients have reason to feel similar qualms about the drugs they are prescribed? What responsibility do nurses have in administering medications and in interpreting their hoped-for effects and potential side effects to patients?

7. Study N. A. Yaroshenko's painting *Sister of Mercy*, shown on p. 108 above. In contrast to Longhi's apothecary, who has the look of an officious quack, Yaroshenko's nurse seems to be the very model of both virtue and savvy. How does the artist achieve that look? Does this nurse remind you of anyone who served as a professional role model—not, perhaps, by her dress or physical features, but by her posture and facial expression? Tell the story of that admired colleague to your classmates.

8. Read the Clinical Voices on pp. 111–14 above. Do any of them seem to "speak" to you, conjuring up memories, reflections, hopes or fears related to your own practice?

4

The Nurse as Patient Advocate and Social Critic

The Prophetic Strand: "No prophet is accepted in the prophet's home town"

LUKE 4:24

Jesus remarks that "from everyone to whom much has been given, much will be required" (Luke 12:48). This saying affirms the connection between a person's power and her responsibility and is especially relevant to professional nurses. Nurses understand they have a great deal of responsibility— this is an obvious part of the professional role. There is also power in being a nurse, but this aspect of the role may receive less consideration. Consider the power of this individual nurse: He works in the perioperative area of the hospital and regularly sees the anxious faces of family members returning for updates after their loved one's surgery. Today, a surgeon intercepts a family in the hallway of the busy day surgery area, where patients, families, and care providers squeeze around one another to go about their urgent business. The doctor greets the family, who stop in their tracks, hopeful to hear good news about their daughter and the high-risk surgical procedure. The nurse knows that the family's awareness of the world around them has shrunk to the point of containing only themselves, the surgeon, and the message about their daughter. That message is dense with critical information and medical language, some of which the family struggles to understand; they don't realize others may be listening too. The nurse is also aware that the group stands in a highly public area, where the surgeon's booming voice may be heard by all. Every moment he delays, there is greater broadcasting of confidential information. He interrupts the surgeon with the words, "I'm sorry to interrupt, but may I move you all to this private room behind you? Then you can have some quiet space to talk together." They all quickly move into the closed room, but the surgeon finds the nurse later to say, "Don't *ever* interrupt me when I'm speaking with a family!" When the nurse mentions the need to maintain privacy, the doctor storms off with a muttered threat to speak to his supervisor. The nurse worries about that interaction. He works hard for the remaining shift to remind himself he did his job well by advocating for the family and patient and upholding the legal requirements for protecting privacy of patient information. He shares the experience with his charge nurse, who voices support and validation for his actions.

This nurse experienced the reality that having power and doing the right thing do not necessarily yield a *feeling* of power and may at times yield additional stress. Having power and responsibility to advocate for others in the daily work of nursing does not always mean that the obviously proper course of action will go uncontested. These microethical dilemmas can be disturbing for the nurse, and even if a decision is undebatable, self-doubt can creep in. The nurse's ethical responsibility to collaborate with others benefits both the individual nurse and those receiving care (ANA, 2015). By informing his charge nurse about the interaction with the surgeon, the nurse received support for his own ethical practice, as well as multiplied the power of the nursing voice in advocating for the patient and family.

Now consider nursing power and responsibility for advocacy expanded to a higher level, affecting many more individuals: In 2019, the Washington state legislature began deliberating a bill protecting meal and rest breaks and eliminating mandatory overtime requirements for certain healthcare workers, including nurses (2019 Wash. Sess. Laws). Nursing advocates had been working for years to get such legislation passed, as research results support the connection between patient safety and well-rested nurses (Washington State Nurses Association, 2019). Those nurses working at the government level in early 2019 were aware that a final vote was imminent, but the vast majority of Washington nurses were not—until a legislator suggested that nurses at certain hospitals did not need protected breaks as they "probably play cards for a considerable amount of the day." That filmed statement spread through social media and news outlets like wildfire, and nurses in the state and across the country became outraged by the suggestion that any nurse had time to sit around and play cards during work. The massive and cohesive outcry by nurses quickly influenced lawmakers, and the governor signed the bill into law just sixteen days after the legislator's comment.

The power of combined nursing voices can effect positive social change. The responsibilities of the nurse can seem overwhelming. After all, the scope of our professional concern ranges from caring well for ourselves to advocating for the well-being of people in our communities, nation, and the world (ANA, 2015). While this scope may be daunting for the individual nurse, consider the potential power of almost four million registered nurses in the United States of America (Smiley et al., 2018). The nurse in her individual role, as well as the combined influence of collaborating nurses and other healthcare professionals, can effect change for individuals, families, the profession and ultimately communities and the world at large. Nurses often consider involvement in professional nursing associations of lesser importance in their professional role (Monroe, 2019). When nurses collaborate and contribute their knowledge and time to nursing organizations, however, they extend their sphere of influence. These combined voices and ideas create synergy and potential to prompt effective changes in healthcare policies.

The present chapter explores in depth what the two stories above illustrate, namely, the relationship between the ethical responsibilities intrinsic to nursing and the social power that nurses wield—or *should* wield—both individually and collectively. It correlates the prophetic strand of biblical moral discourse, in which social justice is a dominant theme, with Provisions 8 and 9 of the *Code* (ANA, 2015), which deal with human rights, health diplomacy, the reduction of health disparities, the public credibility and moral integrity of the nursing profession, and the integration of "principles of social justice into nursing and health policy" (pp. 31, 35).

In section 1, we clarify what we mean—and what we *don't* mean—by "prophecy," explaining why caution is necessary in ascribing to the biblical prophets an interest in "social justice," and then justifying our choice of a passage from the Gospel of Luke and two passages from 1–2 Kings to represent Strand 4. Having addressed these preliminary considerations, we proceed to our argument itself by examining the story of Jesus' programmatic sermon in his hometown of Nazareth. In that sermon, Jesus notes that two early Israelite prophets, Elijah and Elisha, had performed miraculous healings for persons who were "outsiders" to the covenant community.

Jesus thereby connects his own ministry with that of the grand tradition of Israelite prophecy and announces that "healing" and "inclusion" are to be central themes of his own work. After looking at Jesus' sermon, we then backtrack to the two stories he cites. The aim of our exegesis of these three scriptural texts is to establish their relevance for the overall theme of this chapter, namely, social justice in health care. In section 2, we look at Provisions 8 and 9 of the *Code* (ANA, 2015), which, as noted above, highlight the social, economic, cultural and political contexts of nursing, and argue that quality health care should be construed as a human right to which all are entitled, not as a privilege reserved for those who can "afford" it. Sections 3–6 contain the clinical voices and the usual end matter.

PROPHECY IN CHRISTIAN SCRIPTURE

What the Bible means by "prophecy" is easily misunderstood or oversimplified.[1] The most common error is to misinterpret the work of the biblical prophets—to regard it either as primarily fortune-telling or as primarily social criticism. The prophets did sometimes make predictions about future events, and they often fiercely criticized the social, economic and political conditions of their own time. It is important to understand, however, that their predictions about *coming* events were rooted in their analysis of *current* events. They saw that such evils as the oppression of the poor and weak by the rich and powerful, the increasing militarization of the Israelite state, and the worship by "God's people" of pagan fertility deities would lead to disastrous consequences, if not swiftly and decisively corrected. They understood these consequences, however, not as the inevitable outworking of impersonal socioeconomic forces, but rather as righteous divine judgments. Thus, the prophets' predictions about the future were based on their analysis of the present, while their analysis of the present was a function of their absolute loyalty to Israel's God and their profound conviction that God, for all his patience, would not forever allow his law to be flouted with impunity. Accordingly, we should understand the prophets not primarily as prognosticators or social critics but as ambassadors of God to an erring people. They engaged in prognostication *because* they were critics of a society that claimed devotion to God but had fallen far short of the purposes

---

1. The general overview of Hebrew prophecy given here borrows heavily from the works by Bowker (2001), Buber (1960), Peterson (2001), Scott (1968), and von Rad (1965).

of God's law. And they engaged in social criticism *because* they understood themselves to be ambassadors of Israel's God. Their sermons often open with the so-called messenger formula: "Thus says the LORD." The prophets believed that God had delegated authority to them, and they regarded their message as a direct, immediate and very specific word of divine rebuke upon Israel's present conduct and as an urgent summons to Israel to "return to the LORD" (Isa 19:22; Jer 3:12, 14, 22; Hos 14:1–2; Joel 2:12–13; Amos 4:6–11). It is thus equally misleading to think of biblical prophecy either as fortune-telling or as the promulgation of a political program or social agenda. They were not interested in dazzling their contemporaries by their clairvoyance or verbal dexterity. Nor did they possess or promote any general theory of "social justice." The prophets' message was rooted in the concrete story of Israel's covenant with God. They insisted that God's continuing protection of and provision for Israel hinged upon Israel's continuing faithfulness and obedience to God. They boldly pointed out all the ways in which Israel was failing to heed God's sovereign law and saving love, and they warned that dire consequences would ensue if this failure was not speedily remedied.

Just as the prophets were engaged in something "more" than social criticism, so those today who engage in social criticism are not, by that fact alone, being "prophetic" in the full, biblical sense of the term. Secular documents such as the ANA (2015) *Code* may condemn social injustice, but they cannot condemn it *as* an idolatrous betrayal of faith in God. Nevertheless, we may regard the *Code* as "prophetic" in a loose, nontheistic sense, for Provisions 8 and 9 condemn certain aspects of the contemporary American healthcare system, such as its inattention to the social determinants of health, its failure to recognize the value of preventive medicine and public health, and its tendency to regard medical care as a market commodity rather than a human right. The *Code*, like the ancient Hebrew prophets, calls for radical social reform.

The Hebrew prophets are conventionally divided into two main groups.[2] The so-called former prophets include such great figures as

---

2. The Bible mentions several other kinds of prophets, whose ministries differed significantly from the "classical" type to which we are here referring. During the period of wilderness wanderings after the exodus, Moses once "shared some of the spirit that was in him" with the elders of Israel in a ceremony that triggered wild "prophesying," that is, ecstatic speech (Num 11:24–30). Later, in the pre-monarchical period, bands of "prophets," operating at the margins of society, engaged in behavior that we might liken to latter-day dervishes and tongue-speakers (1 Sam 10:9–13; 19:18–24). During

Samuel (eleventh century BCE), Nathan (early tenth century BCE), Elijah and Elisha (ninth century BCE). Their exploits are recounted in the books of Joshua, Judges, 1–2 Samuel and 1–2 Kings. Not much of what the former prophets *said* is recorded in the books devoted to their work, aside from snippets of their conversations and disputes. We learn, however, a great deal about what they *did*, about what they stood for and who they stood against. We know that they mounted a stout defense of ethical monotheism during times when Israel was sorely tempted to worship the fertility deities of neighboring peoples and when power and wealth were being concentrated in the hands of the ruling and commercial classes, to the detriment of villagers and smallholders. In this respect the former prophets paved the way for their successors, who are known as the latter prophets. These include Isaiah (late eighth century BCE), Jeremiah (late seventh through early sixth century BCE), "Second Isaiah," "Third Isaiah,"[3] Ezekiel (mid-sixth century BCE) and the twelve minor prophets, whose careers stretched from the mid-eighth century BCE (Amos and Hosea) through the mid-fifth century (Malachi). The books devoted to these figures consist largely of their spoken words, which they or their disciples subsequently wrote down and collected. Somewhat less attention is given in these books to historical and biographical narrative. The major themes of their ministries—the need for covenantal fidelity to God and the need for social justice—remain consistent with that of their predecessors. But the former prophets generally tend to focus more on the problem of idolatry than on the problem of social justice, whereas the latter prophets give proportionately more attention to the various ways in which the political, social, cultural, economic and religious life of Israel is at odds with God's law.

the period of the monarchy, "prophets" were often part of the royal court, where they were expected, not to burst into ecstatic utterance, but to advise the king on matters of state. Some of these were mere yes-men who did little more than affirm God's approval of government policy (Jer 28:1–17; Amos 7:10–13). Nathan (2 Sam 12:1–15) and Micaiah (1 Kgs 22:1–28), however, are striking counterexamples; they were court prophets who boldly criticized royal actions and ambitions.

3. Most scholars regard chapters 40–55 of the book of Isaiah as the work of an anonymous prophet of the mid-sixth century BCE, who lived among the Israelite exiles in Babylon, and chapters 56–66 as the work of still another anonymous prophet, who lived among the people of Jerusalem after the exiles' return. These two figures are conventionally called Second Isaiah and Third Isaiah, respectively. They are thought to be spiritual descendants of the original Isaiah, and their surviving sermons have been added to those of the master, which are found in chapters 1–39.

To represent Strand 4, we have chosen Jesus and two of the former prophets, Elijah and Elisha, whose ministry he links his own. This may seem an odd choice, for it is the latter prophets, rather than the former, who say so much about social justice, which is the topic of Provisions 8 and 9 (ANA, 2015). In contrast, Elijah and Elisha devoted themselves to preserving Israel's religious and political independence from its pagan neighbors, and the great theme of Jesus' preaching ministry was the rule of God.[4] But all three were notable healers, and the stories of *who* they healed, and *how* they healed, turn out to have profound implications for Christian nursing.

The story of Jesus' sermon in the Nazareth synagogue serves two key functions in the narrative structure of the Gospel of Luke: it provides a compact summary of the central themes of Jesus' ministry, and it offers a glimpse of the combination of wild adulation and fierce opposition that Jesus will arouse in those to whom he ministers. We shall see how these themes emerge as we go along, but let us look first at the story itself:

> [16] *When he came to Nazareth, where he had been brought up, he went to the synagogue on the sabbath day, as was his custom. He stood up to read,* [17] *and the scroll of the prophet Isaiah was given to him. He unrolled the scroll and found the place where it was written:* [18] *"The Spirit of the Lord is upon me, because he has anointed me to bring good news to the poor. He has sent me to proclaim release to the captives and recovery of sight to the blind, to let the oppressed go free,* [19] *to proclaim the year of the Lord's favor."* [20] *And he rolled up the scroll, gave it back to the attendant, and sat down. The eyes of all in the synagogue were fixed on him.* [21] *Then he began to say to them, "Today this scripture has been fulfilled in your hearing."* [22] *All spoke well of him and were amazed at the gracious words that came from his mouth. They said, "Is not this Joseph's son?"* [23] *He said to them, "Doubtless you will quote to me this proverb, 'Doctor, cure yourself!' And you will say, 'Do here also in your hometown the things that we have heard you did at Capernaum.'"* [24] *And he said, "Truly I tell you, no prophet is accepted in the prophet's hometown.* [25] *But the truth is, there were many widows in Israel in the time of Elijah, when the heaven was shut up three years and six months, and there was a severe famine over*

4. What Jesus meant by "the rule of God" (or "kingdom of God") may be summarized as follows: God's rule is *already present among us*, thanks to Jesus' own presence among us, both in his earthly life and through the Holy Spirit that he sent after his resurrection and ascension. But it is *not yet consummated*. As a present reality, it inspires and empowers us to perform concrete acts of loving service to our neighbors, following Christ's example. Yet its final triumph is still to come, something we await with longing and expectancy, and cannot bring about by our own efforts.

all the land; ²⁶ yet Elijah was sent to none of them except to a widow at Zarephath in Sidon. ²⁷ There were also many lepers in Israel in the time of the prophet Elisha, and none of them was cleansed except Naaman the Syrian." ²⁸ When they heard this, all in the synagogue were filled with rage. ²⁹ They got up, drove him out of the town, and led him to the brow of the hill on which their town was built, so that they might hurl him off the cliff. ³⁰ But he passed through the midst of them and went on his way. (Luke 4:16–30)

This episode follows the account of Jesus' baptism by John in the Jordan River (Luke 3:1–22), the record of his regal ancestry (3:23–38), the tale of his temptation in the desert (4:1–13) and a brief notice of the fabulous success of his first preaching tour in the region of Galilee (4:14–15). Taken together, these four stories indicate Jesus' divine sonship, his spiritual authority and his messianic mission. The reader can therefore appreciate the excitement felt by the people of Nazareth when Jesus, whose reputation as a preacher and wonderworker (though not yet as "the Messiah") has clearly preceded him, comes home to preach.

At first things go well: the townspeople are "amazed at the gracious words that came from his mouth" (v. 22). Is this "amazement" due to their appreciation of his eloquence, or are they enticed by the prospect of receiving bounty from the hand of their favorite son? For Jesus certainly does make some attractive promises and claims to be fulfilling an ancient prophecy "in their hearing" (v. 21). He says he was sent "to bring good news to the poor . . . to proclaim release to the captives and recovery of sight to the blind, to let the oppressed go free, to proclaim the year of the Lord's favor" (vv. 18–19).[5] Joel Green (2003) notes, "Within Luke's world, 'The poor' are understood best as 'the marginal,' as those excluded from social and religious intercourse because of any number or combination of factors, such as those related to gender, age, economic destitution, physical malady, or religious impurity" (pp. 1860–61). The Nazarenes apparently imagine themselves to be the rightful recipients of this largesse. For *they* are the ones who are oppressed by their Roman overlords and by the collaborationist temple authorities. *They* are the ones who are afflicted with seemingly incurable illnesses and permanent disabilities. *They* are the ones who are crushed by debts, from which the inauguration of "the year of the

---

5. This quotation blends Isa 58:6 and 61:1–2. Most modern scholars believe that their author was an anonymous post-exilic prophet, whom they have dubbed "Third Isaiah." See footnote 3.

Lord's favor" (v. 19), that is, the Jubilee Year, will release them.[6] All Palestin-ian Jews of that time might have so regarded themselves. But the people of Nazareth regard Jesus as one of them and feel they have a special claim to whatever his fulfillment of this prophecy will entail.

Then Jesus unleashes an unpleasant surprise. He does not revoke the promises he has just made, for these are to be programmatic for his sub-sequent ministry, but he informs the Nazarenes that they shall not be the primary beneficiaries of these promises. "Doubtless you will quote to me this proverb," he tells them, "'Doctor, cure yourself!'" (v. 23). This prov-erb seems to be roughly equivalent to our expression "Charity begins at home" (Caird, 1972, pp. 86–87). But "beginning at home," that is, doing in Nazareth "the things [he] did at Capernaum" (v. 23), is not his plan.[7] Then he quotes another proverb: "No prophet is accepted in his hometown" (v. 24). Jesus thus casts himself in the role of a "prophet in Israel" (Fitzmyer, 1981, p. 537), though it is not immediately obvious why he feels unaccepted by his townspeople, when, until now, they have been an adoring audience. Presumably it is because he assumes that their temporary adoration is due to their expectation that his promise to fulfill the ancient prophecy "in their hearing" (v. 21) means that he will fulfill it *for them* and anticipates their outrage when they realize the truth. He then reminds them of two stories from Israelite history, in which prophets performed miracles, not for the benefit of their fellow Israelites, but for the benefit of pagan outsiders.

At this the people of Nazareth explode (v. 28). We shall look at the stories Jesus cites in more detail below, but here it suffices to note that the Nazarenes' reaction to hearing them referenced proves that Jesus has un-derstood their real motives all too well. But it is important to note that their outrage is due not only to their disappointed greed but also to their offended exclusivism. That is, they are scandalized not only by the fact that they won't enjoy the promised benefits of Jesus' ministry but also by the fact that some of the people who apparently *will* enjoy those benefits do not, in their eyes, deserve them. As Alan Culpepper (1995) notes, "When the radi-cal inclusiveness of Jesus' announcement became clear to those gathered

---

6. The Jubilee Year is described in Lev 25:8–55. This may have been what Third Isaiah meant by "the year of the LORD's favor" (Isa 61:2) and what Jesus understood Third Isaiah to mean in quoting him. See Caird, 1972, pp. 86–87; Culpepper, 1995, p. 106; Trocmé, 1973, pp. 19–76; and Yoder, 1995, pp. 60–75.

7. Capernaum lies about thirty miles northeast of Nazareth. Jesus had been active there shortly before the present story takes place, and a report of his deeds "had spread through all the surrounding country" (Luke 4:14–15).

in the synagogue in Nazareth, their commitment to their own community boundaries took precedence over their joy that God had sent a prophet among them. In the end, because they were not open to the prospect of others' sharing in the bounty of God's deliverance, they themselves were unable to receive it" (p. 108). Thus, the terrible irony of the story of Jesus' sermon in the Nazareth synagogue was not that Jesus stubbornly denied to his townspeople the liberation from sin, debt, poverty and illness that he was generously offering to others, but that because they resented the fact that he was offering these blessings to those whom they deemed undeserving, they disqualified themselves.

With that point in mind, let us look briefly at the two Old Testament stories to which Jesus refers. To understand these stories, a brief word about their historical and literary background is in order. First and Second Samuel tell the story of the tumultuous process by which the Israelite monarchy was established in the late eleventh century BCE and of the reign of King David (ca. 1000–ca. 970 BCE). First and Second Kings narrate the reign of King Solomon (ca. 970–ca. 931 BCE), the catastrophic division of the country into the northern and southern kingdoms after Solomon's death, the vicissitudes of both kingdoms over the next several centuries, the fall of the northern kingdom (= "Israel" or "Samaria") to the Assyrians (ca. 722 BCE) and the fall of the southern kingdom (= "Judah") to the Neo-Babylonians (ca. 587 BCE).

Elijah the prophet, whose ministry is related in 1 Kings 17:1—19:21, 1 Kings 21:1–27 and 2 Kings 1:1—2:12, was active in the northern kingdom during the reigns of Ahab (c. 874–c. 853 BCE) and Ahaziah (ca. 853–ca. 852 BCE). Ahab is remembered by Scripture as having done "evil in the sight of the LORD more than all who were before him" (1 Kgs 16:30), his greatest offenses having been his marriage to the Phoenician princess Jezebel, who was a devotee of the Canaanite sky-god, Baal, and his subsequent introduction of Baal worship into the religious life of Israel. Elijah immediately condemned Ahab's flirtation with paganism and predicted that God would execute judgment upon Israel and its neighbors by sending a severe drought and famine. Knowing that his prophecy had infuriated Ahab, Elijah went into hiding in a remote area to the east of the Jordan River, where, famously, he was fed by ravens (1 Kgs 17:1–7). But eventually even these miraculous provisions failed, and he was forced to flee again. We pick up the narrative at this point:

⁸ Then the word of the Lord came to him, saying, ⁹ "Go now to Zarephath, which belongs to Sidon, and live there; for I have commanded a widow there to feed you." ¹⁰ So he set out and went to Zarephath. When he came to the gate of the town, a widow was there gathering sticks; he called to her and said, "Bring me a little water in a vessel, so that I may drink." ¹¹ As she was going to bring it, he called to her and said, "Bring me a morsel of bread in your hand." ¹² But she said, "As the Lord your God lives, I have nothing baked, only a handful of meal in a jar, and a little oil in a jug; I am now gathering a couple of sticks, so that I may go home and prepare it for myself and my son, that we may eat it, and die." ¹³ Elijah said to her, "Do not be afraid; go and do as you have said; but first make me a little cake of it and bring it to me, and afterwards make something for yourself and your son. ¹⁴ For thus says the Lord the God of Israel: The jar of meal will not be emptied and the jug of oil will not fail until the day that the Lord sends rain on the earth." ¹⁵ She went and did as Elijah said, so that she as well as he and her household ate for many days. ¹⁶ The jar of meal was not emptied, neither did the jug of oil fail, according to the word of the Lord that he spoke by Elijah.

¹⁷ After this the son of the woman, the mistress of the house, became ill; his illness was so severe that there was no breath left in him. ¹⁸ She then said to Elijah, "What have you against me, O man of God? You have come to me to bring my sin to remembrance, and to cause the death of my son!" ¹⁹ But he said to her, "Give me your son." He took him from her bosom, carried him up into the upper chamber where he was lodging, and laid him on his own bed. ²⁰ He cried out to the Lord, "O Lord my God, have you brought calamity even upon the widow with whom I am staying, by killing her son?" ²¹ Then he stretched himself upon the child three times, and cried out to the Lord, "O Lord my God, let this child's life come into him again." ²² The Lord listened to the voice of Elijah; the life of the child came into him again, and he revived. ²³ Elijah took the child, brought him down from the upper chamber into the house, and gave him to his mother; then Elijah said, "See, your son is alive." ²⁴ So the woman said to Elijah, "Now I know that you are a man of God, and that the word of the Lord in your mouth is truth." (1 Kgs 17:8–24)

Several points deserve special mention. First, the widow of Zarephath and her son are Sidonians (i.e., Phoenicians). Presumably they worship the same national deities as the notorious Jezebel, a Sidonian princess and now the consort of King Ahab of Israel. It is astonishing, therefore, that the widow and her son, who are themselves suffering desperately from the famine afflicting the entire region, should provide hospitality to an Israelite prophet fleeing from his own government. The marriage of Ahab and Jezebel had established cordial relations between Israel and Phoenicia, which had long been enemies, but this arrangement apparently depended on Ahab's willingness to permit Jezebel to import her Baalism into Israel. This meant that an enemy of Ahab and Jezebel was also an enemy of Phoenicia. Therefore, the widow of Zarephath is placing herself in danger from her own government by showing hospitality to Elijah.

Second, Elijah has taken refuge from *his* government in the homeland of Baalism, a religion that he fiercely opposes. Furthermore, he asks Yahweh, the God of Israel,[8] to furnish these starving Baal-worshipers with an unending supply of flour and oil, and later, to raise the widow's son from his deathbed. The text is certainly not suggesting that Elijah is accommodating himself to Baalism during this double crisis of regional famine and state persecution. Rather, as Choon-Leong Seow (1999) points out, the text is affirming that "over against Baal, the Canaanite god of life . . . Israel's God is the true Lord of life, with power over the forces of nature and even over death itself" (p. 125; cf. Mariottini, 2003, p. 512).

Third, precisely *because* the God of Israel is the true Lord of life, it is possible and appropriate for those who worship him—including, by the end of this story, the widow of Zarephath—to forge friendships across political frontiers and to transcend religious and ethnic divisions of long standing (v. 24). Jesus was thus perfectly correct in invoking this story to rebuke the exclusionary prejudice of the people of his own hometown. As Seow (1999) notes, "In receiving divine favor, the Phoenician woman becomes a prototype for other Gentile women who receive God's grace through their encounters with Jesus (see Matt 15:21–28; Mark 7:24–30). God's universal love reaches beyond the boundaries of nationality, ethnicity, and even religious affiliation" (pp. 129–30).

Fourth, the woman is "converted" to faith in the God of Israel only after God's prophet restores life to her son, who has just died of some sudden

8. The story of the revelation of God's name is found in Exod 3:13–15. Ancient Hebrew was originally written without vowels, and the name given there was YHWH, a form of the verb "to be." Jews regard God's name as too holy to be spoken aloud, and it is customary for them, when reading Scripture aloud, to speak the word *Adonai*, meaning "the Lord," whenever "YHWH" appears in the text. Similarly, many printed editions of the Bible replace the divine name with "the Lord," often set in small capitals. Most contemporary Christians feel free to pronounce the divine name aloud, and some newer editions of the Bible print the word—with the most probable vowels inserted: thus "Yahweh." (The older spelling, "Jehovah," is now considered incorrect.)

illness, but it is important to recognize that she ascribes her son's deadly illness to some past mistake that she has committed of which Elijah's presence has reminded her (v. 18). This is yet another example of the close connection that many biblical authors, and many characters in biblical narratives, draw between sin and sickness. Yet Elijah does not ask the woman to reveal any details of that sin to him, or to perform any ritual of penitence, or to profess her faith in Israel's God, before restoring life to the boy. Perhaps he waives these conditions out of gratitude for the remarkable hospitality she has shown him, despite her poverty and despite the risks involved. In any case, Elijah simply asks the bereaved mother to give her son's body to him; after Elijah cries out to the Lord, the child revives (1 Kgs 17:19–22). The resuscitation has taken place without any moralizing or "evangelizing" on Elijah's part.

Finally, we may note the exceptionally tactile procedure that Elijah uses in raising the child (vv. 19–23). He shows absolutely no fear of contagion and absolutely no squeamishness about the ritual impurity involved in touching a dead body—and the dead body of a non-Israelite, no less!

Figure 4.1. Bernardo Strozzi, *Prophet Elijah and the widow of Sarepta* [oil on canvas]. (1630s). 106 cm x 138 cm. Kunsthistorisches Museum, Vienna, Austria

The second of the two stories that Jesus mentions in his sermon in the synagogue at Nazareth deals with the healing of the Syrian general Naaman by the prophet Elisha, Elijah's chosen successor (2 Kgs 5:1–19). Elisha's long ministry, which is related in 1 Kings 19:19–21 and 2 Kings 2:1—13:20, stretched from the middle of the ninth century BCE to the early years of the eighth, during the reigns of four successive kings of Israel. Many miracle stories and prophetic legends are told of Elisha, but not necessarily in chronological order, and it is often impossible to determine which events in his career took place in which royal reign. Moreover, in the story of the healing of Naaman, neither the name of the reigning king of Israel nor the name of the reigning king of Aram-Damascus (Syria) is given. It appears, however, that our story took place around the year 842 BCE, when Aram enjoyed military superiority over Israel, but when a temporary truce was in place. For when Naaman, the Aramaean military commander, pays a visit to the Israelite king, the latter fears that the Aramaeans are looking for a pretext to resume hostilities. Not so. Naaman has come, not to pick a fight, but to seek healing for a skin malady from which he suffers.

> [1] *Naaman, commander of the army of the king of Aram, was a great man and in high favor with his master, because by him the LORD had given victory to Aram. The man, though a mighty warrior, suffered from leprosy.* [2] *Now the Arameans on one of their raids had taken a young girl captive from the land of Israel, and she served Naaman's wife.* [3] *She said to her mistress, "If only my lord were with the prophet who is in Samaria! He would cure him of his leprosy."* [4] *So Naaman went in and told his lord just what the girl from the land of Israel had said.* [5] *And the king of Aram said, "Go then, and I will send along a letter to the king of Israel."*
>
> *He went, taking with him ten talents of silver, six thousand shekels of gold, and ten sets of garments.* [6] *He brought the letter to the king of Israel, which read, "When this letter reaches you, know that I have sent to you my servant Naaman, that you may cure him of his leprosy."* [7] *When the king of Israel read the letter, he tore his clothes and said, "Am I God, to give death or life, that this man sends word to me to cure a man of his leprosy? Just look and see how he is trying to pick a quarrel with me."*
>
> [8] *But when Elisha the man of God heard that the king of Israel had torn his clothes, he sent a message to the king, "Why have you torn your clothes? Let him come to me, that he may learn that there is a prophet in Israel."* [9] *So Naaman came with his horses and chariots, and halted at the entrance of Elisha's house.* [10] *Elisha sent a messenger to him, saying, "Go, wash in the Jordan seven times, and your flesh shall be restored and you shall be clean."* [11] *But Naaman became angry and went away, saying, "I thought that for me he would surely come out,*

and stand and call on the name of the LORD *his God, and would wave his hand over the spot, and cure the leprosy!* [12] *Are not Abana and Pharpar, the rivers of Damascus, better than all the waters of Israel? Could I not wash in them, and be clean?" He turned and went away in a rage.* [13] *But his servants approached and said to him, "Father, if the prophet had commanded you to do something difficult, would you not have done it? How much more, when all he said to you was, 'Wash, and be clean'?"* [14] *So he went down and immersed himself seven times in the Jordan, according to the word of the man of God; his flesh was restored like the flesh of a young boy, and he was clean.*

[15] *Then he returned to the man of God, he and all his company; he came and stood before him and said, "Now I know that there is no God in all the earth except in Israel; please accept a present from your servant."* [16] *But he said, "As the* LORD *lives, whom I serve, I will accept nothing!" He urged him to accept, but he refused.* [17] *Then Naaman said, "If not, please let two mule-loads of earth be given to your servant; for your servant will no longer offer burnt offering or sacrifice to any god except the* LORD. [18] *But may the* LORD *pardon your servant on one count: when my master goes into the house of Rimmon to worship there, leaning on my arm, and I bow down in the house of Rimmon, when I do bow down in the house of Rimmon, may the* LORD *pardon your servant on this one count."* [19] *He said to him, "Go in peace." (2 Kgs 5:1–19)*

Three points stand out. First, we can immediately see why Jesus cites this story about prophet Elisha and Naaman the Syrian, along with the previous story of prophet Elijah and the widow of Zarephath, to expose the ethnocentrism of the people of Nazareth. For both Naaman and the widow are outsiders to the religion of Israel, and therefore presumably "unworthy" to receive the grace of Israel's God. But precisely because they are not bewitched by a false sense of entitlement, they possess the only thing required for divine blessing, namely, sincere gratitude. In the case of the widow, Yahweh, through the instrumentality of his prophet, resuscitates a devotee of Baal, the Phoenician sky-god; in the case of Naaman, Yahweh heals a devotee of Rimmon, the Aramaean sky-god (Gray, 1962, p. 507), of a dreaded skin disease. In both cases, the "pagan" beneficiary of Yahweh's grace instantly responds with a ringing confession of *Israelite* faith. The widow of Zarephath says to Elijah, "Now I know that you are a man of God, and that the word of the LORD from your mouth is the truth" (1 Kgs 17:24); Naaman the Aramaean's comment to Elisha echoes that of the widow: "Now I know that there is no God in all the earth except in Israel" (2 Kgs 5:15b). The key theological claim is that the grace of Israel's God extends to those who, like the impoverished Sidonian widow and the great Syrian general, are "outsiders" to Israel, providing only that they acknowledge their need of it. No one "deserves" grace, but neither ethnicity, nor religious affiliation, nor social status, nor age, nor gender disqualifies a person from receiving it. The sole condition for receiving it is humble receptivity to it. In contrast, those who, like the people of Nazareth, imagine they have some sort of "claim" upon the grace of Israel's God disqualify themselves—precisely because divine grace is *never* something that one is "owed."

Second, contact with the God of Israel, via his prophet, clearly has a morally sensitizing effect upon both Naaman and the widow, though the circumstances differ somewhat. In the widow's case, the untimely death of her son, while Elijah is in her home, causes her to remember some old sin she had committed—to which, however, the prophet pays no heed when he undertakes to revive the boy (1 Kgs 17:19–22). In Naaman's case, the healing of his leprosy effects an immediate "conversion" to the Yahwistic faith of Israel, along with a sudden worry that he will be denying his new faith every time he accompanies his king to the "house of Rimmon" (2 Kgs 5:18). Elisha does not formally absolve him, in advance, of the sin of idolatry, but he does bid him without further ado to "go in peace," apparently acknowledging that, under the circumstances, Naaman's "mental reservation" will suffice, especially since his private altar to Yahweh will be built on earth imported from Israelite land (2 Kgs 5:19).

A third point about the story of Elisha's healing of Naaman the Syrian is very significant for our purposes, though it has no obvious analog in the earlier story of Elijah's raising of the Sidonian boy. This pertains to the great general's initial assumptions about what therapeutic regimen he would have to undergo and what fee he would have to pay. He crosses the border between Aram and Israel with a huge baggage-train of goods by which to purchase the services of the local prophet. Moreover, Naaman fully expects the prophet to cure his "leprosy" by means of elaborate rituals and therapeutic procedures.[9] So he is outraged to learn through Elisha's messenger that the prophet will do no such thing, and will not even do him the courtesy of

---

9. Here, "leprosy" probably does not refer to Hansen's disease, but to some other dermatological condition, such as psoriasis, vitiligo or severe eczema (Seow, 1999, p. 193, see footnote 92). These are unsightly and uncomfortable, but they do not render a person incapable of performing the vigorous military and political activities for which Naaman was responsible and which he had been dutifully carrying out all along (Spina, 2005, pp. 76–77).

meeting him face to face. Elisha simply orders Naaman to immerse himself seven times in the river Jordan. When Naaman stomps off in a huff, his servants urge him to come back, very sensibly arguing that, having already traveled this far, he should at least try the prophet's prescribed method. Naaman glumly puts aside his wounded pride, bathes in the Jordan as ordered, and emerges with "his flesh restored like the flesh of a young boy" (2 Kgs 5:14). Delighted, he then goes back to the prophet, intending to lavish upon him all that gold, silver and fine apparel he has brought. This time Elisha speaks to him face to face—but he declines the payment. For Naaman's healing was an act of divine grace, mediated to him through the prophet, and just as the only condition for *being* healed was humble obedience, so the appropriate response to that miracle was his heartfelt gratitude, not the payment of a fee or gratuity (Gaiser, 2010, pp. 63–85).[10]

To summarize: The biblical books representing Strand 4 are traditionally subdivided into the Former Prophets, which contain a good deal of narrative material but few prophetic utterances, and the Latter Prophets, which contain very little narrative material but many speeches. Yet former prophets, such as Elijah and Elisha, and latter prophets, beginning with Amos, Hosea and Isaiah, represent a continuous spiritual lineage which lasted from the ninth through the fifth centuries BCE. Israelite prophecy was dormant during the Persian and Hellenistic periods (although the apocalyptic literature of that period was a kind of offshoot); then it sprang suddenly back to life in the persons of John the Baptist and Jesus of Nazareth. Two closely related themes dominated the preaching of the entire tradition of Israelite prophecy: unswerving allegiance to Yahweh, against the persistent temptation to polytheism and idolatry, and social justice, against the stubborn tendency of the ruling classes to oppress the poor. The stories of the former prophets strongly emphasize the evils of paganism (and of

---

10. The story of the curing of Naaman has a grim epilogue. In 2 Kings 5:19b–27, Elisha's servant, Gehazi, scandalized that his master had refused the lavish payment that Naaman had offered, runs after him, tells him a lie that preys upon Naaman's new and rather naive devotion to Israelite "prophets," and secures for himself a sizable portion of the gifts that had originally been intended for Elisha. Frederick Gaiser (2010) notes that Gehazi's ethnocentric belief that Elisha was wrong in healing an "outsider" for free reappears in the outrage expressed eight centuries later by the people of Nazareth in response to Jesus' synagogue sermon. Both believe "that the nations exist for Israel's enmity and exploitation rather than to share in divine favor" (p. 69). But whereas Jesus merely rebukes the Nazarenes and withholds from them the blessings they believe they deserve, Elisha, who knows all about his servant's perfidy, inflicts upon Gehazi the very disease of which he has just healed Naaman.

political alliances with neighboring pagan states) but give less attention to social injustice. But we *do* find several healing stories told of the former prophets, such as those we have examined above. These indicate the former prophets' belief that God's grace is not restricted to Israelites (as one might suppose them to have believed, given their fierce monotheism) but is available to "outsiders," irrespective of ethnicity, religious affiliation, social class or gender. This is precisely why Jesus, who made the healing of the sick and disabled such a central element of his own prophetic ministry, cited the stories of Elijah and Elisha in his Nazareth sermon (Luke 4:16–30). The latter prophets do speak eloquently about many aspects of social justice, and in that respect might have provided a more direct linkage to Provisions 8 and 9 of the ANA *Code* (2015). They say very little about healing or health care, however, and so we have chosen their predecessors to represent Strand 4.

THE CODE OF ETHICS FOR NURSES, PROVISIONS 8 & 9

Let us now look at Provisions 8 and 9 of the *Code* (ANA, 2015) and determine the ways in which, and the extent to which, they reflect the themes we have observed in the prophetic strand of biblical moral discourse.

Provision 8 (ANA, 2015) states, "The nurse collaborates with other health professionals and the public to protect human rights, promote health diplomacy, and reduce health disparities" (p. 31). The first interpretive statement for this provision affirms that health is a "universal human right" (p. 31). This is oddly stated, as it seems to imply that illness and injury are human rights *abuses*. But the proneness to disease and injury are inescapable aspects of the human condition, not defects in the social order. Fortunately, the *Code* clarifies what it means by quoting an (unreferenced) statement from the World Health Organization to the effect that "the *highest attainable standard of health* [emphasis added] is a fundamental right of every human being" (p. 31). Further, the *Code* frames the "economic, political, social, and cultural dimensions" (p. 31) of this right in terms of *access* to all that people need for maximal health, and implies, without directly stating, that fundamental human rights are violated when a society erects, or fails to remove, legal or economic impediments to such access.

Just as the *Code* (ANA, 2015) stresses that individual and community health are largely socially determined, it emphasizes that teamwork among healthcare professionals and public policymakers is crucial for the promotion of public health, and therefore for the advancement of the common good. The linchpin of the second interpretive statement is the claim that "ethics, human rights, and nursing converge as a formidable instrument for social justice and health diplomacy that can be amplified by collaboration with other health professionals" (p. 31). This interpretive statement goes on to affirm that health diplomacy—that is, high-level international legislation, negotiation and action on matters of global health—should enjoy "parity with other international concerns such as commerce, treaties, and warfare" (p. 32). It adds the proviso, however, that access to the goods and services that promote individual and public health is only one of many fundamental human rights, and that trade-offs among various rights are sometimes unavoidable. For example, imposing a temporary quarantine during an epidemic might be justifiable if it stems the spread of the disease, even if it temporarily restricts some people's liberty to travel; or curtailing certain healthcare services during an economic downturn might be ethically warranted if that frees up funds for other necessary provisions.

The third interpretive statement (ANA, 2015) gives special attention to the "institutional inequalities and disparities" (p. 32) that exist in virtually every nation between those who have easy access to healthcare services but relatively low incidence rates of "illness, trauma, suffering and premature death" (p. 32) and those who have just the reverse. The statement does not specifically indicate that these inequalities and disparities are often a function of endemic racism, sexism, ethnocentricity or religious intolerance, although this seems to be implied in the call given to nurses to "collaborate to create a moral milieu that is sensitive to diverse cultural values and practices" (p. 32). The fourth interpretive statement deals with "collaboration for human rights in complex, extreme, or extraordinary practice settings" (p. 33), that is, settings where healthcare services are affected by political and military conflict, natural disasters and environmental catastrophes. Nurses serving in such settings are bidden to give special attention to "vulnerable groups such as the poor, the homeless, the elderly, the mentally ill, prisoners, refugees, women, children, and socially stigmatized groups" (p. 33).

Provision 8 of the *Code* (ANA, 2015) shares with the prophetic literature of the Bible a deep commitment to the well-being of persons who are often ignored, marginalized or oppressed by the powers that be. Furthermore, the emphasis given in Provision 8.2 to the importance of global health and the attention given in Provision 8.4 to demanding and difficult practice settings recall the willingness of the Hebrew prophets to perform healings in time of famine or war on persons whom their own coreligionists

Figure 4.2. Antonio Bellucci, *St. Sebastian and St. Irene* [oil on canvas]. (First half of the eighteenth century). 110 cm x 129 cm. The State Hermitage Museum, St. Petersburg, Russia

might easily have excluded as "pagans" or "foreign enemies." That said, the language of fundamental and universal human rights, by which the *Code* justifies these positions, is quite different from the prophetic discourse of the Bible, in which the obligation to include "the Other" is grounded in the wideness of God's mercy.

Provision 9 (ANA, 2015) states, "The profession of nursing, collectively through its professional organizations, must articulate nursing values, maintain the integrity of the profession, and integrate principles of social justice into nursing and health policy." Whereas Provision 8 affirms that nurses must collaborate with other healthcare professionals in insisting that access to quality health care is a fundamental human right, Provision 9 delineates the distinctive values of the nursing profession and the crucial role of the nursing voice in health policy discussions. It stoutly maintains that "the promotion or restoration of health, the prevention of illness and injury, and the alleviation of pain and suffering" (p. 35), which have long been central values of "bedside" nursing with individual patients, also have profound implications for and applications to the welfare of society at large.

The second interpretive statement of Provision 9 (ANA, 2015) pertains to the "integrity of the profession" (p. 35). This phrase has two equally significant aspects: First, it refers to the *ethical* integrity of the profession, that is, to the centrality of the values of "respect, fairness, and caring" (p. 35) in nursing practice. Second, it refers to the (ethical) integrity of the profession *throughout the world*. Just as the *Code* affirms itself to be "the profession's non-negotiable ethical standard" (p. viii), so it affirms itself to be "the covenant between the profession and society" (p. 35). Of course, the binding force of a document promulgated by the ANA extends only to *American* nurses, or perhaps only to members of the ANA itself. Yet those professional nurses who acknowledge the authority of the ANA *Code* are expected to "promote awareness of and adherence to" (p. 35) codes of ethics belonging to other nursing bodies, such as the International Council of Nurses.

Figure 4.3. *Mary Eliza Mahoney (1845–1926)*. Photographs and Prints Division, Schomburg Center for Research in Black Culture, The New York Public Library. Mahoney was the first African American to study and work as a professionally trained nurse in the United States and a staunch advocate of the elimination of racial discrimination in the nursing profession.

The third and fourth interpretive statements of Provision 9 (ANA, 2015) reiterate themes introduced in Provision 8 and apply them forcefully to the work of professional nursing organizations. They insist that considerations of social justice be "integrated" into the curricula of nursing schools and the programs and policy platforms of nursing organizations. Because human health is so greatly determined by socioeconomic factors, and because ready access to high-quality healthcare services is deemed a fundamental and universal human right, nursing work *is* social justice work, plain and simple. This is true of all *kinds* of nursing (patient care, education, supervision, administration, research, etc.) and it is true of nursing at all *levels* (individual, community and global). Provision 9.4, titled "Social Justice in Nursing and Health Policy," extends the same point still further, and in two directions. First, the nursing "voice" must be heard internationally in negotiations pertaining to healthcare policy and legislation (p. 36). Second, the commitment of nurses to social justice must not be restricted to *human* flourishing; it must extend to the "health and well-being of the natural world" (p. 37). This is partly because the degradation of local environments and the depletion of natural resources harms human beings, especially the poorest and most vulnerable, and partly because the well-being of the world itself is a positive ethical good to which the nursing profession pledges itself.

It would be a stretch to assert that Provision 9 (ANA, 2015) has any obvious parallels in the three prophetic texts we have examined above, aside from the very general claim that they all share a commitment to "social justice." Given that the nursing profession as we know it did not exist in the ancient world, we cannot expect ancient prophetic texts to have much *direct* bearing on how modern nurses should participate in programs and policy discussions aimed at improving and promoting public health. However, we can at least say that the *Code* and the ancient Hebrew prophets shared the conviction that human flourishing depends on just social arrangements and a healthy environment. Consider, for example, the prophet Isaiah's description of the cosmic transformation that will occur at the coming of Israel's Messiah:

> *⁶ The wolf shall live with the lamb, the leopard shall lie down with the kid, the calf and the lion and the fatling together, and a little child shall lead them. ⁷ The cow and the bear shall graze, their young shall lie down together; and the lion shall eat straw like the ox. ⁸ The nursing child shall play over the hole of the asp, and the weaned child shall put its hand on the adder's den. ⁹ They will not hurt or destroy on all my holy mountain; for the earth will be full of the knowledge of the* LORD *as the waters cover the sea.* (Isa 11:6–9)

Figure 4.4. Edward Hicks, *Peaceable kingdom* [oil on canvas]. (Ca. 1833). Worcester Art Museum, Massachusetts, USA/Bridgeman Images

CLINICAL VOICES

Social justice work in nursing depends upon nurses' willingness to work together as a profession to benefit others and the world around us (ANA, 2015). The "deeper moral vision" (p. 46) and attention of the individual nurse toward improving the health and dignity of others is essential. The positive impacts can increase exponentially when those individuals combine efforts, as well as include other healthcare colleagues. Leadership and interprofessional collaboration are not only expected essential nursing skills but also are powerful means for improving equitable and safe health care, work, and natural environments (Interprofessional Education Collaborative, 2016). These nurses speak to the challenges of historical and existing influences on the profession and the lives of their patients:

Toe Zaw: *Nurse gender and societal messages*

I was designated to float to the Ob-Gyn unit. Just as I was on my way, I was informed that a female nurse was requested and I could

139

remain on my home unit. Initially, I took offense to this request, feeling it impugned my professionalism. However, I understand that some of these patients may be more comfortable with a nurse of the same gender, affecting their comfort level and feeling of ease to overcome the stresses of their illness. Initiating a conversation about this topic with the patient at these times would not be beneficial in helping them overcome their illness. Historically, women have been exploited, disenfranchised, and oppressed, and these issues continue to impact how care is delivered and received regarding women's health. As a profession, we do not do a good enough job of informing the public that great nursing care can be equally provided regardless of gender. Doctors have done a better job of informing the public that great medical care can be received regardless of the gender of provider. We nurses always try our best to accommodate the needs of our patients, making this challenge harder to overcome. As more men enter the profession of nursing, are we responsible to educate the public that great nursing care can be delivered regardless of gender? My answer is yes, and I can do my part to educate the public (including family and friends); we can use our collective voices to help inform the general public—normalizing the nursing care provided by male nurses regardless of setting and shifting critique instead to the care provided, and not the gender of the nurse.

Marit Knutson: *Partnership and advocacy*

I cared for a man who was homeless and had just found out that his partner was pregnant. He wanted to go to Lamaze classes with her, but the prospect of becoming a father was overwhelming because he had recently been diagnosed with metastatic cancer. Additionally, he had a complex psychiatric history and history of polysubstance abuse. I was working with him for two twelve-hour shifts, watching him organize the mess of his room, encouraging him to stay on our floor and try a nicotine patch instead of going out to smoke, reiterating that I had just asked the provider about more pain meds but hadn't heard back, and urging him to wear his brace because he had lesions to his spine. After the second day, I thought about how our society had really truly failed this man. He was definitely an outsider, and our perception of him as a care team was obfuscated by frustration. If only he could just do as we asked of him, then it would be easier to care for him, right? But we had to work to show him utmost respect, which he deserved. We adapted and provided the best care we could, encouraging a partnership with him instead of one in which we were power-struggling. I suggest that rebelliousness is a positive virtue for nurses to have. Being an advocate and ally is a radical thing to do. Standing up for, and at the side of, marginalized communities in struggle bucks the status quo, especially when the notion is that access to health care is a privilege instead of a right. Nurses have been expected previously to be docile, perform tasks, and take orders. This is not the case anymore.

Anonymous: *Regaining trust*

I was employed by the Alaska Native Tribal Health Consortium for many years working with Alaska Native people. I had the honor of being one of their first "direct hire" employees at their facility not being paid by the federal government or other civic organization to just provide care to this underserved population, but I was employed to work alongside this population to improve health and wellness in their communities. The Consortium was made up of the thirteen different "tribes/regions" of Alaska, was tribally owned and operated, and supported native preferential hiring and advancement of their people. It was my honor to be hired to serve this disadvantaged and mistreated population. I learned a lot about myself and the privileges I grew up with, just because of the color of my skin. Seeing how our government had treated this vulnerable population disgusted me. I would often be yelled at by upset patients who would be non-trusting of me because of prior abuse they had suffered at the hands of people who looked like me. I had to work to regain their trust and confidence and let them know that I was not there to "hurt or study" them. This took much patience and perseverance, but I was happy to do this after witnessing the results of many years of mistreatment. I see where my voice doesn't go very far, but when I connect with others who share my values and beliefs, positive change can be made. I do realize that to make a change, nurses must be united and I cannot do it alone—but I can be a "prophet," take a stand for what is right, and promote health care as a basic human right for all.

Gloria Chang: *Language barriers and social justice*

My parents were immigrants who knew very little English. Going to the doctors terrified them because 1) there was a language barrier, 2) it was too expensive, and 3) they knew nothing about health care. I recalled during one doctor's visit my father thought he needed to be on "blood dinners" (eating blood for dinner) instead of "blood thinners." None of the healthcare staff followed up with why my father kept refusing to be on blood thinners, which could have been life-threatening for him. My experience growing up enables me to better understand and relate to the constant struggles of social injustice for low-income, ethnic minorities. I think the hardest part about trying to maintain social justice is to preserve the compassion you have for not only one specific population but for all populations. I have had many experiences where patients would try to manipulate the provider and staff into giving them pain medication. It is difficult to not keep your guard up when this happens. Ever since my clinic started using motivational interviewing, I have found that these patients would open up to me instead of getting angry, because they were being heard. Even though motivational interviewing may not always work, it has allowed me to create better relationships with these patients, which is invaluable progress.

Flannery Moran: *Stigma and advocacy*

I had the privilege of caring for a long-term AIDS patient, who'd originally been diagnosed as a young man, some thirty years prior. He was a light sleeper and would lap the halls at night in his robe, trailing his IV pole, since the constant yells and cries of other patients in such tight quarters kept him awake. We had long conversations about his painful experiences with his disease and its effects on his psychological, emotional, personal and professional life. I was incredibly moved that he was willing to share such personal experiences with me. In particular, his recounting of the evolution and significant setbacks over the years in AIDS care, from the "inside," was stunning. He described the large and detrimental obstacles to progress in HIV/AIDS research over the years because of the stigma surrounding homosexuality and alternative lifestyles, and sat crying over the innocent babies born with HIV whose lives had been lost because of such judgmental attitudes. I honestly will never forget him. As nurses and as future advanced care providers, we have an opportunity not only to make a difference in the lives of those we care for personally but also to call truth and stigma for what they are—and potentially to have an influence on a much larger scale. Being a "prophet" and seeker of social justice is about more than just having insight. When you are unable to right a colossal wrong for lack of opportunity, resources or skill, find a way to be valuable and never stop fighting until your voice is heard.

KEYWORDS

1. Ethical monotheism/Yahwism
2. Exclusion/inclusion
3. Former Prophets
4. Idolatry
5. Latter Prophets
6. Prophecy
7. Social justice

READING COMPREHENSION

1. "What the Bible means by 'prophecy' is easily misunderstood or oversimplified." What *does* the Bible mean by the term, and what does it *not* mean?

2. The exegesis of Luke 4:16–30 offered above concludes with the following statement: "The terrible irony of the story of Jesus' sermon in the Nazareth synagogue is not that Jesus stubbornly denied to his townspeople the liberation from sin, debt, poverty and illness that he was generously offering to others, but that because they resented the fact that he was offering these blessings to those whom they deemed undeserving, they disqualified themselves." Summarize the argument that leads to this conclusion.

3. Summarize the five key points made in the discussion of 1 Kings 17:8–24.

4. Summarize the three key points made in the discussion of 2 Kings 5:1–19.

5. Summarize the content of Provisions 8–9 of the ANA *Code*.

MAKING CONNECTIONS

1. Describe a situation in which you provided nursing care for a person who might be considered an "outsider" to American society by virtue of her race, ethnicity, religion, nationality, native language, gender identity or sexual preference. What did you learn about yourself and your profession from that experience?

2. Does the claim of this chapter that nursing care is "social justice work" shed new light on your experience with the patient you identified in Prompt 1 or reshape your self-understanding as a nurse?

3. Jesus tells the people of his hometown, "No prophet is accepted in the prophet's hometown." In this chapter we have considered nursing as a "prophetic" profession. Have you ever felt misunderstood or ostracized because of your choice of profession or for any actions you have taken in the line of duty?

4. Study the painting by Bernardo Strozzi, *Elijah and the Widow of Sarepta*, shown on p. 129 above, and then reread 1 Kings 17:8–24. Which moment in the story does it portray? What light does it shed on the relationship between Strand 4 and modern health care, particularly on the questions of the patient/provider relationship and the allocation of scarce resources?

5. Study the painting by Edward Hicks, *The Peaceable Kingdom*, shown on p. 139 above. This painting, done in Hicks' characteristically "primitivist" style, illustrates Isaiah's vision of a world restored by God to the purity, innocence and peace of the garden of Eden. It depicts the reconciliation between humanity and the natural world, between predators and prey, and between diverse groups of human beings, in this case Native Americans and the English settlers of Pennsylvania. Imagine this painting hanging over the nurse's station in your unit. What specific changes in patient care and in the relationships among the staff might it inspire, if it were regarded as a symbol of what your unit aspires to become?

6. Read the Clinical Voices on pp. 139–42 above. Do any of them seem to "speak" to you, conjuring up memories, reflections, hopes or fears related to your own practice?

5

Moral Maturity in Christian Nursing

"The Bible was composed in such a way that as beginners mature, its meaning grows with them."

AUGUSTINE, 1998, P. 40

In this final chapter, we unpack the concept of "moral maturity" as it pertains to the Christian nurse. We show how the four strands of biblical moral discourse "interweave" (section 1) and how the corresponding provisions in the ANA (2015) *Code of Ethics for Nurses* must be "integrated" (section 2). The usual "clinical voices" (section 3) and teaching/learning helps (sections 4–6) follow. But let us begin with the story of a nurse who beautifully demonstrated what we are advocating here.

Mae was a clinic nurse in a busy gastroenterology center. A mother brought her school-age son, Ivan, into the clinic for management of encopresis (chronic constipation with fecal incontinence). Ivan was a quiet child and had been cooperative with his medication regimen. His physician determined that the only reason Ivan was continuing to have difficulty was that he had lost sensitivity to sensations associated with bowel movements. Meanwhile, the child was suffering greatly at school and at home from being teased by classmates and his twin brother about the chronic smell of leaking stool. Mae received a referral to conduct biofeedback training with Ivan and proceeded to meet with him and his mother once a week. Between sessions, Mae thought about different approaches she might use to try to connect with Ivan; she didn't seem to be helping him improve at all. In fact, he continued to appear sad and withdrawn. During the sessions, Ivan was able to demonstrate quick and appropriate responses, but his mother reported nothing had changed at home. Clinic protocol required strict adherence to half-hour appointments, but following the fourth session, Mae wondered if there was more to Ivan's story. The lack of progress just didn't make sense. Mae put the equipment away and asked Ivan and his mother if they would be willing to spend a few extra minutes talking.

After Ivan was dressed and sitting comfortably by his mother's side, Mae gently asked how things were going at home. Ivan's mother said they implemented all the strategies recommended by the doctor. "But he just isn't willing to sit for more than a minute on the toilet. No matter what kind of reward is waiting for him from his star chart, or what kind of interesting book he's chosen!" Mae watched as Ivan made himself small and stared at his shoelaces. "Ivan, what's it like for you when you go to the bathroom? What do you think about the books and star chart?" Ivan shrugged and was silent, his eyes filling with tears. "You look sad, Ivan. Is there something you are worried about or afraid of?" Ivan glanced up at Mae with tears running down his cheeks and said, "Well, I just *can't* stay in the bathroom! My brother told me that a rat will swim up and bite me on the *butt!*" Suddenly, Mae understood, and Ivan's mother gasped, "You didn't tell me, Ivan! Oh, your brother is in *so* much trouble!" Mae said, "It sounds like it's pretty scary to sit on the toilet, is that right?" Ivan nodded glumly. "Ivan, would you like to go out to the waiting room and play Nintendo for a few minutes while I talk with your mom?" Mae asked. Ivan scooted quickly out the door, and Mae turned her attention to talking with his mom. Quiet little Ivan had been too afraid and embarrassed to share this bit of information earlier in his medical workup, one critical piece of his story that changed everything. Although greatly over time now in the appointment slot, Mae found the physician to share this revelation and ask for a psychotherapist referral. A couple of months later Mae received a phone call from Ivan's mother, who reported that counseling was indeed helping him overcome his toileting fears and helping the family address his twin's bullying behavior. He seemed to be a happier child, his mother said, and no longer looked sad when it was time to go to school.

Mae found herself challenged to apply all her best nursing care to solve this persistent and puzzling client problem. Although the strands were not literally checked off a list of moral maturity elements, nor did Mae specifically refer to the *Code* (ANA, 2015) in order to address her patient care problem, her processes and actions suggest a foundation of both. As a Christian nurse, Mae considered Ivan's worth as a child made in God's image, in need of compassion, respect, and patient, attentive listening to words and body language. While she maintained an awareness of the time limitations in the clinic setting (Strand 1), she considered the greater value of getting to the root of the problem and identifying a useful solution for the child and family—one that resulted in a long-range savings of time, money, and resources (Strand 3). Through honest self-reflection (Strand 2), Mae realized that she was not having a positive impact on her patient as hoped, which allowed her to admit her own limitations and seek a better patient care approach. She took the information to the attending physician, advocated for a different intervention for the patient, and received positive feedback later of Ivan's success (Strand 4). As Mae considered this series of events, she was able to see how it contributed to her own ongoing moral development; she grew from the experience and became more confident in her situational awareness and decision-making.

Before moving to the question of how one might achieve the kind of moral maturity that Mae displays in this story, two points of clarification are in order. First, we do not suppose that only nurses who are Christians can attain the kind of moral maturity required by the *Code* (ANA, 2015) or, conversely, that all nurses who are Christians display such maturity. Our aim is simply to sketch out what moral maturity in the nursing profession looks like for Christians who enter that profession resolved to allow the spiritual and ethical teachings of the Bible to shape their personal and professional character and guide their personal and professional conduct. We gladly acknowledge the high degree of agreement between the moral teachings of all the world's great religions, and the exemplary work—fully in accordance with the *Code*—done by nurses who practice religions other than Christianity, or who practice no religion at all.[1] Second, we understand moral maturity as a worthy aspirational goal. Yet, like all forms of maturity, it is a *flying* goal, one

---

1. Nurses from other traditions may need to put the *Code* into conversation with whatever moral authorities they acknowledge—though how they would do so is not for us to say. We surmise, however, that a Muslim nurse, who is deemed morally mature according to the Quran and Sharia, or a Jewish nurse, who is deemed morally mature according to the Hebrew Bible and the Talmud, would perform most nursing duties in much the same way as a Christian nurse, who is deemed morally mature according to the Christian Bible. Such differences in religious belief and practice as might exist among them would seldom be noticeable at the level of day-to-day patient care, medical research or unit administration. That does not mean that such differences "don't matter." It only means that what they matter *for* is not something the *Code* uses as an indicator of ethical nursing practice.

that recedes as we approach it, or rather one that constantly beckons us forward. It is really a lifelong *process* of maturation and a career-long process of professional development that we are describing and advocating here. One is always "on the way"—unless one makes the disastrous mistake of imagining that one has "arrived." Moreover, it is a process that, on the one hand, takes place quite naturally as one grows in age and experience, and, on the other hand, requires constant self-reflection, *ad hoc* feedback and constructive criticism from colleagues, willing participation in formal professional review procedures and a good deal of prayer. Or, to recall our analogy of the braid, it is a process of deliberately and conscientiously "interweaving" the insights of the four strands of biblical moral discourse into one's own life, just as those strands are already interwoven within the canon of Christian Scripture.

INTERWEAVING THE STRANDS

In the introduction we argued that the differences in theological outlook and literary form among the texts representing the four strands demonstrate the rich array of ways in which the canon of Scripture in its entirety can shape the lives of Christian individuals and communities. The four strands "gloss" or comment on each other, each interpreting the other three, providing corrections to and qualifications for the excesses and deficiencies to which each of the others, taken by itself, might be prone. The word *gloss* comes from the Greek word *glōssa*, meaning "tongue." It can refer either to the organ of speech or to a spoken language.[2] In the technical terminology of theology, to "gloss" a text of Scripture means to expound upon it. Medieval biblical scholars produced a vast collection of such commentaries, which were collectively titled the *Glossa Ordinaria*. Figure 5.1 below shows a page from that work, in which the biblical text appears at the heart of the page, surrounded by the expositions of various ancient and early medieval Christian authorities. But whereas the material in the *Glossa Ordinaria* was written by later scholars *about* the sacred text, we are suggesting that glossing also occurs *within* the text of Scripture itself—one biblical passage glossing another. Texts representing each of our four strands provide valuable insight

---

2. Both senses of the Greek word *glōssa* (or *glōtta* in some dialects) find their way into English as well. For example, the word *epiglottis* (literally, "upon the tongue") refers to the flap of skin at the back of the throat that prevents food from going into the trachea, and *glossolalia* (literally, "tongue-speaking") refers to the spiritual gift of talking in a language otherwise unknown to oneself (see Acts 2:1–13 and 1 Cor 14:1–40).

into how to read—and how *not* to read—texts representing other strands. This is not accidental. For when the ancient Jewish rabbis compiled the Old Testament, and again when the ancient church fathers compiled the New Testament, they selected works that offered various ways of thinking about the nature and activity of God and about how God's people ought to live in order to honor him. This procedure assured that the biblical canon would contain a rich comprehensiveness of content and an abundance of illustration that would have been missing if texts representing only one kind of moral discourse had been included. Yet it imposed upon *readers* of the Bible the responsibility of interpreting each part of it in light of the whole—or in the case of moral texts, such as we are examining here, of interpreting texts representing each strand in light of other texts representing other strands. This is what we mean by saying that reliable moral instruction is derived from Christian Scripture only when we "interweave" the four strands, that is, only when we let the texts "gloss" each other.

Figure 5.1. *Biblia Latina cum Glossa Ordinaria*. Basel: Froben and Petri, 1498, p. 50. Shown on this page is Gloss on Genesis 1:1 by Nicholas of Lyra. The inset square with the illuminated initial letter is the biblical text (*In principio creavit Deus caelum et terram*) with some interlinear textual notes in smaller lettering. Surrounding the inset is Nicholas' commentary on the verse—beginning with the opening words of the verse, again with an illuminated initial letter. Citations to other biblical verses are given in the margins.

Some readers of the Bible might find this claim disconcerting, fearing that it compromises the Bible's thematic unity. They might suppose that all of its books communicate essentially the same religious message, albeit in a wide variety of literary forms, and that with a few annoying exceptions (which are usually explained away) the religious meaning and moral implications of every biblical verse are perfectly self-evident as they stand. We do not see it this way. We certainly *do* affirm the Bible's overall thematic unity (Bauckham, 2003, 38–53; Rowley, 1961, 15–37). But we understand this unity on analogy with that of a great piece of symphonic music, in which many different rhythmic patterns, melodic lines and instrumental tone colors blend into an articulated but perfectly coordinated whole. Compare, for example, the aesthetic effect produced by a large monastic choir chanting Gregorian plainsong in unison with that of a full concert orchestra playing a Beethoven symphony. If you remove one singer from the monastic choir, you may reduce the volume and tone quality of the music a bit, but you do not change the melody or the lyrics, and there is no harmony to change at all. If, however, you remove the string section from an orchestra, it simply cannot perform Beethoven at all. Similarly, the various "voices" in the Bible offer a richness of meaning that none of them can provide by itself but that all of them together *do* provide, precisely because, different as they are, they ultimately harmonize with each other. Each of the four strands of biblical moral discourse has its own distinctive insights and emphases. To be sure, the insights and emphases of one strand do not directly contradict those of the other strands, but they do provide diverse perspectives on how God's people should comport themselves. Thus, when you read a text that represents one strand—say, the legal strand—in light of the insights and emphases of the holiness, wisdom and prophetic strands, you are less likely to *mis*read it than you would be if you read it *only* in light of other legal texts. Or rather, you are less likely to wrongly apply its meaning to your life that way. The problem lies not in what Strand 1 texts themselves *say* but in what you are likely to think they *mean* if you fail to listen to contrasting texts from Strands 2, 3 and 4. The same point applies to *each* strand: to read it for maximum spiritual benefit, you must read it "canonically," that is, in light of the distinctive insights and perspectives provided by the other strands.

To illustrate this point, let's imagine four Christians, each of whom *begins* his study of Scripture with a deep sympathy for only *one* of its four strands of moral discourse, but each of whom gradually discovers the riches of the other three strands.

Our first reader is prone to legalism. He likes to live in orderly, well-regulated environments, both at home and in the workplace, and he approaches the Bible as a rulebook. Strand 1 texts speak to him, and he speaks passionately—and perhaps a little too stridently—of Strand 1 texts to his family, his friends and his coworkers. But as he goes deeper and deeper into the Scriptures, he discovers far more than rules and regulations. As he works his way through the book of Leviticus, he comes to chapter 17 and suddenly notices a subtle shift in emphasis. It is not that the Holiness Code denies the importance of outward conduct, but it gives greater attention to matters of character than the earlier legislation. This causes our reader to ask himself about his motives for obeying God's law, and equally importantly, his motives for expecting other people to do so. He continues his study and comes to the Wisdom literature, which reminds him that there is more to problem-solving, decision-making and human interaction than stiff conformity to divine and human laws. It insists that that wide experience, emotional intelligence and effective communication skills are all necessary in finding the "right" way forward through life's complexities and ambiguities. Eventually our legalistic reader dips into the stories and writings of the Hebrew prophets and the early Christian apostles and discovers that the point of God's law is not merely to secure social and political *stability*, but also to protect the rights of each person and to promote the common good of all. He catches his breath when he reads Jesus' statement that "the Sabbath was made for humankind, and not humankind for the Sabbath" (Mark 2:27), and he feels deeply convicted when he comes to Jesus' rebuke of the "scribes and Pharisees," who "tithe mint, dill, and cummin, [but neglect] the weightier matters of the law: justice and mercy and faith" (Matt 23:23). Yet in exposing the problems of legalism, all these bracing discoveries have taught him the spirit of genuine obedience. They have illuminated for him the purpose of the law, which is to promote the flourishing of all.

Let us now imagine a different reader, this one troubled by perfectionism, such as the student described in the chapter on Strand 2 above, who thought she had shed her neurotic need to achieve "perfection" by working hard to "improve" herself. The problem with this person is not her quest for holiness as such but the anxious self-preoccupation that drives it, the egotistical need to be *conspicuously* good, or rather, to be conspicuously *better* than others. When she encounters the legal, wisdom and prophetic strands of Scripture, however, her moral horizons are widened—and her egotism is dampened. Strand 1 stresses that individual citizens do not flourish unless the social institutions that regulate public life are functioning properly, and that it is the responsibility of individual citizens to support and uphold those institutions. Strand 3 emphasizes that people who cultivate their own moral virtue without also gaining practical wisdom from daily experience and formal education are likely to look either insufferably arrogant or pitiably naïve. Strand 4 insists that an indispensable part of the quest for personal holiness is self-forgetful service to one's neighbors. Together, Strands 1, 3, and 4 actually aid this reader's quest for scriptural holiness by exposing the error and futility of egotistical perfectionism. She has come to see for herself what John Wesley meant when he observed, "Directly opposite to [solitary religion] is the gospel of Christ. . . . 'Holy solitaries' is a phrase no more consistent with the gospel than holy adulterers. The gospel of Christ knows of no religion but social; no holiness but social holiness. 'Faith working by love' is the length and breadth and depth and height of Christian perfection" (Wesley, 1984, p. 321).

Our third reader is a fan of Strand 3 and consults the Bible primarily to glean tips on "how to win friends and influence people" (Carnegie, 1998). This reader naturally gravitates to the Wisdom literature. But there, amidst all the sound practical advice about solving problems and relating to others, he discovers the following warning: "Do not be wise in your own eyes; fear the LORD, and turn away from evil" (Prov 3:7). Strand 3, he realizes, is actually glossing itself. He proceeds to the prophetic writings and finds a similar warning against "being wise in [one's] own eyes and shrewd in [one's] own sight" (Isa 5:21). Moreover, the Apostle Paul, whose writings interweave all four strands of moral discourse, insists that "the wisdom of God," manifest in the life, death and resurrection of Christ, is the furthest thing from the self-seeking pragmatism that "human standards" often mistake for wisdom (1 Cor 1:18–31). Our third reader profits greatly by expanding his repertoire of Bible reading, discovering that the pursuit of "the good life" means the pursuit of a life of goodness and that "success" is empty without obedience to the law, the practice of virtue, and a keen social conscience.

Our fourth reader is enamored of the prophets' call for social justice and indignant over the historical inability of all human societies to establish it. She desires to speak "prophetically" to a fallen world but fails to distinguish clearly between "difficulties" and "problems." In her fixation with Strand 4 themes, she tends to assume that all human troubles, whether difficulties or problems, are chargeable to the evil conduct or depraved indifference of some person or institution. Although her moral passion is certainly admirable, her view of the world is narrow and simplistic. For not all human troubles *can* be solved, and not all troubles, whether solvable or not, are morally chargeable (Steele, 2018, pp. 24–28). She would benefit by the humility and patience required by Strand 2: "How can you say to your neighbor, 'Let me take the speck out of your eye,' while the log is in your own eye? You hypocrite, first take the log out of your own eye, and then you will see clearly to take the speck out of your neighbor's eye" (Matt 7:4–5). She would benefit, too, from the realism and savvy of Strand 3: "Be not righteous overmuch, and do not make yourself overwise; why should you destroy yourself? Be not wicked overmuch, neither be a fool; why should you die before your time?" (Eccl 7:16–17, RSV). Reading more widely in Scripture will not dampen her prophetic conscience, but it will enlarge her overall moral vision.

Our key point here is that in using the Bible as a guide to action and character formation, we must factor in the distinctive insights of all four strands of moral discourse. These strands gloss each other and, taken together, warn us against the narrowness of outlook and the rashness of action that might befall us if we were to fixate on any of them taken by itself.

INTEGRATING THE PROVISIONS

How does this understanding of the moral authority and use of Christian Scripture apply specifically to Christian nursing? The first thing to observe is that the nine provisions of the *Code* (ANA, 2015), along with their respective interpretive statements, are not "interwoven" in quite the same way as the texts representing the four strands of moral discourse are in the canon of Scripture. The *Code* is an itemized inventory of ethical obligations, which shape the professional life of the nurse who heeds them by sheer accumulation, and not, like the Bible, a potpourri of texts from different settings, composed in different literary styles and genres, which attain their overall meaning and moral force by mutual glossing. This does not imply that the *Code's* provisions do not need to be "unpacked," elaborated and applied. They certainly do, and that is precisely the function of their respective interpretive statements and of commentaries such as Marsha Fowler's *Guide* (2015). It only means that the ethical standards found in the *Code* apply only to professional nurses (not to all Christian disciples in their various walks of life, as do the moral teachings of the Bible) and that its contents are carefully calibrated to current circumstances in society and revised from time to time as those circumstances change. Thus, the provisions and interpretive statements of the *Code* build on each other and reinforce each other, but they do not exactly gloss each other as various passages of Scripture do.

We suggested above that the thematic unity of Scripture was like the musical unity of a great symphony, where the aesthetic whole is greater than the sum of the individual parts. To extend the analogy, the thematic unity of the *Code* (ANA, 2015) is like the musical unity of the sequence of diatonic seventh chords in a C-major scale (see Figure 5.2). It is more tonally complex than the notes of the scale played by themselves, but it is laid out in strict accordance with the rules of harmony, lacks a melody altogether, and possesses little emotional depth or aesthetic charm.

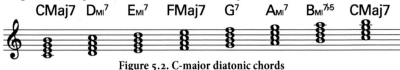

Figure 5.2. C-major diatonic chords

That is just as it should be, given what such a document contains and how its audience will use it: codes of ethics are meant to be obeyed, not relished. Yet the contents of the *Code* (ANA, 2015) certainly *do* need to be integrated into the personal and professional lives of RNs and APRNs. By that we mean that nurses must inwardly appropriate and outwardly apply the nine provisions and their respective interpretive statements. Christian nurses do so in tandem with their appropriation and application of the moral teachings of the Bible—and it has been the aim of this book to help them correlate these two very different authorities. How this process of integration might look is illustrated in Figure 5.3.

This figure is a slightly modified version of Figure 0.3 from the introduction (p. 10). The references to the four strands of biblical moral discourse shown in the earlier chart are replaced by references to their correlative provisions in the *Code* (ANA, 2015), but the color-coding we used to differentiate the four biblical strands is retained. Our point is that morally well-rounded nursing includes the various activities shown in the four fields above. Attaining moral maturity means, therefore, not only that the nurse assiduously performs a wide array of professional functions (as defined by his scope of practice and job description), but quite intentionally strikes a balance in the time and energy devoted to each. Conversely, if a nurse were to avoid performing the activities shown in any of those fields, his practice would be professionally impoverished and ethically deficient.

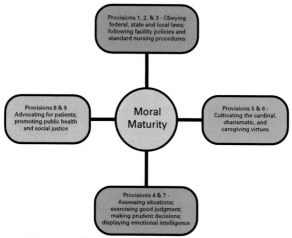

Figure 5.3. Moral maturity and the nine provisions

This can be illustrated by a thought experiment much like the one offered earlier with respect to the interweaving of the strands. Imagine that a nurse concentrated her attention on the matters defined in Provisions 1–3 (ANA, 2015), as shown in the purple field above. Doing so might well be appropriate for a young nurse fresh out of school, but steady professional development involves much more than scrupulously following rules and mechanically performing tasks. A nurse who does not allow the joys and challenges of the work to touch her heart (as Provisions 5 and 6 require), or who fails to "grow into" the job (as Provisions 4 and 7 require), or who cannot see past the immediate needs of her patients to the wider social problems that cause their illnesses and injuries (as Provisions 8 and 9 require), has simply not attained moral maturity. Similarly, a nurse who concentrates on matters of character—the virtues named in the green field in our diagram or the practical skills and strategies named in the red—might be an admirable person, but he would not be a morally mature nurse if he flaunted the rules of the unit or shirked his fair share of the work. Finally, a nurse who possesses an especially sensitive social conscience and vigorously protests the inequities and injustices of our world and their impact on public health, as indicated in the gold field above, might be a wonderful standard-bearer for public health and an effective patient advocate. Yet being a morally mature nurse involves more than social criticism and patient advocacy: it also involves collaborating with other healthcare professionals, dispensing meds, running lab tests, chatting encouragingly with patients, and so forth. Striking a balance among the various matters covered by the nine provisions—that is, expressing the goodness of one's character by the excellence of one's conduct and growing in virtue and skill by performing one's daily tasks with intentionality—is what constitutes moral maturity in the nurse. Doing it all in obedience to God, in imitation of Jesus, by the power of the Holy Spirit, and for the sake of one's neighbor, is what constitutes moral maturity in the *Christian* nurse.

CLINICAL VOICES

Moral maturity requires the nurse to be a reflective practitioner, and we hope this framework of four biblical strands encourages nurses to think about how their vocation is enhanced by the way law, holiness, wisdom, and prophecy interact with the *Code* (ANA, 2015) from a Christian ethics standpoint. When the pragmatic elements of the *Code* are incorporated with this biblical foundation, the result is deep understanding of the full spectrum of nursing care to address sound mind, body and spirit of self and others. These nurses share reflections about their growth integrating professional and biblical moral elements in their clinical work:

Melissa Frondozo: *Conflicting values between nurse and patient*

> I felt my braid unraveling a bit as I was trying to care for a specific patient. I found that although I was trying to care for this patient with all four aspects of biblical moral discourse in mind, she did not share the same ethics. To provide the best care that I could for her, I had to relent in some of my values and come to a compromise with hers so she felt she still had autonomy. This patient suffered a burn, but her medical history included being a paraplegic (independent with wheelchair), and she still displayed symptoms of short-term memory loss, impulsiveness, and focused obsessions on things because of her traumatic brain injury ten years ago. As one small example, all she could focus on was going outside to smoke, while the policy states patients are not allowed outside to smoke. I exercised the first (law), third (wisdom), and fourth (prophecy) strands by kindly explaining the rules of the hospital (law) and why we have such rules (law, wisdom, prophecy). She agreed but said she was going to do it anyway, and her mother (her caregiver) was going to wheel her downstairs. Smoking is unhealthy, doesn't promote health or wound healing, and doesn't align with my personal virtues. Is keeping my moral braid

intact worth it? In my opinion, no, because nursing to me isn't only about my morals, but the balance with the patient's morals as well. The most important thing is listening to the patient and working with them according to what their morals may be. In the case of my patient, she was not willing to stop smoking—but what *was* she willing to work on to attain her optimal, healthy self?

Josephine Eshun: *End-of-life pain management*

As a nurse, I have not always found it easy to reconcile my Christian principles with my daily nursing duties, though I know full well that those two intersect somehow. Law, wisdom, prophecy, and holiness are the means by which the Bible attempts to guide the character and conduct of its followers. It also helps the professional nurse navigate the world of ethics. There have been times when I had to keep my Christian and biblical beliefs behind a personal curtain I have dubbed "not now" because applying them in certain situations makes it all so complicated and crippling. For instance, with my comfort care patients, I often find myself questioning my role in the patient's life and death. By law, I have to keep the patient comfortable by administering the morphine sulfate that is prescribed for such patients. However, I always have an attack of the conscience as one of the Ten Commandments, "Thou shall not kill," pops into my head all the time. How do I comfortably make ethical decisions? Or as a Christian, how do I fulfill both my Christian duty and my nursing duty? Withholding the morphine is unlawful and administering it also does not align with my beliefs.

Anonymous: *The process of learning patience*

When I started my career as a new nurse, I was very impatient about almost everything. I would rush through tasks as quickly as possible just to keep up with the growing amount of work. I would get extremely restless when a colleague was slow to respond to a request, or when a patient was taking too long to do something such as getting up or taking their medications. My lack of patience led me to become easily frustrated and gave me a great deal of stress and anxiety. This affected not only my own work and quality of care but also that of my colleagues. It affected my personal life as well. At that time, my personal character and habits illustrated a frustrated and anxious person. As I gained more experience and grew older, I realized that being patient was so important not only to help me be a better nurse to my patients and colleagues, but also to help me physically and mentally. As I started to gain more patience at work, I noticed my mindset changing. I was no longer so stressed or frustrated by things over which I had no control, which promoted my personal health and well-being. I was able to foster a healthy work environment for my colleagues and myself because I had more time to help them instead of being stressed. Although I am still struggling with being patient, I am constantly reminding myself how far I have come. Christian perfection is meant to be a process of continuing maturation, not of obtaining a certain level of righteousness or virtue. For me, reaching my desired level of patience is going to be an ongoing process of growth and learning.

KEYWORDS

1. Gloss

2. Integrating the provisions

3. Interweaving the strands

4. Moral maturity

READING COMPREHENSION

1. What is the difference between "interweaving" the four strands of biblical moral discourse and "integrating" the nine provisions of the ANA *Code* and their respective interpretive statements?

2. How does this chapter use musical analogies to illustrate the difference between "interweaving the strands" and "integrating the provisions"?

3. What negative consequences does this chapter foresee for a reader of the Bible who failed to "interweave" all four of the strands into her spiritual life?

4. What negative consequences does this chapter foresee for a nurse (or Christian nurse) who fails to "integrate" all nine of the provisions into her professional practice?

MAKING CONNECTIONS

1. Many books on medical ethics contain case studies and offer specific strategies for resolving the moral quandaries that often arise in health care. This book does not. What it offers, instead, are various "clinical voices," reflections by advanced practice nursing students on the material presented in the text. How helpful have you found these reflections in grappling with the content of each chapter and in growing toward "moral maturity" as a nurse? How have the clinical voices in this chapter, shown on pp. 156–58 above, helped you to "take" this book as a whole?

2. How will the approach taken in this book shape your analysis of ethically complex healthcare cases and your role in helping your patients and professional colleagues resolve medical-ethical quandaries?

3. How helpful has the approach taken here been for your spiritual life and for your professional practice as a nurse?

4. Study Albert Charles Challen's portrait of the Jamaican Roman Catholic nurse Mary Seacole (1805–1881), shown below, and do some background research on Seacole's life and career. What qualities of "moral maturity," as described in this chapter, does her story reflect, and how successfully does Challen capture those qualities in his painting?

Figure 5.4. Albert Charles Challen, *Portrait of Mary Seacole* [oil on panel]. (Ca. 1869). 59.7 cm x 88.9 cm. National Portrait Gallery, London, England

Annotated Bibliography

The present work has certain resonances with many of the standard monographs and textbooks in the fields of nursing ethics, medical ethics, bioethics, and spirituality in nursing, as listed below. Yet it also displays significant differences from them. For example, we have said little about the four key principles of modern "secular" bioethics—namely, autonomy, nonmaleficence, beneficence and justice—the validity of which is not presumed to depend on any particular set of religious convictions. Nor have we addressed many of the hot-button issues in modern healthcare ethics, such as the care of persons addicted to opioids or the relation between public health protocols and immigration laws in times of pandemic. Nor have we made much use of case studies, except where these appear in the "clinical voices" section of each chapter. We have deliberately omitted these things from this book, partly because they have been addressed so often and so well in other works, and partly because they did not seem to help us achieve our specific aim. Yet we recognize their importance in any well-rounded course in nursing ethics and address them, via other resources, in our own course for advanced practice nurses. The works listed below *do* address them—and do so extremely well. We gratefully use several of them in our nursing ethics courses, either as required or recommended texts, and we cite many of them above. What we offer here is a brief sketch of the contents of each, along with an account of how they inform, relate to or differ from the present work, and how they might be used in tandem with the present work in a nursing ethics class.

Beauchamp, T. L., & Childress, J. F. (2013). *Principles of biomedical ethics* (7th ed.). New York, NY: Oxford University Press. The first edition of this book appeared in 1977, and the authors have worked assiduously to keep bioethics abreast of the "immense changes [that] have occurred in the field," and in medicine itself, over the past four decades. The book has deservedly achieved the status of a "classic" and a "canonical text," and is so called by those who have endorsed the book on its back cover, including several whom Beauchamp and Childress fondly designate as their own "abiding critics." The book attends to every conceivable ethical issue, and we observe connections between matters that we would classify under each of the four strands of biblical moral discourse and the contents of *Principles*. Nevertheless, Beauchamp and Childress approach bioethics from the perspective of what they call "universal common morality," rather than any of the "particular moralities" (including that of Christianity) to which people (including patients and healthcare providers) might be committed. In that respect, their book is aligned more closely with the ANA *Code* (2015) and the volume by Jonsen et al. (2015) reviewed below than it is with our own. Moreover, *Principles* takes the form of a comprehensive monograph, as opposed to a classroom-friendly textbook. To be sure, it is elegantly written, forcefully argued and richly furnished with concrete examples, but it lacks pedagogical helps such as case studies and discussion questions. We *use* the book in lecture preparation, but we do not *assign* the book in a one-off course in nursing ethics for APRN students. It seems better suited as a foundational work for graduate programs in bioethics proper.

Doornbos, M. M., Groenhout, R. E., & Hotz, K. G. (2005). *Transforming care: A Christian vision of nursing practice*. Grand Rapids, MI: Eerdmans. Doornbos et al. ask the question, "Can nursing be Christian?" and offer a resoundingly affirmative answer to it. Their answer is all the more persuasive for being so richly textured, as the interdisciplinary team of co-authors include a nurse educator (Doornbos), a philosopher (Groenhout) and a theological ethicist (Hotz), and we find ourselves in close agreement with the positions they take on most issues in the theory and practice of Christian nursing. But there are two significant differences between their work and our own. The first pertains to religious outlook. Doorbos et al. reflect a solidly Reformed perspective on Christian ethics, whereas we approach the issue from a broadly Wesleyan frame of reference. Reformed Christians tend to avoid ascribing "holiness" or "virtue" to human beings and approach ethics with a sober sense of human brokenness and sinfulness. Wesleyans, in contrast, tend to emphasize God's power to bring moral healing and restoration to those redeemed by Christ and imbued with the Holy Spirit. These differences in outlook are reflected in our respective approaches to nursing ethics. The second difference pertains to methodology. Doornbos et al. rarely engage the text of Christian Scripture directly in their reflections and make no direct mention of the *ANA Code of Ethics for Nurses* (ANA, 2015). Our own work foregrounds both.

Fowler, M. D. M. (2015). *Guide to the code of ethics for nurses with interpretive statements: Development, interpretation and application* (2nd ed.). Silver Spring, MD: American Nurses Association. Of all the books on the present list, we have depended most heavily on this one. We have cited it constantly in this book and we always assign it as a textbook in our course for APRNs. It offers a detailed exposition of the ANA *Code*, provision by provision. But the book is truly a *guide* to the *Code*, not merely a *commentary* on it, and several features of Fowler's book deserve special mention. First, she provides a brief but incisive account of the historical development of the *Code*, which shows how the *Code* has evolved in step with advances in the healthcare sciences and with the growing professionalization and expanding mission of nursing itself. Second, Fowler lays out "the nursing process in clinical-ethical situations," (p. xxi), which functions as a discipline-specific analog to the decision-making protocols in Jonsen et al. (2015; see below). Third, although Fowler is here writing under the auspices of the ANA, such that her *Guide* mirrors the "secular" or "nontheistic" character of the *Code* itself, she is nevertheless quite alive to the religious roots of modern nursing. She herself has graduate-level training in theology and is currently a Senior Fellow at the Office of Faith Integration at Azusa Pacific University (a sister school of our own institution). In her hands, nursing takes its rightful place in the interdisciplinary field of the medical humanities. Finally, this book includes many teaching/learning aids, along with a photo-reproduction of the *Code* itself, complete with its original pagination, for easy reference.

Grace, P. J. (2018). *Nursing ethics and professional responsibility in advanced practice* (3rd ed.). Burlington, MA: Jones & Bartlett Learning. First published in 2008, and now in its third edition, this work is a standard textbook in graduate-level nursing ethics courses—and deserves to be. It is divided into three sections: "Foundations of Advanced Practice Nursing Ethics," "Common Ethical Issues across Practice Specialties," and "Ethical Issues in Advanced Practice Specialty Areas." To cover the wide array of bioethical and clinical issues the book addresses, Grace has recruited a team of fourteen coauthors. She remains the primary author, however, not simply the editor, and this assures that a consistent stylistic "voice" is maintained throughout. The book is lavishly furnished with vivid case studies (often supplemented by detailed ethical analysis), thought-provoking discussion questions, and visually arresting tables, all of which enhance its use in classroom settings. For these reasons, and also because there is nothing specifically "religious" about its approach to nursing ethics, it contrasts dramatically with the approach and contents of the present volume, and has thus proven to be a perfect companion text in our own course for APRN students.

Jonsen, A. R., Siegler, M., & Winslade, W. J. (2015). *Clinical ethics: A practical approach to ethical decisions in clinical medicine* (8th ed.). New York, NY: McGraw-Hill. As its subtitle suggests, this work takes a solidly "decisionist" approach to medical ethics. That is, it offers a highly refined and flexible method for enabling care teams to make ethically warranted decisions in quandary situations. The approach it takes to resolving such quandaries is illustrated in the famous "Four Topics Chart." To analyze an ethically problematic case, the reader first addresses its "medical indications," then the "preferences of the patient," then the "quality of life" that a specific medical intervention is likely to provide for the patient, and finally the "contextual features" of the case. As the reader moves through this step-by-step process, she applies the standard bioethical principles of beneficence, nonmaleficence, respect for patient autonomy and justice/fairness. The decision-making method developed by Jonsen et al. addresses three of four fields of moral inquiry that we have discussed in this book: "law," "wisdom" and "prophecy." It does not, of course, use those terms, and it assumes that bioethical principles are self-validating and universally applicable. But as one would expect from its conduct-driven approach, this book gives little attention to the moral character and religious convictions of the healthcare provider, that is, to what we would call "holiness" considerations. Nor is anything said here about the quality and spirit of "routine" healthcare work, that is, to patient care in situations that do not involve ethical conundrums.

Lysaught, M. T., Kotva, J. J., Jr., Lammers, S. E., & Verhey, A. (Eds.). (2012). *On moral medicine: Theological perspectives in medical ethics* (3rd ed.). Grand Rapids, MI: Eerdmans. Since 1987, when the first edition of this work was published under the editorship of Stephen Lammers and Allen Verhey, it has been an indispensable treasury of writings offering Christian perspectives on ethical issues in health care. The third edition includes 156 selections, which are organized into six main parts: "Method," "Christianity and the Social Practice of Health Care," "Patients and Professionals," "Vulnerable Persons," "The Beginning of Life," and "The End of Life." Taken together, they richly display the value of "particular moralities" in bioethics—in this case, *Christian* morality—in contrast to the approach taken, for example, by Beauchamp and Childress (2013), who claim to represent a "universal common morality." We cordially recommend this book as a valuable resource, deserving a place on the shelf of all who have a special interest in medical and/or nursing ethics.

O'Brien, M. E. (2018). *Spirituality in nursing: Standing on holy ground* (6th ed.). Burlington, MA: Jones & Bartlett Learning. Two interlocking concerns drive this work: the spiritual character of the nurse and the spiritual needs of various types of patients for whom the nurse provides care. As to the first concern, O'Brien understands nursing as "a caring ministry" and a "contemplative" profession and describes leadership in nursing as "servant leadership." As such, this book has close affinities with our account of the holiness and wisdom strands of biblical moral discourse, though fewer with our account of the legal and prophetic strands. As to the second, O'Brien devotes distinct chapters to the spiritual needs of various patient populations—"the patient with an acute illness," "the chronically ill person," victims of "mass casualty disasters," and persons at every stage of the human life cycle. Her accounts of caregiving to these diverse groups are fortified with a great deal of qualitative and quantitative data—and indeed, she insists that competent, patient-centered nursing care requires both thorough interviewing of individual patients and rigorous psychosocial research into the demographic groups to which they belong. Yet O'Brien certainly does not want nurses simply to "live in their heads" or to imagine that knowing patients well enough to care for them skillfully requires nothing more than knowing a great deal of "objective information" about them. Accordingly, her book is enlivened with touching stories about nurses and their patients, and at times strikes an almost devotional tone. It says little, however, about nursing *ethics* as such, and it mentions the ANA *Code* (2015) only once—in connection with the notion of nursing as "servanthood."

Pellegrino, E. D., & Thomasma, D. C. (1993). *The virtues in medical practice.* New York, NY: Oxford University Press. This book and its companion volume (see following entry) were written in response to two significant and interrelated trends that characterized the field of ethics in the late 1980s and early 1990s. The first was the resurgence of "virtue ethics," thanks largely to the work of Elizabeth Anscombe, Alasdair MacIntyre and Stanley Hauerwas. Ethics had, for several centuries, been dominated by one or another form of "decisionism." The focus here was on people's discrete moral actions and choices, and the moral validity of a proposed decision was determined either by its adherence to some general moral principles or by the value of the consequences that were expected to follow from it. In contrast, virtue ethics sought to restore attention to the agent in her human wholeness, that is, to her character, as it developed throughout her life and as it reflected her participation in and commitment to various overlapping communities of moral discourse (political, ethnic, religious, professional, etc.). The second trend was a growing dissatisfaction with the brand of decisionism that had dominated medical ethics for several decades, namely, the "ethical principlism" of Beauchamp and Childress (2013; see above). Pellegrino and Thomasma applied the methods and insights of modern virtue ethics to the field of medicine, though in doing so they understood themselves to be retrieving and rehabilitating a conception of medical practice that went back to Hippocrates, as well as a conception of the moral good that had been articulated by Aristotle and Aquinas. The authors understand medicine as a "moral community," rooted in time-tested traditions of professional obligation and comportment and oriented to the care and cure of the sick. The specific virtues that Pellegrino and Thomasma here describe—and describe with great relish and richness of detail—are fidelity to trust, compassion, phronesis (= prudence), justice, fortitude, temperance, integrity and self-effacement. This list bears close comparison with the contents of chapter 2 above. Importantly, Pellegrino and Thomasma argue that these virtues must characterize not only physicians but also nurses, dentists, pharmacists and other medical professionals.

Pellegrino, E. D., & Thomasma, D. C. (1996). *The Christian virtues in medical practice.* Washington, DC: Georgetown University Press. In this book, the authors build upon the treatment of virtue ethics in medicine that they had developed in their earlier work but go on to ask whether it "makes a difference" for a medical professional to be a Christian and to cultivate the specifically "theological" virtues of faith, hope and love. As true students of Aquinas, they ask further how the theological virtues shape the cardinal virtues of prudence and justice, and as sensitive commentators on the field of contemporary medical ethics, they also discuss how a Christian medical practitioner might understand such putatively "secular" principles as autonomy and beneficence. Thus, this book, like its predecessor, has close parallels with our account of Christian holiness in chapter 2. Nevertheless, there is a marked difference between the approach taken by Pellegrino and Thomasma and the approach taken here. Although they *appeal* to "scriptural revelation" in their account of the virtues, they give little sustained attention to specific biblical passages but focus mainly on theological and philosophical texts; in contrast, our approach is heavily exegetical—and, of course, specifically concerned with the profession of nursing.

Shelly, J. A., & Miller, A. B. (2006). *Called to care: A Christian worldview for nursing* (2nd ed.). Downers Grove, IL: InterVarsity. A deep religious concern drives this work, namely, that the profession of nursing is in danger of losing its moorings in the "Christian worldview" that animated its founders in the late nineteenth century, and that newer "paradigms," such as materialistic naturalism, postmodernism and New Age spiritualism, are increasingly influencing nursing theory, education and practice. Shelly and Miller seek to defend the contemporary relevance of the traditional Christian worldview against its new competitors and to demonstrate that the Christian conception of reality, and particularly of the human person, is better suited to the kind of patient care that promotes holistic healing or, as they often put it, true *shalom*. Despite this "apologetic" aim, however, the book is rarely polemical in tone. On the contrary, it breathes the warm, confident spirit of authentic evangelical piety, and it includes numerous edifying stories by and about Christian nurses whose practice reflected—sometimes with quiet determination, other times with bold assertiveness—their Christian worldview. Yet the authors are not afraid to speak sharply at times, particularly when describing how the clinical practices which sometimes emerge from the new paradigms possess little scientific warrant and offer dubious therapeutic benefit. *Called to Care* is intended as a textbook for college courses and parish nursing training programs: each of its chapters begins with a statement of its purpose, a list of its objectives, and a list of its keywords, and concludes with prompts for "further thinking" and "theological reflection," case studies, and discussion questions. We find ourselves in deep sympathy with the argument of this book, and we applaud its user-friendliness and engaging spirit. Our primary complaints are, first, that it tends to use passages of Christian Scripture as proof texts (uncontextualized and unanalyzed quotations are common), and second, that its account of complex theological concepts (e.g., *shalom* and the image of God) is somewhat superficial. The book's account of the value of the Christian worldview for contemporary nursing is more successful when it *illustrates* it through anecdotes and testimonies of Christian nurses than when it attempts to *defend* it through conceptual analysis or scriptural exposition.

Thobaben, J. R. (2009). *Health-care ethics: A comprehensive Christian resource*. Downers Grove, IL: InterVarsity. There are three striking affinities between Thobanen's book and our own. First, it shares our evangelical, and indeed, our specifically Wesleyan religious perspective. True, it recognizes the wide array of groups which that "evangelicalism" covers and acknowledges that the differing religious convictions of these groups sometimes yield differing positions on controversial healthcare issues. Yet Thobaben assumes that committed evangelicals of various stripes have enough in common theologically—at least in the area of theological anthropology, that is, the Christian doctrine of human nature—that they will generally speak with a common voice on healthcare issues. Second, when Thobaben addresses these issues, chapter by chapter, he begins with a detailed interpretation of a specific passage from the Bible, usually one of the Gospels. This gives his account of the relevance of Christian Scripture for bioethics greater depth, specificity and nuance than we sometimes find in those works that operate from a more generalized "Christian worldview" (e.g., Shelly & Miller, 2006) or that content themselves with citations of convenient proof texts (e.g., Doornbos et al., 2005). Third, Thobaben understands that a well-rounded theory of Christian bioethics must *integrate* the specific insights and concerns of several different moral philosophies that are often regarded as incompatible. These include the deontological approach of Immanuel Kant and John Rawls (roughly akin to our Strand 1: Law), the virtue ethics approach of Aristotle, Aquinas and Stanley Hauerwas (akin to Strand 2: Holiness), and the utilitarian approach of J. S. Mill (akin to Strand 4: Prophecy). Yet there are also four significant ways in which Thobaben's approach differs from our own. First, he does not show how *Scripture itself* reflects multiple types of ethical discourse, as we have tried to do in our delineation of the four strands. Second, and to his great credit, he tackles specific issues head-on (e.g., abortion, managed care, end-of-life decisions, and assistive reproductive technologies), whereas we have tended to skirt these. Third, Thobaben shows how the normative positions on specific healthcare issues that follow from evangelical religious convictions are generally more congruent with the values of the social contract theory according to which American society operates than the positions taken by various other ideologies and ethical theories currently on offer, such as "scientism" and "privatized therapeutic syncretism." At the same time, he insists that the moral obligation that evangelical Christians have—and should gladly embrace—to care for the preborn, the sick, the disabled and the dying will generally exceed what the laws of a contractarian society can require of all citizens. Finally, Thobaben's aim is to articulate how evangelical Christians in general ought to think, act and vote with respect to specific bioethical issues and healthcare policies, whereas our aim is more narrowly focused on the character and conduct of Christian nurses.

Verhey, A. (2003). *Reading the Bible in the strange world of medicine.* Grand Rapids, MI: Eerdmans. This book is a collection of ten essays that touch on a wide array of bioethical topics, such as genomics, abortion, physician-assisted suicide, and the allocation of scarce medical resources. The essays are held together by Verhey's profound conviction that the Christian Bible has something important to say about how we should think about these diverse subjects, despite the obvious fact that the Bible does not directly address any of them. Verhey sets himself the daunting task of demonstrating the connections between Scripture and medicine. The essay of greatest significance for our own project is the second, which is titled "The Bible and Bioethics: Some Problems and a Proposal." It begins by reviewing the various reasons that his self-appointed task of connecting Scripture and medicine seems doomed to failure. But this is precisely why the essay is so valuable: it does not shirk the grave difficulties of the task, but rather works out a strategy of scriptural interpretation that faces up to them. We have tried to follow Verhey's strategy in our reading of the biblical passages we have selected to represent the four strands.

References

2019 Wash. Sess. Laws. Ch. 296, 1–7. Retrieved from http://lawfilesext.leg.wa.gov/biennium/2019-20/Pdf/Bills/Session%20Laws/House/1155-S.SL.pdf

Allnurses.com. (n.d.). *Stamps commemorating nursing.* Retrieved from https://allnurses.com/nursing-activism-healthcare/stamps-commemorating-nursing-766461.html

American Nurses Association. (2015). *Code of ethics for nurses with interpretive statements.* Silver Spring, MD: Author.

Anonymous. (1890). *Walt Whitman with his nurse Warren Fritzenger, on the wharf, probably near his Mickle Street house in Camden, NJ* [photograph]. Retrieved from http://www.loc.gov/pictures/item/97506894/

Anonymous. (1918, June). *A flower for nurse. French baby at the American Red Cross nursing home near Paris* [photograph]. Retrieved from http://www.loc.gov/pictures/resource/anrc.09169/

Anonymous. (1922, May 12). *Gold key to door of Nurses Memorial Building, Florence Nightingale School, Bordeaux, France* [photograph]. Retrieved from http://www.loc.gov/pictures/item/2017679951/

Anonymous. (ca. 12th century). *Salome and midwife bathing the infant Jesus* [painting]. Retrieved from https://commons.wikimedia.org/wiki/Category:Midwife_Salome

Anonymous. (n.d.). *Mary Eliza Mahoney (1845-1926)* [photograph]. New York, NY: Schomburg Center for Research in Black Culture, The New York Public Library.

Aristotle. (1998). *The Nichomachean ethics* (D. Ross, J. L. Ackrill, & J. O. Urmson, Trans.). Oxford, England: Oxford University Press.

Augustine. (1887a). The handbook on faith, hope and love (J. F. Shaw, Trans.). In K. Knight (Ed.), *Nicene and Post-Nicene Fathers, First Series* (Rev. ed., Vol. 3). Buffalo, NY: Christian Literature. Retrieved from http://www.newadvent.org/fathers/1302.htm

Augustine. (1887b). On the morals of the Catholic Church (R. Stothert, Trans.). In K. Knight (Ed.), *Nicene and Post-Nicene Fathers, First Series,* (Rev. ed., Vol. 4). Buffalo, NY: Christian Literature. Retrieved from http://www.newadvent.org/fathers/1401.htm

Augustine. (1998). *Confessions* (H. Chadwick, Trans.). Oxford, England: Oxford University Press.

Barrett, J. (c. 1856). *Florence Nightingale receiving the wounded at Scutari* [painting]. London, England: National Portrait Gallery.

Bauckham, R. (2003). Reading scripture as a coherent story. In E. F. Davis & R. B. Hays (Eds.), *The art of reading scripture* (pp. 38–53). Grand Rapids, MI: Eerdmans.

References

Beauchamp, T. L., & Childress, J. F. (2013). *Principles of biomedical ethics* (7th ed.). New York, NY: Oxford University Press.

Bellucci, A. (ca. first half of 18th century). *St. Sebastian nursed by St. Irene* [painting]. St. Petersburg, Russia: The State Hermitage Museum.

Benner, P., Sutphen, M., Leonard, V., & Day, L. (2010). *Educating nurses: A call for radical transformation.* San Francisco, CA: Jossey-Bass.

Benner, P., Tanner, C. A., & Chesla, C. A. (1996). *Expertise in nursing practice: Caring, clinical judgment, and ethics.* New York, NY: Springer.

Bok, S. (1982). *Secrets: On the ethics of concealment and revelation.* New York, NY: Vintage.

Bok, S. (1999). *Lying: Moral choice in public and private life.* New York, NY: Vintage.

Bonhoeffer, D., & Bethge, E. (Ed.). (1975). *Ethics* (N. H. Smith, Trans.). New York, NY: Macmillan.

Bowker, J. (2001). *The complete Bible handbook: An illustrated companion.* New York, NY: DK.

Brenan, M. (2017, December). Nurses keep healthy lead as most honest, ethical profession. *Gallup.* Retrieved from https://news.gallup.com/poll/224639/nurses-keep-healthy-lead-honest-ethical-profession.aspx?g_source=Economy&g_medium=newsfeed&g_campaign=tiles

Brueggemann, W. (1994). The book of Exodus: Introduction, commentary, and reflections. In L. E. Keck (Ed.), *The new interpreter's Bible* (Vol. 1, pp. 675–981). Nashville, TN: Abingdon.

Buber, M. (1960). *The prophetic faith* (C. Witton-Davies, Trans.). New York, NY: Harper & Row.

Caird, G. B. (1972). *Saint Luke.* London, England: Penguin.

Calvin, J., & McNeill, J. T. (Ed.). (1960). *Institutes of the Christian religion* (F. L. Battles, Trans.; 1559 ed., Vol. 1). Philadelphia, PA: Westminster.

Carnegie, D. (1998). *How to win friends and influence people.* New York, NY: Simon & Schuster.

Challen, A. C. (ca. 1869). *Portrait of Mary Seacole* [painting]. London, England: National Portrait Gallery.

Chardin, J. B. S. (1747). *The attentive nurse* [painting]. Retrieved from https://simple.wikipedia.org/wiki/The_Attentive_Nurse#/media/File:Jean_Sim%C3%A9on_Chardin_-_The_Attentive_Nurse_-_WGA04757.jpg

Clements, R. E. (1998). The book of Deuteronomy: Introduction, commentary, and reflections. In L. E. Keck (Ed.), *The new interpreter's Bible* (Vol. 2, pp. 269–538). Nashville, TN: Abingdon.

Clements, R. E. (2003). Deuteronomy. In W. J. Harrelson (Ed.), *The new interpreter's study Bible* (pp. 241–302). Nashville, TN: Abingdon.

Cohen, L. M. (2011). *No good deed: A story of medicine, murder accusations, and the debate over how we die.* New York, NY: HarperCollins.

Crenshaw, J. L. (1997). The book of Sirach: Introduction, commentary, and reflections. In L. E. Keck (Ed.), *The new interpreter's Bible* (Vol. 5, pp. 601–867). Nashville: Abingdon.

Culpepper, R. A. (1995). The gospel of Luke: Introduction, commentary, and reflections. In L. E. Keck (Ed.), *The new interpreter's Bible* (Vol. 9, pp. 1–490). Nashville, TN: Abingdon.

Davis, E. F., & Hays, R. B. (Eds.). (2003). *The art of reading scripture.* Grand Rapids, MI: Eerdmans.

References

de Champaigne, P. (1648). *Moses and the Ten Commandments* [painting]. St. Petersburg, Russia: The State Hermitage Museum.

de Lyra, N. (1498, December 1). Gloss on Genesis 1:1. In J. Froben & J. Petri (Eds.), *Biblia Latina cum glossa Ordinaria*. Basel, Switzerland: Universitätsbibliothek Basel.

Doornbos, M. M., Groenhout, R. E., & Hotz, K. G. (2005). *Transforming care: A Christian vision of nursing practice*. Grand Rapids, MI: Eerdmans.

Dostoyevsky, F. (2010). *The idiot* (H. Carlisle & O. Carlisle, Trans.). New York, NY: Signet Classics.

Dürer, A. (1513). *St. Peter and St. John healing a cripple at the gate of the temple* [engraving]. Retrieved from https://commons.wikimedia.org/wiki/File:Albrecht_Dürer_-_Saint_Peter_and_Saint_John_Healing_a_Cripple_at_the_Gate_of_the_Temple.jpg

Ehrman, B. D. (2003). *Lost scriptures: Books that did not make it into the New Testament*. New York, NY: Oxford University Press.

Fadiman, A. (2012). *The spirit catches you and you fall down: A Hmong child, her American doctors, and the collision of two cultures* (15th anniversary ed.). New York, NY: Farrar, Straus & Giroux.

Fitzmyer, J. A. (1981). *The gospel according to Luke (I–IX): Introduction, translation and notes*. In W. F. Albright & D. F. Freedman (Eds.), *The anchor Bible* (Vol. 28). Garden City, NY: Doubleday & Co.

Fitzmyer, J. A. (1985). *The gospel according to Luke (X–XXIV): Introduction, translation and notes*. In W. F. Albright & D. F. Freedman (Eds.), *The anchor Bible* (Vol. 28A). Garden City, NY: Doubleday & Co.

Fowler, M. D. M. (2015). *Guide to the code of ethics for nurses with interpretive statements: Development, interpretation and application* (2nd ed.). Silver Spring, MD: American Nurses Association.

Furnish, V. P. (1972). *The love command in the New Testament*. Nashville, TN: Abingdon.

Gaiser, F. J. (2010). *Healing in the Bible: Theological insight for Christian ministry*. Grand Rapids, MI: Baker Academic.

Grace, P. J. (Ed.). (2018). *Nursing ethics and professional responsibility in advanced practice* (3rd ed.). Burlington, MA: Jones & Bartlett Learning.

Grahame, K. (1961). *The wind in the willows*. New York, NY: Scribner's.

Gray, J. (1962). Hadadrimmon. In G. A. Buttrick (Ed.), *The interpreter's dictionary of the Bible* (Vol. 2, p. 507). Nashville, TN: Abingdon.

Green, J. (2003). Luke. In W. J. Harrelson (Ed.), *The new interpreter's study Bible* (pp. 847–903). Nashville, TN: Abingdon.

Harak, G. S. (1993). *Virtuous passions: The formation of Christian character*. Mahwah, NJ: Paulist.

Harrelson, W. J. (1962). Law. In W. J. Harrelson (Ed.), *The new interpreter's dictionary of the Bible* (Vol. 3, pp. 77–89). Nashville, TN: Abingdon.

Hauerwas, S. M., & Willimon, W. H. (1999). *The truth about God: The Ten Commandments in Christian life*. Nashville, TN: Abingdon.

Hayes, J. H. (2003). Leviticus. In W. J. Harrelson (Ed.), *The new interpreter's study Bible* (Vol. 10, pp. 145–88). Nashville, TN: Abingdon.

Hicks, E. (ca. 1833). *Peaceable kingdom* [painting]. Worcester, MA: Worcester Art Museum.

Hugo, V. (1992). *Les misérables* (N. Denny, Trans.). London, England: Penguin.

Interprofessional Education Collaborative. (2016). *Core competencies for interprofessional collaborative practice: 2016 update.* Washington, DC: Author. Retrieved from https://hsc.unm.edu/ipe/resources/ipec-2016-core-competencies.pdf

Jameton, A. (1993). Dilemmas of moral distress: Moral responsibility and nursing practice. *AWHONN's Clinical Issues in Perinatal & Women's Health Nursing, 4*(4), 542–51. Retrieved from http://www.aodp.org/

Jeremias, J. (1966). *Rediscovering the parables* (S. H. Hooke & F. Clarke, Trans.). New York, NY: Scribner's.

Johnson, L. T. (1998). The letter of James: Introduction, commentary, and reflections. In L. E. Keck (Ed.), *The new interpreter's Bible* (Vol. 12, pp. 175–225). Nashville, TN: Abingdon.

Johnson, S. (2006). *The ghost map: The story of London's most terrifying epidemic—and how it changed science, cities, and the modern world.* New York, NY: Riverhead.

Jonsen, A. R., Siegler, M., & Winslade, W. J. (2015). *Clinical ethics: A practical approach to ethical decisions in clinical medicine* (8th ed.). New York, NY: McGraw-Hill Education.

Kaiser, W. C., Jr. (1994). The book of Leviticus: Introduction, commentary, and reflections. In L. E. Keck (Ed.), *The new interpreter's Bible* (Vol. 1, pp. 983–1191). Nashville, TN: Abingdon.

Kowalczyk, L. (2013, May 19). For bombing suspect's nurses, angst gave way to duty. *The Boston Globe.* Retrieved from https://www.bostonglobe.com/

Lewis, C. S. (1962). *The problem of pain.* New York, NY: Macmillan.

Longhi, P. (ca. 1752). *The apothecary* [painting]. Retrieved from https://commons.wikimedia.org/wiki/File:Pietro_Longhi_-_The_Apothecary_-_WGA13411.jpg

Luther, M. (1959). The large catechism (T. G. Tappert, Trans.). In T. G. Tappert (Ed.), *The book of concord* (pp. 357–461). Philadelphia, PA: Fortress.

Lysaught, M. T., Kotva, J. J., Jr., Lammers, S. E., & Verhey, A. (Eds.). (2012). *On moral medicine: Theological perspectives in medical ethics* (3rd ed.). Grand Rapids, MI: Eerdmans.

Mariottini, C. F. (2003). 1–2 Kings. In W. J. Harrelson (Ed.), *The new interpreter's study Bible* (Vol. 10, pp. 479–569). Nashville, TN: Abingdon.

Mark the Ascetic. (1979). On the spiritual law (G. E. H. Palmer, P. Sherrard, & K. Ware, Trans.). In G. E. H. Palmer, P. Sherrard, & K. Ware (Eds.), *The philokalia* (Vol. 1, pp. 109–60). Boston, MA: Faber & Faber.

Matthews, V. (2000). Law. In D. L. Freedman (Ed.), *Eerdmans dictionary of the Bible* (pp. 793–96). Grand Rapids, MI: Eerdmans.

May, W. F. (1991). *The patient's ordeal.* Bloomington, IN: Indiana University Press.

May, W. F. (2001). *Beleaguered rulers: The public obligation of the professional.* Louisville, KY: Westminster John Knox.

Mayer, J. D., Salovey, P., & Caruso, D. R. (2008). Emotional intelligence: New ability or eclectic traits? *American Psychologist 63*(6), 503–17. doi: 10.1037/0003-066X.63.6.503.

Meier, J. P. (1979). *The vision of Matthew: Christ, church, and morality in the First Gospel.* New York, NY: Paulist.

Mendenhall, G. E. (1970a). Ancient oriental and biblical law. In E. F. Campbell, Jr., & D. N. Freedman (Eds.), *The biblical archaeologist reader* (Vol. 3, pp. 3–24). Garden City, NY: Doubleday. (Original work published May, 1954).

Mendenhall, G. E. (1970b). Covenant forms in Israelite tradition. In E. F. Campbell & D. N. Freedman (Eds.), *The biblical archaeologist reader* (Vol. 3, pp. 25–53). Garden City, NY: Doubleday. (Original work published September, 1954).

Merton, T. (Ed. & Trans.) (1970). *The wisdom of the desert: Sayings from the Desert Fathers of the fourth century.* New York, NY: New Directions.

Mohrmann, M. E. (1995). *Medicine as ministry: Reflections on suffering, ethics, and hope.* Cleveland, OH: Pilgrim.

Mohrmann, M. E. (2005). *Attending children: A doctor's education.* Washington, DC: Georgetown University Press.

Monroe, H. A. (2017). *Education and experience in nursing professional values development* (Doctoral dissertation). Retrieved from ProQuest Dissertations Publishing. (Order No. 10601014).

Monroe, H. A. (2019). Nurses' professional values: Influences of experience and ethics education. *Journal of Clinical Nursing, 28*(9–10), 2009–2019. doi.org/10.1111/jocn.14806.

Muilenburg, J. (1962). Holiness. In G. Buttrick (Ed.), *The new interpreter's dictionary of the Bible* (Vol. 2, pp. 616–25). Nashville, TN: Abingdon.

National Nursing Workforce Study. (2017). Retrieved from https://www.ncsbn.org/workforce.htm

Newbigin, L. (1995). *Proper confidence: Faith, doubt, and certainty in Christian discipleship.* Grand Rapids, MI: Eerdmans.

Nicholas of Lyra. (1498). *Biblia Latina cum Glossa Ordinaria* [photograph of Gloss on Genesis 1.1]. Universitätsbibliothek Basel, Switzerland. Retrieved from https://www.e-rara.ch/bau_1/content/pageview/5083816

Nienhuis, D. R. (2007). *Not by Paul alone: The formation of the Catholic Epistle collection and the Christian canon.* Waco, TX: Baylor University Press.

Nightingale, F. (1863). *Notes on hospitals* (3rd ed.). London, England: Longman, Green, Longman, Roberts, & Green. Retrieved from https://archive.org/details/notesonhospital01nighgoog/page/n7

Nightingale, F. (1992). *Notes on nursing: What it is, and what it is not* (Commemorative ed.). Philadelphia, PA: Lippincott.

Nightingale, F. (2002). Florence Nightingale's theology: Essays, letters and journal notes. In L. McDonald (Ed.), *The collected works of Florence Nightingale* (Vol. 3). Waterloo, Canada: Wilfrid Laurier University Press.

Nightingale, F. (2010). Florence Nightingale: The Crimean War. In L. McDonald (Ed.), *The collected works of Florence Nightingale* (Vol. 14). Waterloo, Canada: Wilfrid Laurier University Press.

O'Brien, M. E. (2018). *Spirituality in nursing: Standing on holy ground* (6th ed.). Burlington, MA: Jones & Bartlett Learning.

Olin, J. (2011). Historic stamp still important today. *RN Central.* Retrieved from http://www.rncentral.com/blog/2011/historic-stamp-still-important-today/

Otto, R. (1950). *The idea of the holy* (2nd ed.). (J. W. Harvey, Trans.). London, England: Oxford University Press.

Pellegrino, E. D., & Thomasma, D. C. (1993). *The virtues in medical practice.* New York, NY: Oxford University Press.

Pellegrino, E. D., & Thomasma, D. C. (1996). *The Christian virtues in medical practice.* Washington, DC: Georgetown University Press.

Peterson, D. L. (2001). Introduction to the prophetic literature. In W. J. Harrelson (Ed.), *The new interpreter's study Bible* (Vol. 6, pp. 1–23). Nashville, TN: Abingdon.

Peterson, E. (2002). *The message: The Bible in contemporary language.* Colorado Springs, CO: NavPress.

Pieper, J. (1966). *The four cardinal virtues.* Notre Dame, IN: University of Notre Dame Press.

Pieper, J. (1997). *Faith, Hope, Love.* San Francisco, CA: Ignatius.

Ramsey, P. (2002). *The patient as person: Explorations in medical ethics* (2nd ed.). New Haven, CT: Yale University Press.

Raphael. (1515). *The miraculous draught of fishes* [painting]. Retrieved from https://en.wikipedia.org/wiki/Miraculous_catch_of_fish#/media/File:V&A_-_Raphael,_The_Miraculous_Draught_of_Fishes_(1515).jpg

Reinders, H. S. (2008). *Receiving the gift of friendship: Profound disability, theological anthropology, and ethics.* Grand Rapids, MI: Eerdmans.

Richardson, C. C. (Ed. & Trans.). (1953). *Early christian fathers.* Philadelphia, PA: Westminster.

Riesner, R. (2001). James. In J. Barton & J. Muddiman (Eds.), *The Oxford Bible commentary* (pp. 1255–63). Oxford, England: Oxford University Press.

Roberts, R. C. (2007). *Spiritual emotions: A psychology of Christian virtues.* Grand Rapids, MI: Eerdmans.

Rowley, H. H. (1961). *The unity of the Bible.* Cleveland, OH: Meridian.

Schiedermayer, D. (1994). *Putting the soul back in medicine: Reflections on compassion and ethics.* Grand Rapids, MI: Baker.

Scott, R. B. Y. (1968). *The relevance of the prophets.* New York, NY: Macmillan.

Seow, C.-L. (1999). The first and second books of Kings: Introduction, commentary, and reflections. In L. E. Keck (Ed.), *The new interpreter's Bible* (Vol. 3, pp. 1–295). Nashville, TN: Abingdon.

Shakespeare, W. (2016). *Othello* (Rev. ed.). London, England: Bloomsbury Arden Shakespeare.

Shelly, J. A., & Miller, A. B. (2006). *Called to care: A Christian worldview for nursing* (2nd ed.). Downers Grove, IL: InterVarsity.

Smiley, R. A., Lauer, P., Bienemy, C., Berg, J. G., Shireman, E., Reneau, K. A., Alexander, M. (October, 2018). The 2017 national nursing workforce study. *Journal of Nursing Regulation, 9*(3), S1–S88.

Spina, F. (2005). *The faith of the outsider: Exclusion and inclusion in the biblical story.* Grand Rapids, MI: Eerdmans.

Steele, R. B. (2000). Unremitting compassion: The moral psychology of parenting children with genetic disorders. *Theology Today, 57*(2), 161–74.

Steele, R. B. (2010). Christian virtue and ministry to persons with disabilities. *Journal of Religion, Disability and Health, 14*(1), 28–46.

Steele, R. B. (2013, Week 2). Wisdom literature: A prudential motive. Retrieved from https://blog.spu.edu/lectio/a-prudential-motive/

Steele, R. B. (2013, Week 3). Wisdom literature: An optimistic attitude. Retrieved from https://blog.spu.edu/lectio/an-optimistic-attitude/

Steele, R. B. (2013, Week 4). Wisdom literature: An empirical method. Retrieved from https://blog.spu.edu/lectio/an-empirical-method/

Steele, R. B. (2013, Week 8). Wisdom literature: Against empiricism; Divine transcendence and divine revelation. Retrieved from https://blog.spu.edu/lectio/against-empiricism-divine-transcendence-and-divine-revelation/

Steele, R. B. (2018). Disability and the beloved community. *Journal of the Christian Institute on Disability, 7*(1), 19–34.

Steele, R. B. (2018, May). From a moral to a theocentric stance on a life's work. *Presented at the Association of Theological Schools' Roundtable Seminar for Midcareer Faculty.* Retrieved from https://www.faithandleadership.com/richard-b-steele-moral-theocentric-stance-lifes-work?utm_source=FL_newsletter&utm_medium=content& utm_campaign=FL_feature

Strozzi, B. (ca. 1640). *Elijah and the widow of Sarepta [Zarephath] (1 Kings 17:7)*[painting]. New York, NY: Art Resource.

Thobaben, J. R. (2009). *Health-care ethics: A comprehensive Christian resource.* Downers Grove, IL: InterVarsity.

Tournier, P. (1960). *A doctor's casebook in the light of the Bible* (E. Hudson, Trans.). New York, NY: Harper & Row.

Trocmé, A. (1973). *Jesus and the nonviolent revolution* (M. H. Shank & M. E. Miller, Trans.). Scottdale, PA: Herald.

Truog, R. D., Brown, S. D., Browning, D., Hundert, E. M., Rider, E. A., Bell, S. K., & Meyer, E. C. (2015). Microethics: The ethics of everyday clinical practice. *Hastings Center Report, 1,* 11–17. doi: 10.1002/hast.413.

Turner, J. (2014, Summer). Sexual orientation and gender identity in nursing. *Minority Nurse,* 8–12. Retrieved from https://minoritynurse.com/minority-nurse-summer -2014/

van Gogh, V. (1890). *The Good Samaritan (after Delacroix)* [painting]. Retrieved from https://commons.wikimedia.org/wiki/File:Van_Gogh_-_Der_barmherzige_Samariter.jpeg

van Rijn, R. (1649). *Christ preaching and healing the sick (or The hundred guilder print)* [etching]. Retrieved from https://www.rijksmuseum.nl/en/collection/RP-P-OB-602

Verhey, A. (2003). *Reading the Bible in the strange world of medicine.* Grand Rapids, MI: Eerdmans.

von Rad, G. (1965). *The message of the prophets* (E. Haller, Trans.). San Francisco, CA: HarperSanFrancisco.

von Rad, G. (1966). *Deuteronomy: A commentary* (D. Barton, Trans.). Philadelphia, PA: Westminster.

von Rad, G. (1972). *Wisdom in Israel* (J. D. Martin, Trans.). Nashville, TN: Abingdon.

Waddell, H. (Trans.) (1998). *The desert fathers: Translations from the Latin.* New York, NY: Vintage.

Wall, R. W. (1997). *Community of the wise: The letter of James.* Valley Forge, PA: Trinity Press International.

Washington State Nurses Association. (2019). *Rest breaks* [Position statement]. Retrieved from https://www.wsna.org/legislative-affairs/2019/guarantee-rest-breaks-and-limit -mandatory-overtime-1

Watzlawick, P., Weakland, J. H., & Fisch, R. (1974). *Change: Principles of problem formation and problem resolution.* New York, NY: W. W. Norton.

Wesley, J. (1984). Preface to hymns and sacred poems. In T. Jackson (Ed.), *The works of John Wesley* (Vol. 14, pp. 319–322). Peabody, MA: Hendrickson. (Original work published 1739.)

Wesley, J. (1985). Christian perfection. In A. C. Outler (Ed.), *The works of John Wesley* (Vol. 2, pp. 34–70). Nashville, TN: Abingdon.

Whitman, W. (1881). *Leaves of grass*. In *The Walt Whitman Archive*. Retrieved from https://whitmanarchive.org/published/LG/1881/poems/169

Yaroshenko, N. A. (1886). *Sister of mercy* [painting]. New York, NY: HIP/Art Resource.

Yoder, J. H. (1995). *The politics of Jesus* (2nd ed.). Grand Rapids, MI: Eerdmans.

Index

Note: Locators in *italics* indicate figures in the text.
Footnotes are indicated with a lowercase n.

Made in the USA
Columbia, SC
30 June 2020